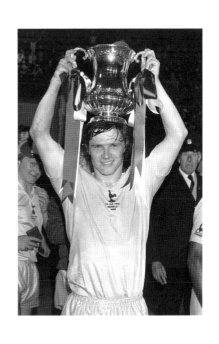

White Hart Lane Legends

Legends

Volume One

White Hart Lane Legends - Volume One

Authors Keith Palmer & David Lane
Concept and Production David Lane

Published by
Legends Publishing
22 Park Road
Hampton Hill
Middlesex
TW12 1HF

E-mail info@legendspublishing.net
Website www.legendspublishing.net

Copyright 2005 by Legends Publishing

ISBN: 0-9543682-5-8

First Edition

Printed by EUROPRODUCTION Sp. z o.o. Warsaw, Poland

Foreword
& Contents

I believe it's fair to say that Spurs have enjoyed many more great individuals than great teams and that one book alone could never do justice to them all. White Hart Lane Legends - Volume One, introduces some of the men who placed Tottenham Hotspur on the football map, while relating their stories frankly and first hand. In various, no-nonsense interviews, some of our past icons reveal their lives and stories behind the scenes; lives that, to this day, have largely remained under wraps.

I take great delight in introducing this group of men and genuinely hope that you will share the feelings and emotions behind their achievements and careers – as well as their total honesty. Many have lifted the lid on stories previously untold, and bared their souls for us the fans to read. Some may well have opened old wounds, but none side-stepped the all-important issues, or the truth behind them.

In thanking each of the following for their time, generosity, and openness, I would also like to pass on the following acknowledgements.

> **Legend**: *A traditional story from the past, which may or may not be true. Popular but unfounded belief.* The concise Oxford Dictionary

Thanks to; *Tommy and Jean Harmer*

For the personal use of Tom's compelling scrap-book, and for your collective hospitality and warmth - and the copious supply of coffee and doughnuts that punctuated my visits.

Cliff Jones

For your expressive love of life, passion for club and country, and uncomplaining nature whenever I needed help. Great player, great man.

Ron Henry

For your humour, help, and hospitality; It's easy to understand why the 'Double' team was so difficult to beat.

Graham Roberts

For helping to kick start this book, for your giving nature, and for not thumping me during its production. Your overwhelming passion for Spurs was inspirational.

Phil Beal

With Greaves, Jennings, and Perryman one of my own personal heroes. Thanks Phil, we genuinely appreciated all your efforts and incredible humour - and always will.

Morris Keston

For your incredible support, intelligence, and backing. If impressed by your lifetime story before, I'm absolutely stunned now!

Keith Burkinshaw

Thanks to Steve for introducing me to a man of integrity and steel, and to Keith for his characteristic honesty. As we spoke, I could see the Wembley scoreboard flashing, 'Tottenham Hotspur – Centenary FA Cup Winners 1981' – Unbelievable memories.

Gary Stevens

For your open expressive nature and strength of character; From heaven, to hell, and back . Apart from compiling your story, I also learned from it.

Pat Jennings

Thanks again Pat. I'm forever in your debt for the time you afforded me, and for your reassuring and meticulous attention to detail. The man certainly matched up to the Legend.

Steve Perryman

Sincere thanks for never complaining when I called you late at night; for creating time and effort to introduce me to many of my old Spurs heroes; and for opening my eyes to the true meaning of leadership and loyalty. The spirit of Nicholson lives on through your eyes and heart.

Eddie Baily

I'm indebted to Steve for our initial introduction and remain mesmerised by the dynamo behind many a great Spurs victory. Eddie, your incredible wit, knowledge, and fighting spirit will live with me forever. No Spurs fan should ever under-estimate the effect those qualities had on our great club.

Jo

Thanks for your faith in me during the rough times, and added belief through the rougher ones; for your support and love.

Keith Palmer

Tommy
Harmer

Era 1950-1960 as a pro. Signed Amateur forms in 1945
Appearances 205 **Goals** 47

If ever a player epitomized the image of the archetypal Tottenham player it was Thomas Charles Harmer; endearingly known to the football world at the time as "Harmer the Charmer". Born in Hackney, London on 2nd February 1928, Tommy represented Spurs both as an amateur and as a highly acclaimed professional.

With scintillating ball skills, allied to a diamond-edged footballing brain, this jinking, body-swerving, imp of a man was sadly denied the glut of international caps that most other countries would have fallen over themselves to award.

A million words have been written about the mercurial forward, but none more pertinent than those penned by the late, great, Danny Blanchflower, a friend and team-mate of Tommy's from those amazing glory nights which have underpinned Tottenham's illustrious history.

These words were taken from Danny's own 'Right Inside Soccer' column in 1958-59. I believe they do the little man full justice and were found in Tommy's personal scrapbook.

Nothing Can Stop Tommy
by Danny Blanchflower

"Harmer the Charmer" is sweetly on song. Throughout the changing conditions of this soccer season; the green grass of early season, the deep mud, the heavily sanded, circus-ring-of-a-pitch at Newport, and last Saturday's hard, slippery surface of slow thawing frost, Tottenham's diminutive Cockney genius has given performances laced with cheeky skill, proving that his subtle magic is highly potent whatever the state of the pitch.

Tommy Harmer, phenomenal gnome, is unique in English soccer. Our style demands much vigour and strength, speed and stamina. Harmer survives and prospers on sheer skill.

Most little players are fast running and nimble. To beat their men they rely on short, quick strides, acceleration, and a fair degree of ball control. Harmer, lacking speed, relies solely on his brilliant ball control, and to my mind this is the greater art. The little fellow may be slow moving, but he's quick-witted. Like the bullfighter, he mesmerises his opponent. Moving with graceful rhythm he takes the ball with perfect control impudently close to the bewildered enemy; and continues past him with leisurely ease.

Harmer grew up in East London, his playground the humble streets of Hackney. There he joined the traditional battles for the bouncing ball. With social conditions changing, he will be among the last of the truly great players to graduate from street football. But through-

out his career critics have doubted his effectiveness. They have made much of his lack of physique and done scant justice to his skill. I have played with and against many great inside-forwards, very few have been better than Tommy Harmer.

His timing and delivery of a ball through the middle for an on-running, scoring forward is one of the most deadly things I've seen in football. I know that occasionally he is swamped into obscurity in a game that has too much endeavour and too little design. But I would gladly fight these battles for him, knowing that more often than not, one little magic twinkle from him is likely to turn the game in our favour. It is characteristic of the England team selectors, who seem to prefer brawn to brain, that they should ignore Tommy Harmer. - I wish he were an Irishman." Danny Blanchflower

Tom, after all these years you still live on Tottenham's doorstep. Have you always been a Spurs man?

Yes, although as a lad, I had the chance of going to the Arsenal too. I went to school in London Fields and have always lived locally. We've been here in this house, which was a Spurs club house, for over fifty years now and have never considered moving elsewhere. We have all our friends and all our memories here, and Spurs are just down the road.

Was it always going to be football for you?

I was, and still am, football mad. I'd always be out with my friends kicking a ball around, although I was always the smallest, and the bigger lads couldn't get the ball off me. I did an early apprenticeship in the print with a company called East and Blades, and then went back to the City after my playing days, working for Bank Hapoalim as a messenger. I'd spend mornings in the print and then my afternoons were totally taken up with football.

What was it like in those early days in football?

We used to have a lot of respect for our clubs in those days. The money wasn't as important as turning on a top display on a Saturday. When I got married I was on £10 per week during the summer, and £12 in winter. Despite earning more than the average man in the street we were always realistic about what could happen later in life.

Jean and I have been together for over fifty years now. Despite my football career, she worked everyday as a dressmaker for a company called Jaqmar of Grosvenor Street, W.1. They made luxury dresses for royalty and the aristocracy. Then she spent twenty years working in a shoe shop in Wood Green. We simply wouldn't let the fame and notoriety affect us in any way. It just wasn't like that in our day. The camaraderie in football back then was special and nobody was allowed to get above his station. I'm not so sure that's the case these days. The rush to over-reward some quite average players is ruining today's game.

You were constantly reminded of your diminutive size during your career. Did it affect your game and what did you go through to try to get your weight up?

It's not so much about what I went through as what went through me! Yes, I was a little fella, but my main assets were my ball-juggling skills and will to win. It sometimes seemed more important for members of the press to remind people that I was five foot five and nine stone four rather than concentrate on what I did best. Spurs put me on a diet of steak and cod liver oil pills and hours of weightlifting, all to no avail. Whatever they pumped in to me didn't work. I just remained the same old Tommy, not that it bothered me. You don't have to be a giant to play the game well!

You mention your frustrations with the Press, but there must have been some who judged you on more than height alone?

Oh yes. One stands out like a shining beacon. I was great friends with the sadly departed Reg Drury. What a gentleman Reg was, and if you told him something in confidence, it never got out. He was a man true to his word and all of us players trusted him with our lives. He's sadly missed. What a lovely man he was and the consummate professional.

Who was the earliest influence on your football career?

The first one was my Uncle Ted. Often he would pop round from home, or from his job in a grocery store to show me as many skills as he could. We'd make him a cup of tea, then he'd spend most of his spare time showing me how to control the ball, and how to use it properly. He taught me the back-heel trick which became one of my favourites. Our training ground was the small garden at the back of the house.

Tell us about your Spurs League debut?

It was a home match against the unbeaten League leaders of the time, Bolton Wanderers. Peter Murphy was unfit so Arthur Rowe, the then manager, drafted me into the team at inside left.

We won two-one and the papers were full of comparisons between myself and Eddie Baily, another Hackney-born Spurs man. Team-mates on the day included Billy Nicholson, Ron Burgess, Les Bennett, all playing against Wanderers and the great Nat Lofthouse. All this in front of 61,000 screaming fans. I'd been given one hour's notice to play in a very important game.

1945–46 Harmer [front row second left] and the Tottenham Juniors show off their silverware

The Little & Large Show — Bobby Smith scores for Spurs, Tommy Harmer turns to celebrate

In the space of eight days, I represented the club in 'A' League, the reserves, and the first team, and thoroughly enjoyed the experience. In retrospect, Arthur Rowe really protected me that day. He'd only told me at short notice that I'd be playing. He simply didn't want me to worry or get butterflies!

Who was your toughest opponent?

There were many, but the one who sticks out in my mind was a diminutive lad from Europe. His name was Adolf Hitler!

Tom, please explain!

I loved Hackney and my life there, but Adolf had other ideas. The area was smashed to pieces during the War so I was evacuated to a small village in Norfolk. Everyone there was very kind to me but we had little time or opportunity to play football. After a year, I returned to Hackney and London Fields School.

My parents thought I'd do well as a cabinet-maker, that is, until I found myself doubled up in pain at the smell of polish. So another job was found for me and I moved to become a messenger with a big firm of printers. Walking home from work one evening I met an old friend who was playing football for the Shoreditch Naval Cadets.

It turned out they were short of players so this pal invited me to turn out for them. I enjoyed the game which, by a chance in a thousand, was against the Hackney Naval Cadets, who were then a very powerful side.

Eleven of their players were Tottenham Hotspur juniors and, although we were beaten, I seemed to make quite an impression. Johnny Westwood, who later became a Spurs professional himself, told Tottenham officials that I was worth a trial and was duly invited to play a match for them. They seemed happy with me and that's how I signed on the dotted line as a Spurs amateur, despite young Adolf.

Next step was the Army. What was that like?

I'll never forget being called up for my National Service medical. The doctor looked at me, I looked at him, he shook his head and my legs trembled. My seven stone, seven pound frame really seemed to hypnotize the doc.

In due course he called in two more medical men. The three of them then proceeded to walk round me hardly believing their eyes. When the inspection finished I expected to be told to go home and grow up. Instead they said "A.1" and I was dispatched to Colchester to learn the soldiering business.

Were they happy days for you?

My days in the Army were mainly happy ones because I learned the full meaning of team spirit and the value of good friends. I had quite a few laughs too. A sergeant strode into the classroom at Hillsea Barracks one afternoon and announced I was wanted at once in the guardroom. All eyes were fixed on me, while I wondered what crime I'd committed, and imagined all kinds of impending punishments.

But it was nothing like that. The barrack's team, being a man short, wanted me to turn out for them. I did, and wore two pairs of thick socks to fill the boots they gave me to play in. Because they were two sizes larger than my feet, the lads gave me a good ribbing.

Whenever I see a Guardsman now I have a little chuckle to myself for it was in an Army XI, which included ten six-footers, that I played my first representative game. I looked, and felt just like a small boy who had stumbled across the game by accident - despite that we won eight-one.

I understand you nearly went to Bournemouth before Spurs?

Yes, that was in 1948. Bournemouth had seen me play for the Army and offered to sign me as a professional. They even said it could be arranged for me to finish my apprenticeship down there, but I declined and played as an amateur for Finchley. I simply didn't want to leave my London home. My partner up-front in those days was George Robb, the great England amateur international, and one of the most gifted players I ever met. Spurs then offered to sign me as a part-time pro. I agreed and became a full-timer in 1949.

You scored many goals from dead-ball situations, but weren't you once castigated for the way you took penalties?

Yes I was. In one three-all draw with Newcastle, I approached the ball, pretended to kick it and stopped. I repeated this again and then comfortably stroked the ball past keeper Ronny Simpson, who later went on to become a big Celtic hero.

The papers were full of questions asking whether I should be allowed to do this or not. Fortunately, the referee decided that there was nothing in the rules to stop me so he let the goal stand.

So were you the David Beckham of your day?

[Laughs] ...Without the cars, houses, or the money.

Any other vices?

I smoked like a trooper, even in the dressing room!

It is said that yourself and Eddie Baily split the fans at Spurs. Some preferred your own more flamboyant style, and others took sides with your team-mate. How did you see it?

Tommy warms up for the match with Tottenham manager Arthur Rowe

Well, let me start by saying that Eddie and I always got along very well. It was the manager's job to decide who played, and the supporters didn't always agree with those decisions. My game was built around ball-juggling, misleading and mesmerizing opposing defences, while Eddie's involved keeping the ball moving.

Eddie didn't kill the ball like I could, a fact appreciated by many of the fans, and a growing band of admirers outside the club. It was just that we were two different kinds of player, with our own ways of affecting a game. Eddie was first class, and an exceedingly strong player.

You felt compelled to seek a move away through lack of games?

As much as I loved my time at Spurs I was forced to seek a transfer to boost my career. I received so many positive accolades from around the world but was constantly overlooked in favour of others, invariably this was put down to my size.

I must admit, I never wanted to leave but couldn't bear being left out of the side for long periods. In the end I was extremely happy that certain individuals talked me out of leaving earlier. I loved my Spurs years.

So wasn't this just yet another case of the little guy being cast aside for somebody more robust?

There are some in football who think you have to be big framed to be effective. I hope that there is a long enough list of players who have slipped through the net to prove that adage wrong. Johan Cruyff wasn't exactly a giant, nor was Maradona.

So are you trying to tell me that size doesn't matter?

Sifting through my career scrap-books I've found a number of descriptions regarding my size, or lack of. Things such as 'Tiny Hero', 'Tom Thumb', 'The Wonder Midget', 'Mighty Atom', 'Spurs Imp', and 'Fly-weight'. The Press guys loved to paint me that way, although I looked after myself out there on the pitch in the same way that the smaller rugby lads do against their larger opponents.

Their descriptions didn't hurt me. I just used to think that they were concentrating on the wrong part of my game. Comments like, 'The build of a thirteen year old', 'Fragile as a ballerina' and 'The circus act in football boots' were more to flower their reports than a fair assessment of my skill.

In one fifth-round cup game against Doncaster, I was played on the right wing, while five foot three Terry Dyson played on the left – the little squirt [laughs]. Both of us played like giants that day.

Team-mates on tour: Tommy, Harry Clarke, Charlie Withers and Ron Burgess take it easy

What was your relationship with the fans?

Excellent. They always treated me very well and were very eager to let me know that they were completely behind me. It really upset some of them that I wasn't more of a permanent fixture in the side, and some thought I should have been given an England chance. Alas, that's all in the past now, but I'm a fan of Spurs as well as an ex-player.

Did you get to know many fans personally?

I grew very close to two particular Tottenham fans. One is Morris Keston, the other a chap called Ted Willis, who many older fans will know by reputation. Ted was born in Tottenham but moved south of the river at the end of the War. Jean and I often used to see Ted and Audrey socially and got on exceptionally well with them. Ted, of course later became Lord Ted, and was the man behind "The Blue Lamp" and "Dixon of Dock Green". The series was a British institution during the fifties, sixties, and seventies. Unfortunately Ted died in 1992 at the age of seventy-four. He was a big Tottenham fan and is still deeply missed.

Morris is still around and keeps in contact with Jean and I to this day. He is an extremely kind and generous man who is as loyal to Tottenham Hotspur now as he was back in the old days. It's a pleasure to have known both of them.

Pitches were terrible in your day Tom. How did you cope with ankle-deep mud being the type of player you were?

In some ways it was in my favour. I didn't weigh very much so didn't get bogged down as much as some of the bigger, heavier lads. Thing is, you had to make do with what clubs had available at the time. We never questioned the state of pitches then as much as they do now and there was no under-soil heating as such. If you're a good pro you should be able to play on anything!

I remember a game against Newcastle where four footballs were used due to the mud and terrible conditions; two white ones, and two orange ones. It didn't stop us from turning on an exciting game for the fans, although we were all ankle deep in mud at the time. We just got on with it.

You played in Bill Nicholson's first managerial league game at White Hart Lane, that famous ten-four victory over Everton. What memories do you have of that one?

I'd been dropped for the preceeding four games and went out on the pitch that day with a lot to prove. I felt that, with a new manager, I had a golden opportunity to show what I could do and therefore bolt down a more regular place in the side. Everton's first choice keeper had been injured on international duty for Eire the week before and was replaced by understudy Albert Dunlop.

Poor old Albert must've suffered severe backache from picking the ball out of the net so many times that day, and I'll never forget scoring my goal in the 78th minute. A left-foot screamer into the net from the edge of the penalty box if I remember rightly.

Everything fell right for us that day, although we made most of our own luck. It was a marvellous way to welcome Bill to the managership too. Ten-Four... The highway patrol game!

And what of Bill Nicholson himself?

I always got on extremely well with him and saw him over at White Hart Lane right to the end. He was an exceptional manager whose achievements were never really officially acknowledged. I understand there was a campaign to get the man a knighthood. He deserved something like that.

Did you ever consider management after your playing career?

No, not really. My last contact with football was at Chelsea where, having played for the first team, I went on to coach the reserves. I actually scored the goal which clinched promotion for them in a one-nil win at Sunderland in 1963.

Which players did you work with?

I helped train lads like Peter Osgood and Alan Hudson under the managership of Tommy Docherty. When he left the club in 1967, I was offered the chance to take over as manager at Torquay United, but decided I didn't want to move from London, and wasn't altogether sure if I fancied management.

At most clubs there's always somebody trying to interfere with what the manager is doing. I always loved my football and never felt under any sort of pressure. I'm happy being the same way to this day.

During your Spurs years you were connected with many other clubs. What stopped you moving during what must have been very frustrating times?

I was born and bred in London and my ties here with family and friends were very strong. I didn't want to break that all up. Torquay was a hell of a long way away for a London lad.

As a player, certain newspapers were always linking me with other clubs, such as Arsenal, Charlton, Ipswich and Orient when Eddie Baily took charge there. A number of clubs abroad were apparently interested too. At one time, it was reported that up to twenty clubs were in for me.

It was really frustrating knowing that the Press and fans of many other clubs were pushing my name for international recognition, but I couldn't always get in to my own club side! I did represent England at 'B' level, but I'd have loved to have pulled on the white shirt for the first team.

Do you remember your transfer fees when you moved clubs?
Yes, when I moved from Spurs to Watford it was for £6,000. Then, when I moved on to Chelsea they paid £3,500 for me. Spurs got me as an amateur so it cost them the grand sum of a tenner a week to sign me.

I used an article by Danny Blanchflower as part of Tommy's introduction in the book, and with their kind permission, I've replicated an article by Frank McGhee in the Daily Mirror of Tuesday, April 23rd, 1957 to conclude. Spurs had beaten Charlton six-two at White Hart Lane, and the England World Cup squad for 1958 was about to be announced. I believe it ably sums up what a lot of Tottenham fans were thinking at the time.

Harmer's the Charmer For England

"England's selectors meet later this week to name the party of players who will make up our World Cup squad for games against Eire and Denmark next month. I wish I could have forced them all at gunpoint to turn up at Tottenham yesterday. I would cheerfully have pulled the trigger on the whole bunch after the match if they had still refused to recognise that there is one man who must not and should not be ignored by them again.

No prizes for guessing who – it's Tommy Harmer the Tottenham charmer, that little genius whose frail frame is packed with sheer shining soccer talent. This game was folding up fast at half-time. Spurs were ambling along, apparently content with their one goal scored by Robb, and Charlton, fumbling along, unable to do anything about it. Then Harmer took over.

After missing a penalty in the forty-sixth minute [he hit a post] Little Tommy grabbed this game by the scruff of the neck, shook it up, and made it great. Timetable of his wizardry reads; Great goal fifty-two minutes; A great right-foot goal. Fifty-six minutes; A brilliantly judged through pass for inside-left Johnny Brooks to score. Sixty-five minutes; Another inch-perfect pass for outside-right Terry Medwin to make it 4-0. Sixty-seven minutes; Harmer goes it alone for his second goal. Eighty-eight minutes; A nonchalant back flick gives centre-forward Bobby Smith number six. In between the fifth and sixth goals, right-half Danny Blanchflower put one through his own net and Charlton inside-left Stuart Leary broke away to score his side's last goal in the First Division.

Spurs' fourth goal, scored by Medwin, marked a mile-stone in the record books. It took the club total to 100 – the first time a First Division club have done this for twenty years." Frank McGhee

Graham
Roberts

Era May 1980 - December 1986
Appearances 276 **Goals** 36

Simply hearing his name still sends a ripple of excitement down the spine. After years of defensive weaknesses, Graham represented our first serious centre-back option since the days of iconic stalwart Mike England.

'Robbo' was a fighter; a man who would not consider the word defeat, and thoroughly warranted his media tag as Spurs' hard man. His formidable partnership with Paul 'Maxie' Miller destroyed the notion that Spurs were an easy touch and nothing more than 'Southern Softies'. I can promise you, they certainly wouldn't have said it to his face!

Graham's early career began at hometown club, Southampton, eventually enjoying spells with fellow South-coast sides Bournemouth and Portsmouth. Believing that opportunity had not exactly beaten his door down, Roberts went on to sign part-time for non-League Dorchester and Weymouth, doubling as a shipyard fitter's mate. Subsequently, a chance meeting, and an uncanny twist of fate would see him plying his trade with Tottenham Hotspur, later appearing in the Centenary FA Cup final, minus two teeth, just a year later.

With that inimitable swagger and trademark barrel chest, Roberts went on to yet another FA Cup final win a year later. He also won seven international caps, including one as captain of the England 'B' side, and, at the time of writing, was the last Englishman to lift the UEFA Cup aloft. Not bad for an amateur with a spanner.

Graham was sadly sold on to Glasgow Rangers in 1986 not long after David Pleat took over the helm. In the eyes of many, he had a good few years left in him in for Tottenham Hotspur. The fans' consensus being that, in the long term, we never ever replaced him. Unsurprisingly, Graham went on to further successes in the Glasgow giant's colours, later moving on to Chelsea and West Bromwich Albion, who, ironically, had thought they'd secured his services just before he'd signed for Spurs. Truth is, he never really wanted to leave.

Off the pitch Graham Roberts is exactly what you saw on it; straight, direct and passionate. He's a man who would gladly walk through walls for the cause of Tottenham Hotspur Football Club.

I'd like to take this opportunity to thank the following; Graham's parents for always having total belief in him, Bill Nicholson for his intuition, and the nameless man who recommended him. He should be made honorary Chief Scout!

Important things first Graham. You're not going to hit me are you?
Not now. There's plenty of time left for that.

So where did it all start for you?
As a player, it all started at my hometown club, Southampton. Before that I'd adopted my dad's favourite team, Everton, and followed them home

and away with him. Saints were my second club having been born there, although allegiances change drastically when you've played for a club like Spurs. I'm Tottenham through and through now, and always will be.

Dad and I are very close. We saw many games together which gave me a great awareness of what fans want to see. In my opinion, some modern day players don't acknowledge or reward their fans enough. After a four or five hundred mile round trip it doesn't take much to go over and clap them, or to sign as many autographs as it takes. Supporters appreciate you more when you appreciate them. What does it cost you, half an hour of your time?

If I were a League manager, I'd make sure my team acknowledged their fans for their support and all their efforts, win, lose or draw. A club is nothing without them.

Things didn't go too well at the beginning of your career. Did you ever lose heart?

Definitely not! I strongly believe that the harder you work in football the more you'll get out of it. If you really want something enough, hard work will nearly always get you there. In fact, it was the set-backs that inspired me to succeed.

All of the truly world class players, now and back then, work tirelessly for their teams. That ethic certainly worked for me. I saw some players just fall by the wayside or under-achieve because they felt they'd already arrived. Maybe it was too easy, or they simply didn't want to put in the required effort to get to the top. I saw some extremely talented lads drop out of the game because either their attitude was wrong, or they couldn't, or wouldn't apply themselves.

You looked comfortable wherever you played. What was your favourite position?

I started out life at centre-forward, so playing the odd game a bit further up the field never really bothered me much. I felt I was a reasonable ball player, and always performed with a passion that the fans could associate with. I played with the same fire and spirit whether at the back, midfield, or up front. I even played in goal once for Spurs, although I'm best remembered for my role at centre-back. You just never know what's round the corner in football. My non-League days, either side of being a pro have taught me that. The ethics are simple; never let your head drop, never stop working or learning, and never lose heart.

So you were a ship-builder's mate. Didn't you have any pals of your own?

[Laughs] I signed schoolboy forms with Southampton but ended up playing as an amateur for both Bournemouth and Portsmouth. After I broke an ankle at Pompey, I drifted into non-League with Dorchester. Weymouth then put in a £6,000 bid for me. That suited me as they allowed me to sign part-time and keep my ship-fitting job.

Spurs weren't the first senior club to come after me at Weymouth. I'd already had chats with Oxford United and I'd actually gone up to The Hawthorns to see Ron Atkinson. But then the name Tottenham Hotspur came in to the mix.

While playing for Weymouth against Telford, I spotted big Ron Atkinson and Mick Brown in the crowd. I knew Ron from Kettering and he soon cornered me and said he'd like to sign me for West Bromwich Albion.

I travelled up with my first wife, had a look around, and was asked if I'd like to play in an up-and-coming testimonial match. I believe a fee of £35,000 was agreed. As I was about to put pen to paper, I was told that Spurs wanted to sign me. When the great Bill Nicholson wanted to see you, the 'no' word was not an option.

Big Ron was absolutely furious and immediately flew into a rage, trying his best to stop me leaving his office. He was going absolutely mad, but what made it worse is that my wife wanted me to sign for West Brom.

I have massive respect for Albion as a club, especially considering I ended up playing there after my Chelsea days, but when a club of Tottenham Hotspur's stature comes a-calling the least you can do is go and listen to them. The thought of such a big club, with that superb support, won me over but I still often wonder what it would have been like playing alongside Bryan Robson every week. But I was lucky in my career, I played with, and against, some of the best players in the world.

It must have been an awkward situation with Ron Atkinson, what was said?

After escaping from Ron's office, the wife and I argued all the way back down to Southampton! The missus still wanted me to go to West Brom, while it was firmly struck in my mind that I wanted Tottenham. I felt sorry for Big Ron's cat that night.

Next day we travelled to White Hart Lane, and twenty-four hours after that I trained with them. We looked at houses more or less immediately. When I first met Keith Burkinshaw the first question he asked me was what position I played in. Bill Nicholson had conducted the signing, while Keith had really never heard of me.

When we got back to Southampton that night the domestic dispute continued. Personally, I'd already made my mind up - it was no contest, so I rang Keith and agreed to sign for Spurs the following Monday morning. It was a great move for me, and one I've never regretted.

Wasn't there a great story behind Bill Nicholson finding you?

There certainly was. Bill was on en route to the West Country to look at another player. He found himself sitting on a tiny, countryside station one evening patiently waiting for his connection when a local man sat next to him. Instantly the stranger recognised Bill and asked where he was off to.

Bill said hello and explained his scouting mission to the guy. The man on the platform then went on to tell Bill not to waste his time, adding "The only player worth looking at in these parts plays for Weymouth".

This is what made Bill such a fantastic man. Impressed by such a glowing report from the local man, Bill re-routed to Weymouth and ended up signing me. How many other men would have the humility to redirect their journey? Spurs subsequently matched West Brom's offer, which was the largest paid to a non-League club at that time, and my life changed forever.

You said that you never regretted joining Spurs, can you elaborate?

Quite simply, it was such a fantastic family club. All the players, their wives and families, and all the staff pulled in the same direction. And I think that came across in the way we played. The friendliness of everyone was simply astounding. Tea ladies, cooks, players, backroom staff, every-body; they made it a truly homely feeling; a 100% family spirited club. That was a very special time in my career. Keith and Bill had created a true club spirit and everyone regularly met up at the club, or off-site. I still have many friends associated with Tottenham, and hopefully always will.

A football club is like any other business, there are personalities who will always naturally mix, and there are others who wish to remain a little more withdrawn. The squads that I was associated with were dedicated and focused professionals, and always aware that we were lucky to be playing for such a great club as Tottenham.

Being influenced by such great professionals as Bill, Glenn Hoddle and Steve Perryman, how could it be any other way? I had fantastic, fun times at Spurs, times I'll never forget as long as I live.

Who were your mates, and any secret enemies?

There were no cliques at Spurs. We had a professional job to do and I hope that was reflected in our results and performances. Of course, we had our extroverts, especially my defensive colleague Paul Miller, who always had something up his sleeve for training sessions and trips away. I sincerely meant what I said, we were all mates and mucked in together.

In reality, they'll always be disputes, a bit of pushing and shoving at training, or clashes of personality. At Tottenham we had very few, and people always laughed and mixed together whatever the heat of the moment produced. After all, football is a physical game played by competitive individuals. The chances of absolute harmony are more of a dream than reality. I played for a number of clubs, Spurs was always the happiest. I grew to think of it as my home.

Did you enjoy training?

Again, it was fun and varied, and the guys made it a pleasure to be there. I played under some great coaches in my years as a pro. They always made it hard but interesting, which usually paid off on match day.

Who was the biggest influence on your career?

It was always my Mum and Dad, who showed deep faith in both me and my career. They have both encouraged me through my whole life. I owe them everything.

As a professional I'd say Peter Shreeves and Keith Burkinshaw. Both helped me immensely after taking that giant leap from non-League to the top flight. Both never stopped prompting and trying to improve my game. I went on to win six full England caps and captained the 'B' team once, so they must have done something right. [laughs]

What are the strong and weak points in your personality?

I love kicking people who ask daft questions [laughs]. Strong points? I'm a good motivator. My record in non-League football speaks volumes for that. I hated losing. When I went out on that pitch I didn't care who I was playing against. It could've been the best player in the world. I knew what my game was about and wouldn't let an opponent change it. I guess I'm a very strong-willed character.

My weak point was listening to too many people, and I took too much bad advice. I gave some individuals too many chances. They took advantage of me and it taught me to be my own man.

Any funny moments stand out in your mind as a player?

There was one from my England days that makes me chuckle even now. Bobby Robson had picked me and I'd joined with a number of other new-comers. I was standing next to Ray Wilkins when Bobby asked "Who's that coloured lad with the ball?" The player was Luther Blissett.

Ray casually turned to him and said "Bloofer, that's Bloofer". All the lads looked at each other knowingly while Mr. Robson innocently boomed out, "Come on Bloofer, you must get on the end of these crosses quicker".

Most of the lads just collapsed with laughter. He did have a bit of reputation for mixing up player's names at the time, like in Hungary, when Bobby read out the team to us, and was filling in our respective roles. "Hoddle, I want you to take all the free kicks" he said. "Oh yes", he went on. "Hoddle, you can take all the throw ins." "And Hoddle, I want you to take all the corners". Kenny Sansom stood up and chipped in. "Well thanks boss. As Hod's doing so much, the rest of us might as well go back to England!" Despite those lapses in memory, Bobby remains one of football's true gentlemen.

Did you agree with your 'hard man' tag at Tottenham?

Well, to call me the only hard man at Tottenham is really a slight on my colleague, Paul Miller. He was like granite, but what a partnership. I always played better when Paul was in the team. It was a partnership in the true sense of the word. He used to flick 'em up, I used to volley 'em off the grass [smiles]. We played very well together.

Who were the toughest opponents in your era?

We usually went out in the first ten minutes to put our name on the game. Opposing forwards knew who we were and that we'd fight back if they started dishing out the dirt. There were some very tough players then. People, believe it or not, like Kenny Dalglish and Ian Rush.

Despite being great players they could both look after themselves when push came to shove. I also had tough games against the likes of Gary Thompson of Coventry, Peter Withe from Aston Villa, and big Cyrille Regis.

I remember passing an opposing centre-forward once while changing ends. We'd won the toss and as we crossed paths we also swapped a few words. He didn't come near me for the rest of the game, which we won four-nil. [laughs]. It's a tough game for tough people.

British football has always been based on the physical side and probably always will. You can watch a game on TV and never realise half the things going on out there. Shrinking violets lose. Even the most artistic and stylish of sides need a strong character to keep it all together. Dave Mackay's role at Spurs was a good example of that.

Spurs had some rough and tumbles with the emerging Wimbledon team in your day. Any particular memories from those matches?

They had taken the view that they were going to muscle their way to the top, and woe betide anybody who stood in their way. It wasn't the Spurs way, but you have to do what's needed on limited resources.

When it came to confrontations with Spurs, they saw us as 'fancy Dans'. The big-time Charlie's who'd roll over when it came to the rough stuff. Short-term it worked for them. Long-term their intentions have blown up in their faces, as their current predicament proves.

There was one infamous game where I got myself sent off on a stretcher. It was more like Rollerball with tackles flying in all over the place, which were mainly leftovers from previous matches. I remember going in exceptionally hard on Lawrie Sanchez, who I felt had been dishing it out for too long. The Press said I'd purposefully used my elbows.

I dispute that. Sanchez had swung a vicious kick causing me to crash to the ground. It was one of those heat-of-the-battle moments that often happen. Sometimes they get picked up, sometimes the ref misses them or even turns a blind eye.

After dismissing Sanchez, the referee, David Axcell, made sure that I was next on the red card list by standing over the stretcher and pointing to the dressing room. The great Bobby Moore, writing for his column in the Sunday Sport said, "It's the first time in my life I've seen a player sent off on a stretcher".

Yes, those games used to get a bit spicy, but we had two options; lie back and play to the media's image of soft-southerners, or stand our ground and fight back.

It was never in my nature to back down. Wimps don't win trophies and Wimbledon knew that as much as I did. In truth, I was the kind of player that opposing fans said they hated, until I signed for them that is. Everybody respects a winner in the team.

You got your teeth kicked out in the 1981 FA Cup Final, do you remember exactly what happened?

Well, it was like this. Lean forward. Only joking... It happened in the first half of the first game. Somebody knocked the ball down and Chrissy Hughton swung his boot and connected with me. There was lots of blood and I didn't know where I was for a few minutes.

By half-time my eyes had glazed over and the Doctor said I mustn't go out again. No way was I going to miss such an important game. I managed to slip quietly away to the toilet, then sneaked out of a side door and back on to the pitch before he could stop me.

I was supposed to go to hospital afterwards but celebrated so hard that I didn't need an anaesthetic. I was supposed to be out for about an hour and a half but woke up nine hours later. Apparently, my then wife had been up and down the ward showing off my medal and chatting with all the patients while I was spark out. I've got a bridge now. [Laughs] A daily reminder of a great Cup Final win.

How tough were those 'Derby' games against Arsenal back then?

The first one I ever played in was a one-nil home win in the old League Cup. We were ecstatic, and totally pumped up by the fantastic buzz in the ground. That night I felt so proud to be a Spurs player. I remember looking over to the Arsenal contingent and thinking, "Great, stuffed yer".

It's the extreme rivalry that makes football the great game it is. With thousands in our grounds, there are millions more at home depending on the result of a single match. Take that ultra-competitive rivalry away and you might as well close the stadiums.

It seemed to me that while the Spurs-Arsenal matches were in progress, sheer hatred was never far away. You could see it in the eyes of the fans; hear it in their excited voices and the way they inter-acted.

Half of the trouble with the way football rivalry is interpreted nowadays is down to the Press. On quiet days they can blow a story out of all proportion; at busier times they love to dwell on negativity.

Explain?

Take the situation where Arsenal and Manchester United were fighting it out for the championship in 2004. It's damned obvious that there's not a Tottenham fan alive that actually wanted Arsenal to win the title. Do turkeys vote for Christmas?

Unfortunately, the Press, radio and media were tripping over themselves to portray Spurs fans as 'disloyal' or 'bitter' because they actually wanted Manchester United to win on a one-off basis. Of course, if that title hadn't been at stake there's no way in the world that Spurs fans wanted United to take the game, and tell me one big-City club fan who would actually want their bitter rivals to celebrate the title?

What they never seem to understand is that if Arsenal win the League it seriously affects the swing of power in north London. Thousands of new youngsters will be attracted over to Highbury for the glamour of being associated with their success. Thousands of kids who could have supported Spurs defect in favour of the enemy down the road. Spurs subsequently suffer financially and lose droves of potential lifetime supporters.

It's not as simple as just wanting Arsenal to lose a game. It's more about protecting and building on club history, rather than a knee-jerk reaction to a single situation. Just ask the fans of Everton, Manchester City and Sunderland what I mean. When are the Press ever going to get real and acknowledge that fact?

Do you think the Arsenal rivalry has changed in recent years?

I have a lot of friends who support Arsenal. Looking at the bigger picture, I want Tottenham to top them in every way. They're the same with us. As much as some arrogantly state that we're no longer their rivals, you always know in your heart that we're the side they'd like to give it to the most. It's natural, and all part of human instinct.

In the seventies and eighties there were Spurs shirts everywhere. Now, all you ever see is red and white. I hate to see London kids wearing red. We need to reverse that trend and bring back the pride in being seen in a

Tottenham shirt. Apart from the fans, the Spurs logo is the most treasured asset of the club. It should be marketed to a wider audience and pushed in the same way that Manchester United did with theirs. Arsenal winning the League does our cause untold damage.

Do you think it's the same for the players?
Seriously, I've actually got a very high regard for Paul Merson for his loyalty to Arsenal. He was apparently offered the chance to go to White Hart Lane twice and turned it down because of his love and affection for the Highbury outfit and their fans. I'm the same. Once a Spurs man, always a Spurs man in my book and I just couldn't be seen in red. Crossing the great divide is not an option. I just can't understand why anybody would want to do it.

Tell me about 'that' tackle on Charlie Nicholas?
To be honest, I actually saw it as more of an accidental nudge, but his momentum took him high and fast over a hoarding. It looked much worse than was actually intended, and to be fair, it was Tottenham versus Arsenal at Highbury, not some Mickey Mouse game that didn't matter [smiles].

Given the same situation now, I'd probably challenge the same way as I did then, although the funny thing about it was getting punished twice. As Charlie ran towards the ball I slid in to dispossess him, then ended up on the ground. Their physio ran over to me, landed on top and proceeded to punch me in the face. Then I got booked.

I don't know how many people noticed that, although I bet Arsene would have missed it! I had a nice shiner the next day I know that. Like I said, it was a North London Derby. I took my punishment and got on with the game.

How did Charlie take it?
Charlie and I have worked together for SKY TV. We often share a laugh about that day. Let's be fair, as much as that tackle is brought up from time to time, he had the last laugh in the amount of goals he stuffed past us. He knows the score, and took it as an occupational hazard.

I was recently doing a commentary on a Ranger-Celtic game and the subject of that tackle came up yet again. As Charlie's face came on screen, Jim White said in the background "Well, at least he's still sitting in his chair at the moment".

Those incidents never leave your life and Charlie and I have laughed about it on many occasions. Once the on-pitch rivalry has gone we all remain good friends afterwards. I loved the 'derby' games. They bought out the best in me. I hope the fans realize that those games meant as much to me as they still do to them. I wasn't just a player; I was also a fan.

What about the drink culture in football then?

It was always there, but just a matter of personal discipline and how much you wanted to get drawn in. I liked a drink then as much as anyone else, although I'm nigh on a tee-totaller now. If anything, I get drunk on atmosphere and people's company more than booze.

I remember the first time I was picked for England. It was away at Hampden and I'd travelled up from London the day before. I decided to hit my bed early in preparation for the big day ahead when Alvin Martin and Bryan Robson came in and congratulated me on my inclusion in the squad. The pair of them skilfully talked me in to going out with the rest of the lads. I got back to the hotel at around three o'clock in the morning!

Thing is, you just can't do that anymore. Apart from there being a whole new thinking process behind soccer fitness and preparation now, the Press hover like vultures, waiting to blow a story out of all proportion. Most of the time about fifteen of us used to go to a bar - not for anything outrageous; just having a laugh and a chat and building on team morale. If that were now it'd end up headline news and everybody would be screaming for the manager's head and saying how disgraceful we were.

Now it's totally different. A lot of the fun and camaraderie has been taken away. It's sad in a way but that was then, and this is now. Yes, there was a big drink culture then, but the whole country has one!

Who were the great players you played with, and against?

The ones that stand out in my mind are people like Ruud Gullitt, Karl-Heinz Rummenigge, and Kenny Dalglish. Graham Souness was also a top quality player, and of course, Glenn and Ossie. Rushy was a very difficult player to mark. He always sat on your shoulder and used that devastating burst of speed to nip in for goal chances. Without doubt, he was the best striker of the time. What price any of them in today's game?

Others that come to mind were Ally McCoist and Terry Butcher at Rangers, and Ricky Villa, Stevie Archibald, and Steve Perryman at Spurs. But the guy who'd top my list every time is Glenn Hoddle. He was simply a class above, and it's a crime how he didn't go on to get a hundred caps. Michel Platini once said that, had Hoddle been a yard or so faster, he'd have been the best player in the world for his time.

Having had the honour of sharing a pitch with the man, I can only endorse those sentiments. I've been so lucky in my career. One minute playing part-time and thinking that would be my lot, and then scooped up out of the blue to face household names. Somebody up there must love me - sometimes!

Returning to Tottenham matters, what was life like with the two Argentines?

Ossie proved a very funny, highly intelligent and articulate man who'd try his best to speak like the rest of the lads. Unfortunately, "Totting-ham' was the closest he ever got to a real English word, that is, until he started to grasp more of the language than we had originally given him credit for.

As a player, the man just skipped across the turf like a spring lamb and, although only slightly built, put himself where others feared to tread. He had tremendous ability and was a real thinker on how the game should be played. He really was world class.

Ricky was also a very, very strong individual, who often said how proud he was to wear the white shirt. He quickly latched on that the crowd loved his flair and expressiveness and was deceptively skilful for such a big man - and what about that goal in the final against Manchester City eh? They both loved Tottenham Hotspur with a passion and still do to this day.

How did it feel taking to the pitch with those two boys?

The whole balance of the team, especially with those two lads on board was brilliant. What strikes me most about those days was waking up early on match days with butterflies in my stomach. You could feel the energy, excitement and anticipation even before reaching the ground.

Invariably, we'd drive down the motorway to White Hart Lane, watching the fans with their scarves flapping from their car windows, knowing that we'd be running out with such a strong side. How exciting was that?

With respect to my fellow non-Leaguers, I'd gone from humble Weymouth to the world famous White Hart Lane, and playing with guys that I'd only seen on a TV screen. Quite frankly, life doesn't get much better than that.

I've chosen three characters from that time; Bill Nicholson, Steve Perryman and Glenn Hoddle. Can you tell us what they were like behind the scenes?

Let's face it, Bill was, and always will be, Mr. Tottenham Hotspur. Why he wasn't knighted for his services to football is just beyond me. Talk about turn the fortunes of a football club around. Bill was a thinker, and his philosophies still exist in the players and people that he influenced over his career. Although he originally signed me, I didn't work with him much directly, but it was clear how much he was loved and revered throughout the game.

He was high up in an elite group of English managers of the day and never quite received due credit for his achievements. Bill did much the same job for Spurs that Shankly had achieved at Anfield, but without the accolades and in a much quieter way.

'Stevie P', or 'Skip' as he was generally known, was the best. Stevie was one of those players that boosted your confidence when you saw his name on the team sheet. Make no mistake, he was as tough as they come on the field, but a real ambassador off it. He loves Spurs, and his loyalty to the club should never be forgotten or underestimated. He could have joined Leeds or Liverpool when both were at their peak, but chose to stay loyal. You don't get many of those to the pound these days. And as for those record appearances, who's going to break that little record then?

Glenn was truly a phenomenon. He could do things with a football that other players only dream about. Of course, managers then should have built teams around him instead of slaughtering him for 'not running back' or 'getting a foot in'. Players like Glenn come around once in a lifetime. Why waste his talents asking him to do donkey-work?

What was Keith Burkinshaw's influence on you and the club?

Keith had a major influence on my career. He reminded me of Bill in that he was a quiet Yorkshireman, with a very dry but subtle sense of humour, and like Bobby Robson, was one of the game's gentlemen. At times he was too honest for his own good.

Keith once pulled me in to his office to tell me that I wouldn't make a midweek League Cup team, but would definitely play in his FA Cup side on the Saturday. I wasn't pleased, but realised the man had a difficult decision to make and that was his job. Although I felt pretty down, I worked hard to battle my way back in to the team. I absolutely hated missing matches.

We went on to lose the League Cup game three-one, but had Leicester City to look forward to in the semi-final of the big one at Villa Park. We beat them two-nil, and everyone geared up for Wembley. We even went away to do one of those embarrassing Cup Final songs. Graham Roberts singing. Yeah, really! Mind the double-glazing.

Keith was great for me. Although he carried on buying players in my position, they never quite removed me from office. But that's life in football, one minute you're the flavour of the month, next minute, who knows? It's a thin dividing line between enjoying being at the top and sinking into obscurity. Keith welded together a good side with quality running all the way through. Even the sub's bench had top names on it.

Tell me about the Championship that got away in 1984-85 and Keith's parting comments?

It's a crying shame that we never went on to win the League. I honestly feel that a stack of cup games was our eventual stumbling block. That team should have been Champions, and I guess it'll rankle with me forever that we didn't make it. Nobody's fault, just a sideline of being in so many competitions at once. I feel that Keith was one of the last real football men before 'the suits' came in to change the game.

Irving Scholar had great hopes for Spurs, and wanted to turn us into a massive European power. I feel that he genuinely had the club at heart but sometimes went a little over the top in the amount of power he wielded.

"There used to be a football club over there", Keith said at the time, words that may live on for a lot longer than anyone thought! Keith felt restricted by this and those parting words were directed more at the board than anywhere else. Keith is a dyed-in-the-wool football man, and when the football side is infringed on, it's time to go.

What was it like winning the FA Cups with Tottenham?

Un-be-lievable! If becoming a pro wasn't fantastic enough, to go on and win two FA Cups was just out of this world. The noise and emotion drummed up during those Wembley finals was just amazing. Spurs fans really know how to turn up the volume on the big occasion. At that particular time it seemed as if we were there every other week, what with FA Cup finals, replays, and Charity Shields, so they probably got more practice than most. Even so, nobody will ever be able to take those away from me.

Do you remember much about the games?

Basically, we got out of jail in the Saturday game in 1981. We were average in the first half and Manchester City looked like they had our measure. Tommy Hutchinson put them one up, then the same player 'fluked' an own goal with ten minutes left on the clock, just as it seemed we were dead and buried.

The second game was a complete contrast. That was a great spectacle of football played in an absolutely electric atmosphere. I've heard it said that a lot of Manchester City fans couldn't afford to travel for the Thursday replay, but even so, what a night!

What was the feeling in the dressing room before the replay?

The whole team had something about it that night. There was a collective feeling that, whatever happened, we'd win. A never-say-die approach that eventually won us the cup, and we know all too well what a great part the fans played in that final. Even when Steve Mackenzie scored his wonder goal, we still knew we'd win. We had the strength, the ability, and a steely determination that I'd rarely witnessed before, and the feeling that collectively, we were unbeatable.

After the Saturday game Ricky was distraught, and rightfully so. None of us had played particularly well and knew we hadn't performed to our ability. If everything went wrong in that first game, it certainly perked up in the replay. Keith simply told Ricky to buck up and look forward to doing the business on Thursday.

After all, we had a second bite at the cherry. I later learned that Stevie Perryman had told Keith to drop Rick because he felt that trooping off like that in the first game was wrong. Luckily Keith made up his own mind, and thank God he did.

Manchester City certainly helped make it a final to remember, eh?

That game contained some great goals and yes, City certainly played their part. They were dogged and scored some excellent goals which got somewhat overshadowed by Ricky's solo effort.

That goal must go down as one of the all-time great Wembley strikes. In my own opinion, I think Mackenzie's volley should join it.

How did you feel as the replay neared the ninety minute mark?

As the first match went into extra time I felt as strong as an ox, and was ready to run through walls to get my hands on that trophy.

Then I mentioned to Pete Shreeves that I felt hot so he decided to throw a bucket of water over me! Suddenly I just felt like somebody had let all the energy out of my body. I felt drained, but luckily I managed to play through it.

Was the 1982 Final vastly different?

Nineteen eighty-two was similar in that the first game was dour. Having drawn on the Saturday, we were under the cosh for large parts of the replay. I think there was a simple reason for that. We were basically, well, knackered. We'd played so many matches that it finally caught up with us.

Were there any special tactics used to win the replay?

QPR seemed to be pressing the game but we got the impression that they were really trying to contain, then hit us on the break, or at the very least, take it to extra-time again. Then in a minute of inspiration, the ball came to me and I decided to go on a run. I'll never forget it.

I just kept running towards the gaps and brushing off challenges. It was almost as if the Red Sea had parted. As I zoomed in on goal, Bob Hazell tried to upend me, before Tony Currie finally hacked me down. The ref blew for a penalty. Glenn stepped up and casually stroked the ball past Peter Hucker in the Rangers goal.

Okay, so it didn't have the excitement and end-to-end flair of the previous year, but we were happy to take the cup back to White Hart Lane. I loved the cup runs. They're so special to everyone associated with the club. Spurs have a great cup history, let's hope those days return, and soon.

Tell us about the players in those cup runs?

From the back, we had two top class keepers. Ray Clemence's record speaks for itself, while Milija Aleksic was probably the most underrated keeper in the country in 1981. Then there was 'Maxie' and I at the back; the two gentlemen of the team [laughs], with Stevie Perryman and Chrissy Hughton as full-backs. Chris was a good footballer; a quick, tough player who definitely took no prisoners. Again, so underrated, yet thoroughly professional.

The midfield was simply world class; Ossie, Ricky, the tireless Tony Galvin, and gifted Glenn. I felt so sorry for Mickey Hazard at times to be around in the same era as those four, especially when you consider what a special little player he was. In most other times Mickey would have become an absolute White Hart Lane hero. Up front we had Garth Crooks and Steve Archibald. How could you better that at the time?

Crooksey latched on to anything coming from over his shoulder, and Archie did so much running for the side. That was a team packed with internationals, and it showed. We've had class internationals since, people like Gazza, Chrissy Waddle, and Richard Gough, but with respect, no Spurs team since have come close to what we had then.

You're the last Englishman to hold the UEFA Cup aloft. What are your memories of that time?

What people forget is that we had some tough ties that year, and after a straightforward opener against Drogheda of Ireland, six-nil and eight-nil, we were matched against Bayern Munich. Unfortunately, we lost the first leg to a Michael Rummenigge goal near the end. It was a freezing cold night but things really heated up on the pitch.

The ref was kept busy doling out yellow cards but we felt confident of getting them back down the Lane and putting them out. We won the second leg two-nil with goals from Archie and Mark Falco. Mark was another under-rated player I thought. Next up was Austria Vienna. They'd had us checked out the Saturday before against Stoke City and thought the same team would turn up. How wrong were they?

I remember their coach being very upset about our aggressive approach because in their League they just weren't used to it. Magyar, the Vienna midfielder, went on record saying, "As for Miller and Roberts, they are both wrong in the head." Poor chap. What I really think he meant was, "As for Miller and Roberts, they are both in the next round of the cup". Funny old game isn't it?

We drew the second leg two-all, with goals from Alan Brazil and Ossie. That was one of our best performances of the season and set us up for the semi-final with Hadjuk Split.

The last Englishman to hold up the UEFA Cup with Tony Parks, who made the winning penalty save

A nice holiday by the Adriatic, eh?

Hardly! The first game was played out against a backdrop of fireworks and driving rain. Mark Falco hit the first but they rallied to beat us two-one. Keith had told the papers that when Split came to White Hart Lane they'd find out what noise was all about.

Right on cue, the crowd lifted us to a one-nil home victory, inspired by Micky Hazard's first European goal of the season. We were in the final, and had the chance to repay Keith for all the hard work and faith he'd invested in us as a team, and as individuals. It couldn't come soon enough for me.

The Final nights were so compelling yet so different. How do you remember them?

They were both explosive for different reasons. There were thousands of Spurs fans in Brussels for the first leg, and word got back that there'd been a shooting in the City centre.

On the pitch it was an extremely sad night for Stevie Perryman, picking up the booking that meant he'd miss the big party back in London. We all genuinely felt for him but it didn't stop Steve joining in the celebrations after a very tough first game.

That's the kind of man Stevie is. He's a team player who wouldn't let personal disappointment get in the way of what was best for Tottenham. The noise back at White Hart Lane I'll never forget.

You were made Skipper for the second leg. How did that feel?

Yes, I acted as stand-in captain for the match at White Hart Lane, and what a game it turned out to be. Anderlecht had some excellent players in their ranks. People like Morten Olsen, Frankie Vercauteren, Rene Vandereycken and Enzo Schifo, who was being hailed as Europe's new super-kid at the time. There were even rumours circulating that Anderlecht were interested in signing me. But why should I leave when I was so happy playing for Spurs?

Apparently, they approached Irving Scholar, although nothing came off it. As much as I respected them, and the excellent team they'd built, I'd become a Spurs man through and through and wanted it to last forever. It felt great leading the lads out to victory but somehow all of us had at least part of our hearts and mind on Stevie P.

What a truly fantastic night that was Graham!

Oh, It still sends shivers down my spine when I watch those games. Back at White Hart Lane they battled very, very hard. We knew they'd be dangerous being the cup holders, and so it proved.

Again, we were just one game away from giving Keith the send off he deserved. And the team that night wasn't all superstars either. Marvellous Mickey Hazard came in for the crocked Ossie, although Oz did get on for a while. Ally Dick and Mark Falco played, and the now infamous Tony Parks took over in goal for Ray Clemence.

Spurs didn't get off to the best of starts did they?
No, the night looked like it was going to go all wrong. Anderlecht scored first through Czerniatinski. They played very well but I managed to go through and score with six minutes left on the clock. The place went absolutely wild.

Do you remember much of the crowd scenes that evening?
I've rarely witnessed scenes in a football ground like that but didn't want the emotion of the moment make us lose concentration. We had to stay very strong and focused for the remaining minutes.

What had turned out to be a fantastic night nearly got soured before it had begun. We were in a bonus dispute with the club and it took intervention by Stevie Perryman to resolve the issue. Without diplomatic and speedy negotiating, we might never have played that final at all. Stevie stuck to his guns, we backed him, and the rest is history.

You clearly have a lasting admiration for Steve's captaincy?
Steve was a fantastic captain in my eyes - the king of them all. He made sure we did everything properly on and off the field. He kept our feet on the ground when it would have been easy to get sidetracked, and he made us focus on what we were supposed to be doing.

I actually asked him to go up and lift the cup, but he didn't feel it was right. He was club captain and all the boys would have loved to see him raise the trophy. Even so, I don't think UEFA would have allowed it due to the fact that he was officially suspended.

So tell us about your goal in more detail?
Even now I can still see Mark Falco pushing the Anderlecht lad out of the way. They would have cleared the ball had he not got his little nudge in. The ricochet hit my chest and off I went to equalize, but without that intervention we'd have lost our final chance of a trophy.

Overall it was a night of great emotion, but Anderlect weren't our only opposition that night. There were the bonus disputes, the disappointment of Steve's suspension and going one down, Danny Thomas' spot-kick miss, then of course the nerve-jangling penalty shoot-out, culminating in Parksey's save! Eventually the cup was ours.

We knew we'd be saying goodbye to Keith, but what a fantastic way to mark his time at the club. It really was so important to the whole squad to give him our 'going away present'. That was the best way to show our respect to him.

How did Keith react afterwards?
For once the tough exterior was down. Tears flooded Keith's eyes as he put his hands on the trophy. The celebrations went on long into the night, but I remember I had to be at the club at nine the next morning for a photo session, then off to the airport to fly to Scotland with the England squad. I'll never forget that night as long as I live. In fact, it was so good I wish it was tomorrow!

Talking of England, you went on to cap your career by representing your country. That must have been an amazing period in your life?
I like to think that all the hard work paid off, and the right people rated me highly enough to get to the top. I'm an extremely patriotic person so my England caps mean so much to me. I wore the shirt with immense pride.

But all good things come to an end, what was life like after Spurs?
After Spurs, I never thought I'd find another club with so much passion. Rangers were the perfect team for me and they'll always have a place in my heart too. They are another family club and once you've played for one of the large Glasgow giants it's very difficult to break that loyalty. Even now, I get Rangers fans asking if they can come and see me.

When I was managing Carshalton, a fanatical Rangers fan called asking if he and his mates could visit on a Saturday night. We agreed dates and he said a coach load of them would come. How shocked was I when two hundred and fifty turned up?

They spent the night emptying the bar, and the rest of it sleeping it off in the club house. The sight of those guys waddling back on to their coaches next morning really bought it home what loyalty is all about. It wasn't just me who was impressed, the local brewery had a good time too.

Tell us about the hat trick against Southampton in March '82?
It was a classic full set; the bobble, the miskick and the own goal! I was played in midfield due to injuries and wasn't popular back home that night.

Given the Spurs Manager's job, how would you change Tottenham's fortunes?
Personally, I'd lay my cards out from the beginning. I'd point out the prevailing financial situation in football, with a promise of new players

mixed with a good set of youngsters. We have some great kids coming through and some deserve a chance.

I'd explain that it was my mission to put Tottenham Hotspur F.C. back where they belong; and that's at the top of the tree of European football. I'd want the supporters to get behind us and pull together like they did a few years ago. Then I'd go out and employ winners; people who have tasted success and want to bring it back to White Hart Lane. The fans would then realise our intentions and where everyone stood.

What's the thinking behind that Graham?

With everyone pulling together, and I'm talking about the board, the management, and the fans, at least we'd have a united club with a proper sense of direction.

Fans may remember me as a combative, passionate type of player. That's what I'd try to instill back into the club. I've played at the highest standard under managers like Keith Burkinshaw, Bobby Robson, Peter Shreeves and Graham Souness. A big part of each of those men has rubbed off on me. I've won things as a player and I've won things in my time as a manager. I'd tell them that, if we all pull together, we'd pick this football club up by the laces and put it back where it belongs- at the top. Treat people with honesty and dignity, and they'll react to you. Keep them in the dark and all kinds of suspicions and accusations will come your way.

Do you have any lingering worries about Spurs?

If I had any minor complaint about Spurs in a long and happy association with them, it's in the way that they've seemingly forgotten some of the older players. The previous regime froze a lot of us out, and in an attempt at resurrecting some of that old Tottenham family spirit, I'd love to see all the old faces return.

There used to be a feeling about the place of building for now, and for the future, and of recognising what our great past was all about. I feel that maybe, some of that has been forgotten, and that much of the new era is more about money and commercialism than people.

Of course, much of that is necessary, and without wishing to dwell on the past, Spurs illustrious history is world recognised. You can't just dismiss it without understanding how important it is to the fans, and what an integral part we've played in world football. We're all part of a great club. Let's work together to make it even better.

Do you still have contact with Spurs?

No, I've sadly never been contacted by the club, or included in playing in certain benefit matches and testimonials. I'd have loved somebody to ask me and to have been more involved. Spurs are my club, and the way fans have reacted to me over the years makes me want to return and put something back in.

I remember some time ago when my mate wanted to buy a box at Spurs. While being shown around, one of the hostesses was asked questions about the names on the list of Spurs' England internationals. Somebody pointed out my name, and she went on, "Oh yes, he was a hard player by reputation; but I don't really know him". I was standing right next to her!

Those are the kind of situations that shouldn't happen. There are a lot of us ex-players who'd like to be involved at some level, or at least made to feel more a part of what's going on. After all, we are part of the club's recent history. In a lot of cases we love the club as much as the fans.

Hypothetically, and to answer your question honestly, if I were installed as manager tomorrow I wouldn't ask for much. Like everybody else I have a mortgage and bills to pay, but I'd walk back on broken glass to be involved at Tottenham.

Was there anything you *didn't* like at Spurs?

Easy, letting people down. I remember losing four-one at home to Burnley in the League Cup. That was the night I managed to score two own goals, both from crosses.

Trevor Steven's first skidded over and hit the bottom of my studs. Ray Clemence went one way, the ball went the other. I don't know who was the most surprised. The second one skimmed off me in to the net. We ended up having an absolute disaster that night and Burnley went on to play Liverpool in the semi's. Obviously those results happen to the best of teams. Even the greatest sides have their off-days. That was definitely one of ours.

To play for Spurs is any schoolboy's dream come true. To have all those expectant fans, and the eyes of the football world watching you at your lowest moment, tears you apart. I always worked doubly hard to put right any mistakes I'd made and tried my best not to let it effect me. My only consolation was that I'd made most of mine in the same game!

So what of the future Graham?

I recently became the new Manager of Clyde Football Club in Scotland. Having won much at non-League level, I felt it was a good time to step up to a League manager's job. I am still ambitious and you never know what the future will hold. What I can say is that I genuinely loved my time at Tottenham Hotspur, and always will.

Eddie
Baily

Era Player 1946-56, Assistant Manager 1963-74
Appearances 326 **Goals** 69

ddie began life as a small, bespectacled Cockney kid kicking a ball around the backstreets of Hackney, but he would later emerge as one of the true Spurs entertainers, becoming a driving force in the armoury of the great Bill Nicholson. Stocky, strong, and confident, Eddie fought off larger opponents with ease and was first spotted by a scout who doubled as a funfair dodgem controller. Quite apt really as Baily was a player who passed opponents for fun and electrified crowds all at the same time!

And it was those great Spurs performances that won Eddie his nine England caps, contributing five goals in his first handful of representative games. But Eddie wasn't just a player. He worked under some of the great managers of his era, and was known throughout the game for a spontaneous and rapier wit which remains to this day. "The Cheeky Chappy" could slay them with his tongue as well as with his feet.

Eddy Baily is now eighty years old, and the picture you may harbour of the average octogenarian should be dismissed straight away as I was left in little doubt that he could still coach or manage given the chance.

Eddie's forthright and brusque manner often disguised a sharp, calculating tactical brain. He knows he upset some, and is equally aware that he inspired others, but whatever Eddie did he loves the game of football to the core. Edward Francis Baily certainly inspired me.

You were first spotted by Spurs scout Jim Joyce playing for Hackney Boys, and according to some reports, wearing glasses. Is that true?

I was an under-fifteen playing for Hackney boys against Edmonton in the Corinthian Shield back in 1938. I was only a little skinny boy and did wear glasses then, but not while I was playing as documented in some reports. After our win, a little fellow introduced himself and asked me if I wanted to train with Tottenham. I looked at him and thought 'Who the hell are you?'

That man turned out to be 'Dodger' Joyce, who was actually in charge of the dodgems in a travelling fairground unit. He invited four of us to train with Spurs that day. I simply needed to know how I was going to get there and when.

I understand 'Dodger' had to visit your house afterwards to try and convince you to sign?

To be honest, I'd forgotten all about our meeting. Then one night there was a knock on the door at the family home at Inver Road, Clapton. It was Dodger again. I had four brothers and two sisters, and the last one in our 'ouse pulled the ladder up [laughs].

Dodger invited me to train on Tuesday's and Thursday's, offering to pay me a couple of shillings to get there. Luckily I had a bike at the time and cycled from Clapton to Tottenham on training evenings. On arrival the first person I laid eyes on was George Hardy, the old trainer. He was a big man with a big voice. He wore a trilby hat and a big white coat and welcomed me with a booming, "What's your name son?" That was my introduction to Tottenham Hotspur back in 1938.

Were you confident that you'd made the right decision to join Spurs as a youngster?

I was very cocky and confident in everything I did. I was the youngest in the family. My brothers were always trying to get me to run errands and do jobs for them, but I always told them to do it for themselves. I suppose I was always confident in sticking up for myself in that way.

Do you have any particular memories of those early days?

Dodger ran the Spurs youth side that played in the Edmonton Senior League. We were kids playing against grown men, because there were no junior Leagues in operation then. We played our games at the Norseman ground at Edmonton, which still exists to this day. I remember playing Crossbrook during the War with Spitfires and Messerschmitts above involved in a noisy dogfight. We simply went to the dressing room and carried on when the raid was over.

Where did the 'Cheeky Chappy' tag come from?

I don't know how that came about but I always seemed to have an answer for everything. If somebody said something I'd always be the first in with a quip. There were a lot of Cockney sayings in those days. I used to say things like, "If me Aunt had balls she'd be me Uncle" – innocent little Cockney sayings that we grew up with.

Did that sense of humour ever get you in trouble?

No, not really, because in that day and age people accepted banter and that kind of humour. I simply answered in my own way.

I understand you were a real sports all-rounder as a kid?

In 1938 I played cricket for London boys, then later on, started a couple of minor games for Essex seconds. I played to a reasonable standard too, and would seriously have preferred cricket for a living over football. As much as I loved cricket the problem was my poor eyesight.

How could you prefer cricket over 'The Beautiful Game'?

When you play cricket you're on your own. It's you against the bowler or vice-versa, whereas football is more dependent on the team. Batting was more individualistic. I could go out as a batsman and do my own thing. Essex sent me to Alf Gover's Academy where Andy Sandham, the famous opening Surrey batsman, used to coach me. I always remember him telling me that I'd never make a batsman because I didn't hit the ball right. He said I didn't have the co-ordination of left arm, left elbow, left eye.

He would tell me that my whole stroke play was out of synchronisation and that they'd get me out too easily. "You'll never get on in the game of cricket son" he used to say.

Apparently, I used to hit the ball from the off to the onside, which was a little unconventional in their eyes. I simply fell by the wayside unfortunately. So football it was!

You left school at fourteen and soon found yourself working on the Stock Exchange, did you enjoy that time?

After school, I went to work at the same firm as my brothers, Hunt Partners, who were a local printing company. I stayed for a year or so and learned all my fire-watching and air raid drills. Most people were being called up for the Army, so the companies filled positions with anybody who showed an aptitude, which was how I got my chance to move.

I knew somebody from the Exchange and went to work for Gustav Ellison in Draper's Gardens. At the age of fifteen I was doing Ledger work and Dividends, things that I didn't know my brain could handle. It was a thoroughly enjoyable experience.

Did you consider going on to become a Stockbroker?

I did at one time. The dealers were entrusting me with more and more work to do and had clearly taken to me. They seemed to be grooming me for the next step up.

They'd buy something in the morning and sell it back in the evening for a big profit. I thought this couldn't be too bad, and they were all making a good living out of it!

You signed for Spurs at seventeen but almost immediately went out to Europe to do your National Service. What was that experience like?

I left Tottenham and was called up to Colchester for six weeks. Then a posting came up. After I'd done my primary training, I got sent to join a Scottish Regiment in Edinburgh; the 79th Battalion of Royal Scots. I remember thinking, "Christ, what's this all about?"

We were preparing for the invasion of Norway, which got cancelled, and ended up going to Belgium, Holland, then through to Germany, where we were stationed just outside Bremen in a little place called Oldenburg. All of my service years were with the infantry.

I was very lucky with my timing because the German's were running away more than coming towards us by that stage of the War. Of course, it was a great experience and my two brothers were in the Artillery just down the road. Their unit was always supporting our forward divisions so consequently I saw a lot of them.

Those Army teams had lots of good pro's in them didn't they?

When the War was over, the Army started to think about football. Being in a Scots regiment they used to love a match on New Year's Day between the Scots and English in the unit. We used to have some bloody good games.

I'd been quite useful in the unit side so one of our officers recommended me to the British Army on the Rhine [BAOR] football team. I joined them in Hanover in early 1946 at the age of twenty-one. I found myself mixing with the top Army names of the time. People like Les Compton, Reg Lewis of the Arsenal, Billy Steel and Jimmy Cowan of Morton, Stan Rickaby of West Brom, George Lee, all famous and established players.

When did you rejoin Spurs?

I'd played in the BAOR side with Alec White, Chelsea's full back. It was Alec who suggested that his manager Billy Birrell would be interested in offering me a place at Stamford Bridge.

My trial coincided with the greyhounds having theirs around the perimeter track, and although two of my brothers were bookies, I didn't really know much about what was going on. Alec's feeling was right though because Billy offered me a non-contract form after the session. Players knew nothing about the implications of contracts then.

On the way home I bumped into Jack Chisholm, who was playing for Spurs at the time. Jack was on his way to Tottenham and asked if I fancied going with him.

When we got there we met Jimmy Anderson, who later went on to become Spurs Manager. Jimmy wanted me back and promptly phoned Chelsea to tell them that Spurs still held my registration from before the War.

Do you ever regret that?

I can't say I regretted it, because you never know how things would've worked out.

I thoroughly enjoyed playing with the lads at Tottenham and was glad that Jimmy had sorted the situation out with Chelsea. I might have missed out on a great opportunity.

If you'd gone off and played for Chelsea I guess that would have been deemed illegal?

I knew nothing about regulations then. All I knew is that they said they had my registration so I simply went by the tone of that conversation. In fact, I think I remember him offering me a tenner at the time to sign on. That seemed a lot of money then.

One name that peppers the history of that post-War era is that of Arthur Rowe. What do you remember of the Spurs manager?
Arthur was a good manager in the way that he encouraged you, and the way he made you feel. He wasn't nasty like some, but contrary to rumour, he never really coached us or showed us what to do. He thought there was no need, so we did a lot of it ourselves as there was a natural telepathy between the players already.

Arthur took over for the last game of the 1948-49 season. We won it five-nil but had long been recognised as one of the top passing sides of the time. Obviously, being an old Tottenham player he knew the club history, then he went over to Hungary for a while, where he'd been preaching a similar passing game.

He once said that he was glad he came back to manage Spurs because they played the way he loved the game to be played, which is passing the football. I said to him once, "Well you know why we pass it to each other? It's because we all play in the same colour shirts!" '
'Well thought!" he casually replied.

In your opinion, when was the defining moment that Tottenham's famous 'Push and Run' style was born?
I don't think it was ever born as such. To me, we'd joined a football team where ninety percent of our passing game was totally ingrained. I put a lot of it down to the fact that we all carried tennis balls in our pockets as kids and used to go up the road one-twoing them off walls, which taught us close skills from an early age. But nobody actually ever taught us to play that way at White Hart Lane, it just happened.

So why was the style attributed as a Tottenham invention?
I don't know why. The Press wanted to create a story I suppose, especially with the manager having been in Hungary. They just put two and two together and made twelve. I assure you, it was our own natural passing game caused by movement off the ball.

We simply never allowed the ball to stop. There were changing room sayings in those days like, 'A rolling ball gathers no moss'. 'Make it simple, make it quick'. Those things knitted us together as a team and had us all thinking the same way. The 'Push and Run' tag came in the fifties when we won the Second Division.

Eddie Baily jogging during training with Les Medley at White Hart Lane

Everybody was acknowledging it as a new game, but it wasn't really, it was the fact that we made ten passes as opposed to a traditional long one. But people used to appreciate it, and opponents would say, "I'll have you. I'll get you next time". We used to laugh and reply that they had to be quicker, much quicker. Because we had a natural flow to our game, we even used to pass to players who were already marked, which then was an unconventional thing to do. We just believed in keeping it moving. The opposition had to do the rest.

You were involved in a very controversial goal in 1951-52 against Huddersfield. Do you remember that one?

We'd won a late corner down the left-hand side, which the linesman claimed I hadn't placed properly. Consequently, the ref came running over and told me to move it. As he turned away, I took it as quickly as I could. Unfortunately, all I could see was his back. On hearing the whistle, I sent my corner-kick over, but the ball hit the ref square in the back of his head. He went sprawling, landing flat on his face in the mud, and the ball came straight back to me. Call it a reflex action if you must, but I chipped it back in and Len Duquemin scored. As we returned to the centre circle, the poor old referee was still picking himself up, wiping the mud away.

You hit him accidentally of course?

No, he just happened to be in the line of fire [laughs]. Of course, the goal stood and I shouldn't have played the ball twice, but the linesman shouldn't have given the goal either. I felt sorry for the ref in as much as it was all over before he came back round.

Did you feel sorry for Huddersfield, because they got relegated?

I agree, it did affect them going down but their situation was caused by results over a season, my corner was merely a reflex action. As it came back to me, I hit it like anyone else would have. As for the consequences of it, no, I didn't sit at home and cry.

Did you always assume you'd move into coaching at Spurs?

I had no idea I was going to coach when I was a player, no idea. All I knew was that I wanted to play football. After bumping into Jimmy Hill one day, I was invited to his coaching school in London, and commended me afterwards for doing extremely well.

I then did my full badge at the same time as Roy Bentley, the old Chelsea captain, and Walter Winterbottom, the ex-England manager. I passed both the written tests and full coaching badge at a college in south London, and there was me thinking I'd never be a coach. In my last season at Orient, at the age of thirty-eight, they gave me the job of team coach. That was the first Orient team to win promotion to the First Division in their history. Strange, but coaching was something that I fell into accidentally.

Although you hadn't pictured yourself as a coach, maybe your peers had spotted your promise?

My basic premise about being coach was making people feel happy. I was always interested in passing on knowledge and making them feel confident. I also felt that they'd have more belief in a coach who could play a bit himself. I don't believe I ever made it a grind and rarely moaned at them. In fact, we always had a laugh. Sometimes I'd call 'em a dopey so and so, but it was done in a way that was accepted with a large dose of humour applied. I simply wanted it to stimulate and interest them and provoke thought.

So how did the Tottenham job come about?

Bill Nicholson came over to Orient one day out of the blue and asked me to join Spurs as assistant manager. He'd lost his own assistant, Maurice Evans, who'd died, and proceeded to praise me for what I'd done at Orient. I accepted his kind offer to work at Spurs not quite realising what I was undertaking. To me, at the time, it was just a job... A better job, obviously, but still just a job.

Did you take anyone with you from Brisbane Road?

No. I just left the O's and thanked them very much. They had a good Chairman in those days, he simply shook my hand and thanked me for my efforts. I liked The Orient. They were my team as a kid, and I used to bunk in there with all my mates [laughs].

They sound marvellous days Eddie. It really opens your eyes up to just how different things were and your level of expectation when you returned to White Hart Lane.

Oh, they were magical days, but I'd gone from the dear old O's team to cracking the whip with Dave Mackay, Cliff Jones, and Danny Blanchflower - all the top stars of the day. Not that they worried me as such, in fact one of my first remarks to them was, "Whatever you can do, I can do better" [laughs]. I remember Danny saying to me "You've got a hard job here y'know. Most of us are on the way out." I just replied, "We'll see."

How was the transition from Orient to working with the kings of the double side?

I never let things affect me like that. I knew I could handle them and had been as good a player as many - better in some cases. [laughs]

Did you find any of them difficult to handle?

There was a lot of happiness around playing football at that time. Few had money worries and everyone was focused on the playing side of things. Personalities rarely affected us. Of course, we all get on someone's nerves at some time, but overall it was an extremely happy place to be. It wasn't in our natures to hate anyone, we all just mucked in and got on with it.

The Tottenham players were a great bunch of lads, especially the younger ones like the Steve Perryman's and Derek Possee's. They were all pushing on trying to break into the first team.

Obviously I had a lot to do with the reserves in those days but when Bill wasn't around I used to run the lot.

Was Graham Souness a big loss when he left?

He was one of those lads who thought he was good enough for the first team at fifteen, such was his nature. But as you're on the subject of difficult lads, I remember throwing a coat at him one day. He was playing for the reserves when he gave the ball away outside our box. Our opponents scored and when he came back to the changing rooms I let fly at him.

We had a bit of a hullaballoo, the coat went flying, and Graham got up and walked out. That was certainly one occasion that stood out.

Since then, whenever we see one another we always share a laugh and a joke, but Graham was a hard nut. He always thought he had to be the king and I suppose he's proved himself right ever since. What a great career the lad had.

So was it the petulance of youth, or merely impatience?

Things just couldn't happen quick enough for Graham. Charlie Faulkner, my old scout, had to go up to Edinburgh once to get him back. Charlie's long dead and buried now, God rest his soul, Souness had gone back up to Scotland after another of his outbursts. The trouble with Graham was that he wanted Friday to come before Monday was over.

Tell me about the young Steve Perryman?

Steve always appeared slow in movement to me but his attitude was genuine and honest. I believe he used to like me because he could always see my jokes, and I could always see his thoughts.

Overall, I would say he was a good lad and a good player, and it's marvellous that he never got above his station. He didn't think he was the greatest and knew exactly where he fitted in.

But he was as good as anyone else out there once he took to the pitch. The lad even played on through injuries. That's a sign of a character, especially in the modern day game.

Were there any other lads who should have come through but didn't quite make it?

It was extremely difficult to break through in those days. The first team was so full of quality regulars that it was hard to emerge unless there were lots of injuries. Derek Possee and Keith Weller made it. Then there were boys like Colin Brittan and Ralph Wetton who didn't. They were promising wing-halves who maybe could've survived given the chance. Lots of youngsters simply lost heart. Lads were only on yearly contracts then and got a free transfer if missing out on the first team. It was much easier to fall by the wayside in those days.

Who conducted the releasing of young players, you or Bill?

This issue came up every year. It was something that was discussed between all the coaching staff. Normally first-teamers were kept on and lots of lads at the bottom of the pile got released. It was a horrible thing to have to agree on, but that's life. The club had to move on and go with the players we thought had the most potential.

Spurs bought well then, poaching some big name players from our biggest League rivals. Tell us about some of them?

We used to watch a lot of players in those days and once identified, we'd probably buy one a season that we felt would do a job for us. Players like Cyril Knowles at Middlesbrough, Mike England at Blackburn and Ralphy Coates at Burnley.

We watched Ralph at Chelsea playing in ankle-deep mud once. He was like a tank that day and agreed that he was our type of player. Unfortunately, apart from the League Cup final, he never quite fulfilled his potential at Spurs. Ralphy was a great lad who got teased a lot by his team-mates, but it was only banter. Lots and lots of banter that went towards creating a special team spirit. Even when scoring the League Cup winner the boys promised to put his foot in plaster as a memory. [laughs]

You were married on the 20ᵗʰ December, 1952.

How well I remember it [laughs]

And you played against West Brom in the afternoon. What I want to know is, how did you get away with it?

How well I remember that too [laughs]. We got married at the old Clapton Church. After the ceremony, we went back to my new wife's flat in Southwold Road, Clapton, climbed the stairs and went inside. We just had time for a quick peck on the cheek and was I promptly whisked back to Tottenham by two Directors, Mr. William Merrit, and Mr. Dewhurst Hornsby.

October 1951: Ramsey, Baily, Medley, the three English Lions, versus Welsh Dragon Burgess

October 1951: Eddie Baily equalises for England against Wales at Cardiff in a one-all draw

It was a dull and murky December day but they got us back in time for a 2.15pm kick off.

Your team-mates must've given you some stick?

I remember hitting a shot over the bar from about ten yards and the whole team laughing that I must be drunk. After the game, about seventy of us went back to celebrate in two small rooms. All the food and drink was supplied by our two great friends Len and Denny Mancini from the boxing world. There was beef and lamb, which were all on ration at the time, they really did us proud. It was the funniest, happiest night ever, although there was absolutely no space to breathe. That was my wedding day and night, and Elsie never forgave me for it. [laughs]

Who were the most colourful characters from your Tottenham days?

There were so many in those days. Johnny Brooks, Alfie Stokes, Tommy Harmer and Derek King were all Hackney and Clapton boys who used to travel to Tottenham together every morning. None of us had cars. It was all public transport then so we'd all meet up on a 653 trolley bus and share lots of banter.

Alfie often got on pleading that he had no money for the fare. The conductors and drivers all knew us, so one day Alfie tried the same stroke and none of us would pay up for him. We convinced the conductor to chuck him off for a laugh. We were all local boys and that helped form the basis of a strong team understanding.

Were there any problems between the Londoners and others players in that team?

Certainly not, background just didn't matter. Ron Burgess, our old captain, was one of the best footballers we ever had... It didn't matter that he was Welsh. Everyone was equal in our eyes. I compare him easily with all the best players I've ever seen at Tottenham Hotspur. The wing-half was expected to go past his inside-forward in those days, but if he went past me in training I'd say, "I'll wait for you to come back Ron." His energy was boundless and was a truly superb player. To me Ronny was the best.

Bill Nicholson once said that Burgess was the best player that ever pulled on a Spurs shirt. Why didn't he get the accolades he deserved?

In fairness he was an international of great stature, but quite why he didn't get more recognition I'll never know. You can talk about your Matthews' and your Beckhams', but here was a man who played his career out in pain. He used to suffer from stomach ulcers and was sick before a game quite regularly. Ron was outstanding and always stuck in my mind as one of the all-time great players. He had energy, he had vision, he tackled, Ron did everything. Great, great, player and massively underrated.

When Bill left the club were you disappointed that you didn't get the managers' job, or did you think it was time to move on?

I was disappointed in as much as the players had been getting Bill down a lot at the time. Results were poor, and he let it slip that he'd had enough on returning from a mid-week game at Sheffield Wednesday. He told me he felt like packing it all in because he wasn't getting the required reaction from the players anymore. I asked him to reconsider, but he said he was adamant.

Bill mentioned that I'd be looked after and that I'd probably be asked to help choose the next manager. He had hoped that Danny Blanchflower would follow but the directors of the time didn't want Danny. I think he'd have been a marvellous choice.

I asked Bill if he'd put my name forward. He said that I'd had my fair share of run-ins with the Directors, and that they wouldn't entertain me. I'd have loved the opportunity. Problem was, I'd been exceptionally forthright in my views on occasions when I'd taken the team over in Bill's absence. That didn't go down too well with them.

So you were too aggressive for them?

If I have got one fault in life it is that I always tell the truth the way I see things. I could be very blunt but simply felt compelled to tell the truth, warts and all. Yes, I was disappointed. Danny was a no-go, then they interviewed Johnny Giles; but Sidney Wale ended up informing us that Terry Neill was coming from Hull City. I said to Bill, "So that's exactly what they thought of you mate. You were supposed to be helping to pick your replacement and they've gone and picked their own - an ex-Arsenal man at that!"

So Neill came in and you were out the door?

Terry Neill literally took over training the day he joined. I asked what was going to happen to me, and he answered that Bill would look after me. On the Friday I asked again where I stood. He simply repeated Bill's words that the Directors would see me right. I said that they hadn't looked after me yet, so why would things change now?

I left with three months wages, which came to £3000 or so, I took my things home and wasn't too pleased about the way I was being treated. I'd played and worked with Bill, and got chopped because he had decided to go. The directors blanked me, although old Reg Jarvis, the company secretary, said a few words to me, but it was all very matter-of-fact. Managers get fortunes when they pack in now. I went and signed on the dole!

How did you cope going from the glamour of Spurs to the dole queue?

All the blokes at the Labour Exchange knew me. Some of them had a laugh with me and said "Oh hello Eddie. Down here with the rest of us now mate?" They were joking and I accepted it that way. All the same it was very demeaning, but I'd paid my taxes up and was entitled to it.

I still couldn't help feeling that I'd been pretty badly treated both professionally and financially. Okay, it happens in football, an occupational hazard you might say. But the actual parting was very, very disappointing.

Do you think Spurs became too high and mighty in their actions?

Tottenham were always a big club, and mainly because the players put 'em there. I didn't know what the Tottenham thinking was after Bill packed in, but there suddenly seemed to be a different agenda.

Bill had been trying to put Danny Blanchflower in place, a man who understood the status and stature of the club, but Sidney Wale, who I never liked, decided that he was going to sail the ship his own way - by rejecting anyone we fancied to manage the club.

He was arrogant and the instigator of the end of the Nicholson era in my opinion.

When did this happen?

That was in 1974. Shortly afterwards I got a call from Ron Suart, who was a great mate of mine. Ron asked me to scout for Chelsea and to do match reports. I used to borrow my mate John Welch's car and go scouting for them. At much the same time I become a sports master in a school in Enfield, working there from nine in the morning, and scouting for Chelsea in the evenings.

I also coached at Corinthian Casuals for a while. Then, completely out of the blue, Bill Nick left West Ham and Ron Greenwood asked me to replace Wally St. Pier as chief scout, as he was retiring. Bill was returning to Tottenham to work for Keith Burkinshaw.

I told him I'd be round in one minute. To be honest it was too good to be true and I became Chief Scout for West Ham and enjoyed one of the best periods of my life. I worked for some of the most decent and honest people, especially John Lyall.

During this time, had you formulated in your mind what you would do given the chance to manage Spurs?

No, I wasn't thinking that way at the time. All I knew was that I wanted the job and given it on a Tuesday, I'd start implementing my own personality the same day.

What did you think of bringing in an ex-Arsenal man at the time?

In my opinion, that was 'arse-upwards' as they used to say years ago. After the ignominy of the sack I began to get my life back on the rails, thanks in no small part to Ron Greenwood. I was at West Ham from 1976 to 1992 and worked closely with him, and a few years later John Lyall. Two excellent gentlemen who were always fair and open.

Did you unearth any gems at The Hammers?

One of the best prospects around at the time was a young Alan Devonshire after Charlie Faulkner had joined me. Ron Greenwood always said that if we fancied a player all we had to do was let him know.

Charlie had spotted Alan playing for Southall and thought he was an excellent prospect. Alan had already been watched by a number of clubs, but none of them had yet made a move. We went over to watch the lad and spoke to their manager Geoff Taylor after the game. He accepted my offer of £3000, subject to paper work, and I then asked if I could meet the player.

As Alan trotted over to me I couldn't believe how thin and pale he was. He didn't look a footballer in the flesh, but during the game seemed to have everything. Alan subsequently left a job in the Hoover factory and became my first real capture. It was good to work with new faces at West Ham, we picked up some well-deserved silverware during some very successful years.

It seems you were always in the background at clubs, prompting, probing and bringing on top players but rarely receiving much credit.

Every manager needs top staff behind him. At least I can say I worked hard for Bill Nicholson, and for Ron and John at West Ham. I really like to add my weight to the person. That's what partnerships are about. Although you like the clubs you work for, it's the people there that count more. I'd fallen out with the Directors at Spurs because I felt they didn't have warmth, and had shown few signs of generosity in my time there. That was my opinion. They may have treated others differently.

Football clubs cannot exist without the down to earth people who work tirelessly for their managers. Bill Nicholson was fortunate in that he had Johnny Wallis, Cecil Poynton and myself at Spurs. We were all good, dedicated men who never got what we deserved.

John Lyall was great to his staff. He had every belief in me to produce, and I was allowed the time and freedom to do just that. There isn't a manager on earth who can do it all on his own.

Were you more effective as a coach or a player in your view?

Tactics are one thing, playing in a game is another. There were always certain games where you felt you'd made a big input. One was a seven-nil thrashing of Newcastle United, who were one of the top two teams at the time, with Jackie Milburn and a host of top players in their ranks.

I feel I had a big influence in the game having made a lot of good passes that led to goals. Then we played Sheffield Wednesday a little after and we hit six against them. I was always prominent and made a similar contribution.

And as a coach?

Overall, we actively encouraged new ideas at both West Ham and Tottenham. Some of those ideas were adapted for matches, little things that might seem insignificant to some, like restarts. Against AC Milan we left four up front when defending a corner just to test them. In the end they left five back to combat it, so their corners left only one up front attacking us. Then we decided to take every corner short, no long ones. We constantly needed to invent new things to stretch other sides.

How would you change the thinking of today's modern players?

Modern day players put a wall up to defend free kicks. Every time they do it someone comes along who curls it over the wall and into the net. My question is why bother putting the wall up in the first place? They might as well let the keeper see it and tell him to stop it. Our old keeper Ted Ditchburn used to demand sight of the ball. "If I can't see it, I can't stop it.", he used to say. It doesn't matter if it's from ten yards, or forty yards, he needed to see the damn thing before he could save it!

I simply can't understand some modern thinking. Our intention was to stop ninety percent of what a certain players' game was about. If that's a tactic, yes we did it successfully. We used to advise players to constantly change positions. If opponents see you doing different things it'll confuse them and cause them to make mistakes. Football is all repetition, so as a coach you have to be constantly devising new ways of making the opposition think again.

So players generally reacted well to your ideas?

Yes, people like Cyril Knowles used to pick up on our ideas first time. In fact most of them eventually got the idea and responded during games.

What was Cyril Knowles like?

Cyril was a good lad. Honest, strong, good left foot. He was very quick and loved coming out with little quips that made the other lads laugh. I think he was good enough to have played for England a number of times.

And Pat Jennings?

Good 'keeper Pat. I used to train him with a rugby ball. In coaching, the monotony of training is commonplace so I used to introduce different ideas to keep them interested. I always used a rugby ball for the goalkeepers.

With the rugby ball you never knew which way it was going to bounce and they had to adjust their body accordingly. Goalies have more occasions where they had to guess the bounce. It was interesting to see three keepers in training and which one would guess the bounce best. The idea was to simply make people adjust.

Who was best, Jennings or Ditchburn?

In posing that question it makes you realise how spoilt we've been over the years. It's a tough decision but I'd have to go for Ditchburn, I think Ted had more to his game. Pat was better at out-jumping players, although overall I feel that Ted just shades it. Ted used to win games on his own. He'd bring out fantastic saves, but in saying that you had to take into consideration the ball and the conditions then.

There were three players that I consider enigmas at Spurs. Can you tell me about Alfie Conn, Terry Naylor, and Johnny Pratt?

Alfie? Funny boy... I could never work out what he was going to do next. He certainly wasn't predictable. The lad did things that nobody could pre-empt. He was a moody player that left you wondering where the hell some of his stuff came from. I must say he was a crowd-pleaser, but there's more to a game of football than meets the eye. He had very good ball control and yes, the crowd loved his flair at Tottenham.

As for Terry Naylor, he was honest and hard working. Never a great player but a good player. Terry was a real trier and an absolute joker off the field, but played the game honestly. He used to try some quite elaborate step-overs, but if they didn't come off he'd just laugh. He'd moan when people didn't do what he thought they should be doing, and he was right. Terry was a typical Cockney joker and they loved him for his jokes and personality. He was the kind who'd buy things just to cause a laugh.

I remember once in Mauritius he and a few of the lads had bought finger puppets. They'd sit round the pool, pick on someone, and ask the puppet questions about him. This was followed by staccato laughter, with everyone around falling about laughing. I often used to wonder how the Argentines coped with that kind of thing.

Finally, there was John Pratt?

John was another Terry Naylor; always there for you, eager, and gave his best on the pitch without being the star. But if they weren't on the pitch you'd soon know that they weren't there. John had honesty, integrity and was totally straightforward. That to me in a footballer is ninety percent of

August 1949 : Eddie is marked by Brentford's number five, Ron Greenwood, at Griffin Park

the battle. Of course you'd love them to have loads of skill, but you'd rather they were with you rather than against you.

What do you remember of Glenn Hoddle?

I remember Glenn as a thirteen-year-old, chipping the ball everywhere and showing off those skills. In a game he reminded me of Martin Peters, great when he had the ball, but often relaxed with his defensive duties. His overall involvement needed working on.

He used to love to have the ball. His production side was brilliant and he was fantastic in tight situations. I used to say to Martin Peters, "You are allowed to tackle y'know." Mackay and Burgess used to tackle and pass, but there are some players who only stand out when they get the ball.

There are only three ways of getting a football in a game; a direct pass, a tackle or a mistake. There aren't any others. So if you can't tackle that's a third of your game gone. If you can't show for the ball that's two thirds, so you spend the rest of your game waiting for a mistake to occur. There were lots of players, like Mackay and Burgess, who had that concept of getting it, using it, and being more involved.

Do you feel you missed out on any top players?

Not many really, at least few come to mind. You'd watch games and see someone a bit quick and think, yeah, wouldn't mind him. But we bought in enough to do the club justice. To be fair, you only have eleven places to fill. If anyone slipped the net it was Graham Souness, especially the way he played for Liverpool during their best years.

Graham was a great player but had proved difficult to handle in his earlier Spurs days. I suppose it was his own self-belief that caused the problems, because up to the time he left he'd actually achieved very little. He'd really become quite a nuisance, so at the time, it was a relief to let him go.

Is there anything you'd changed about your career Eddie?

I guess it all revolves around money I suppose. The rewards in my heyday were comparatively very poor, but when you look back everything is relative. I don't think I regret anything because I was fortunate enough to be earning a living out of something I loved to do, which I don't think is always appreciated by the modern day player.

We thought it was a privilege to play in front of big crowds, like on Boxing Day, and even like you said, on my wedding day. When I took up coaching I helped to put a lot of lads on the road to a good future, or to making a good living out of the game. Not necessarily all at the very top, but even those who survived at a lower level.

Do you remember much of your international matches as a player?

My first was as a member of the 1950 World Cup party that went to Rio de Janeiro. It was the first time England had been involved in the World Cup and inclusion was by invitation only. Until then, only the South American teams, and maybe one or two others had taken part. Our team had Tom Finney, Billy Wright, Stan Matthews, Alf Ramsey, Ted Ditchburn, and Stan Mortensen - all famous names in the game. Ted, Alf, Billy Nick and myself were chosen from Tottenham.

England beat Chile two-nil in the first game, then lost one-nil to America, although if truth be known, we should have won twenty-nil. It was incredible how that game went.

Walter Winterbottom later told me he'd blood me against Spain in our third game, which would be in the Maracana stadium. It was like a new world. There were oxygen tanks in the underground changing rooms, there was a moat around the pitch, and there were fireworks going off everywhere in the ground, which held in the region of 110,000.

Stan Matthews played outside right and I was told that if I got in trouble I was to give it to him. There were few tactics in the early days and that was my introduction. We lost one-nil and came home. That was the end of our World Cup.

Did you get much of a look in after that?

After that I played against Wales and Austria, which was a huge game to play in. Having drawn two-all at Wembley, we then had the rematch in Vienna. That was the game where Nat Lofthouse became the famous 'Lion of Vienna' and I've often laughed with Nat about that. I asked him on several occasions how he became so famous.

I joked that it was me who stuck the ball through the middle for him to run on to. He simply ran after it, got there before the goalkeeper, and both fell arse over head. As they fell, the ball bobbled into the net, and they went on to call him 'The Lion'!

I don't know about a lion, I said, what about the little fella who pushed the ball through? I think we got about £20 fee then, and £60 in the World Cup if I remember rightly.

Was it very different playing against foreign players in those days?

The biggest shock I had was touring for England 'B' against Italy 'B' in 1950. Italy had some world class names in their team and we simply never saw the ball. Wherever you went on the pitch the ball had already been passed. They were lightening quick, great passers of the ball, and well and truly stuffed us five-nil. I couldn't help thinking to myself that they played exactly the same method as Tottenham Hotspur. What I wasn't used to was the body checking. They used to do things that you wouldn't encounter in British football. They allowed ice-hockey style body checks where they stuck their body in the way. But they fouled you before you could get yours in. I learned a lot from that game. I came off thinking about the way they'd used themselves to block us out. [Laughs] It was certainly educational.

And the Brazilians?

While in Rio for the World Cup I saw some amazing things, which underlined my view that there's simply no answer to skill. You just can't beat it. We used to go down on to the Copacabana beach and watch them doing all kinds of things. Some with make-shift footballs and some juggling with fruit or orange peel. They were flicking it up and over the nets. That's the answer to it all, skill.

I did a similar thing with a tennis ball when I was kid. It was a hundred yards to the school gates and I used to go along flicking it up the wall practising my skill. I guess I was doing the same as the Brazilians but in slightly different surroundings. They had the beach, I had the East End.

What was your weakness as a player?

I was a weak tackler. In fact, I couldn't tackle at all. People like Jimmy Scoular and Joe Mercer used to say, "I'll have you today".

I used to reply, "You'll have to be quick", because I based my game on lightening thinking, and being first. If they missed you they'd say, "I'll get you back next time".

I was lucky, I had Ron Burgess and Bill Nick as wing–halves, both ball winners. They could always give it back to you. I was a bit like Hoddle I s'pose…only better [laughs].

You must have bundles of fun memories?

There were many on our travels, and some that I just couldn't repeat. Once, when driving in Germany, our wheel went flying past us on the motorway. Although the coach leaned over slightly it was a hilarious sight watching it bounce into the distance. So funny in fact that we hadn't considered the implications of driving on three wheels. On another trip our plane engine caught fire. I told my wife Elsie that the best place to go was the toilet at the back of the plane, because that normally stayed intact when it hit the ground.

I'll also never forget a journey up from the South Atlantic on a big boat. They were battening down the hatches on the ship as I asked a crew member what was happening. "You'll find out in about ten minutes" he said. "We're about to hit a force nine gale" When it hit us everyone started to panic. Alf Ramsey said that we'd never get home. He kept on repeating

Sonny Walters watches Eddie displaying his ball juggling skills at White Hart Lane

it over and over. I told him, "God will look after you Alf. I don't know about me, but he'll definitely look after you."

And at Tottenham?

There used to be two old ladies who gave out the half-time tea. Les Medley and I were great mates and always swapping banter. One of the girls shouted out for me to "Leave old Les alone". I called back, "Ain't it time you went home to cook the dinner?"

Of course, if that was now I'd be meeting a lawyer on Monday, but everyone laughed and it was all part of the moment. People didn't ridicule players in those days like they do now and you didn't have to worry about upsetting everyone or being sued!

How would you turn around the fortunes at modern day Tottenham?

As far as the football side is concerned you can only get money one of two ways. Borrow it, or do what Chelsea have done – get in a rich benefactor. The decision making was terrible for years at Spurs. They've bought in a panic, not watched players for long enough before buying, or players have simply not produced the goods in a white shirt.

Also, too many have been permanently injured and it didn't seem to be a team effort any more. Once the slide begins, it's very difficult to turn it around. The playing side should be dictated by three factors; system, common sense, and effort. You can't have one without the others. And when I say effort, I don't just mean lots of running about. It should be about ideas, thinking, and implementing those thoughts.

How do you view the modern game?

Nowadays, the business of being a Trainer is so more advanced. To me, an ankle is an ankle and a ligament is a ligament. Whatever it is, it's the same injury as years ago.

The modern game produces more joint injuries than ever before. Of course, players are much fitter than in my day, but that doesn't mean they are better players.

The size of the pitch is still the same, the circumference of the ball is still the same, the actual skill factor is still the same. You still have to head it, pass it, control it etc., and the equipment is far different from when I was playing. We never had a pitch with grass on after November. It was always wet, and then come April, it was dry and dusty with no grass. You had grazes all over your body from slide-tackling.

I'd love to see how the modern player would cope with second-rate pitches, six inches of mud, and the ball and boots that we had to use. It's so difficult to judge who was better because the circumstances and equipment are so far superior now – and the modern ones get millions of pounds for simply adding their names to a product!

Would you agree that dietary changes make up for much of the difference now?

I accept that. Our team had about seven smokers. After every home game we'd all go in the pub and have a couple of pints of beer. Our wives used to come and watch us with the kids, then we'd get the old trolley bus home together.

Our Saturday nights used to be indoors with fish and chips doing a jigsaw. We didn't have televisions then. At the end of the day it was a basic, simple life, although we were as famous as some of the modern ones are today.

You had to play on with injuries back then too, didn't you?

In our day there were no substitutes so if you got injured they used to stick your leg in a bucket of ice and tell you to go out and 'make yourself a nuisance'. We'd then hop up and down the wing and used to get the dead needle if someone passed the ball to us. We'd call 'em stupid so-and-so's if they passed to us, because we couldn't run properly and were only out there to keep a defender busy.

The tackling years ago was tougher too. You get yellow cards for nothing these days. I can't remember anyone actually being sent off back then. When you got in bed at night you couldn't sleep on one side because the grazes stuck to your lint, it was really painful.

Eddie you've certainly experienced life.

Yep, played with the best, worked with the best. What more could you wish for? As a player I worked for Arthur Rowe, who was very conscientious, and an extremely nice man. Then there was Freddie Still at Port Vale, who was very superstitious. He used to tell us that he'd keep the same socks on till we lost. So the boys used to try their hardest to win just so he'd have to go around with stinking feet.

Then I was at Forest with Billy Walker. He used to do his tactics on a snooker table. Billy Nick was another honest man, as were Ron Greenwood and John Lyall. They were all good people and I loved working for them all.

Pat
Jennings

Era 1964 - 1977
Appearances 591 **Goals** 1

Pat Jennings - just the mention of those two words evoke awe and respect in sizeable proportions. Pat illuminated the football world for over four decades; growing up just wouldn't have been the same without hearing his name called out over the tannoy system at White Hart Lane every other weekend.

Anyone who has experienced even the briefest flirtation with the 'beautiful game' will know his name; and if you are a fan, you'll appreciate that this is one legend whose playing colours remained completely irrelevant. Popularity and respect followed the man's distinguished career path, as did the eyes and ears of a generation of adoring fans.

From the lumber mills and mines of Northern Ireland, to the pinnacle of world football, Pat's journey was a truly incredible one. Over a twenty-three year career, his trademark laid-back approach, gentle demeanour, and modest manner, belied a burning desire to succeed, allied to an inner passion to do it in style. An exterior as cool as ice masks a determined and dedicated professional, who will live in the hearts of the White Hart Lane faithful forever. But Pat was more than just a Spurs star. The man became a veritable football icon, with a list of international superstars queuing around the corner to praise his considerable achievements.

In the late Sixties, early Seventies, Spurs fans would chant the names of their heroes in team order before every game, with unique personal reverence allotted to each one. Although it was seldom necessary to chant for any other than 'Big' Pat first, what a massive void it left if a rare injury deprived us of his services for those all-consuming ninety minutes. Apart from being 'Mr. Dependable', Pat became a colossus between the Spurs posts, and most would agree that we failed to replace one of the few uncastigated players to cross 'The Great Divide'.

Keepers came and went over the years, but nobody, since those heady days of the imposing Northern Irishman, has anyone ever really stamped his moniker on the green jersey - Pat Jennings was, and always will be, our number one.

For a man who casually states that he'd "Never really considered playing pro football", that "He didn't know the opportunity was open", and that he merely liked "Throwing himself about a bit", his list of achievements is truly astounding.

At Spurs alone, Pat picked up an FA Cup winner's medal in 1967, two League Cups in 1971 and 1973, and played in two UEFA Cup finals, winning one in 1972, finishing runner-up in 1974. And just for good measure, he received a deserved Footballer of the Year award in 1973, followed by an MBE in 1976, topped off by his most treasured accolade in that very same year, a PFA Footballer of the Year award. High praise indeed to be voted by the very opponents that he'd dedicated a lifetime in thwarting. It begs the question, how much would the man with the legendary hands be worth in today's insane transfer market?

Pat's Tottenham career coincided with a plethora of superb and memorable players; Dave Mackay, Jimmy Greaves, Cliff Jones, Cyril Knowles, Alan Mullery, Steve Perryman, Martin Chivers; names that trip off the tongue like a who's who of British sport. Yet still the name Jennings is up there with the best of them all, and deservedly so.

UEFA, in an attempt at topping off their 50th anniversary celebrations, recently scoured each European country to determine their best player over the last fifty years. Six Northern Irish football heroes were listed, with the name P. Jennings rising to the top with an overall 57% of the vote.

The poll soon took on the look of a two-horse race, with Pat's impressive tally beating that of even George Best's 33%; the remaining 10% being shared by Peter Doherty, Peter McParland, Jimmy McIlroy and that other doyen of the lillywhite shirt, the late, great, Danny Blanchflower.

For me, BBC Northern Ireland's poll produced two of the most pertinent of quotes. These were supplied by a pair of Irish fans... "Pat Jennings gets my vote for services to the Northern Irish teams and for being a great ambassador for the province". The next was posted anonymously but was equally pragmatic, "Best showed no loyalty to any team, least of all Northern Ireland. Jennings is a legend". The case for the defence rests.

Was it always going to be football for you or did you ever consider other sports?

I attended a Catholic school in an era when local schools were keen to promote Gaelic sport and games. Therefore it was mostly Gaelic sports up to the age of eleven, as soccer was considered 'foreign'. My first competitive soccer tournament was as an eleven-year-old playing in a competition for under-nineteens.

Believe it or not, we used to get around 1,800 people coming to watch those early matches, for what were basically street teams. The venue we used was called Rooney's Meadow in those days and had the most modest of facilities. I'm proud to say they now call it Jennings Park. Strangely, it was my size that was a problem in the early days. I was small, and couldn't even reach the crossbar. Still, it didn't stop me competing as the Gaelic game had toughened me up somewhat.

Who was the local Irish hero of the time?

That was Peter McParland, the ex-Villa and Wolves winger. Coincidentally, we lived a couple of hundred yards from each other at opposite ends of Chapel Road in Newry. They certainly love to reward local boys made good in my old home town as Peter now has a sports complex named after him. I still love the Gaelic game, and I've been quite a boxing fan over the years too. It's a tough place that bred tough sportsmen.

Who did you support as a lad?

I didn't really have an allegiance myself. Most local lads followed which-ever club Peter McParland played for, so I guess it was Villa or Wolves in the early days.

My dad was a labourer. He didn't earn a fortune but always managed to get us tickets for the big International games at both soccer and Gaelic football. With his support and prompting it was difficult not to love sport. I owe him a lot for inspiring and nurturing my interests.

I understand your brother greatly influenced your early career too. What was his advice?

Yes, my big brother Brian had been trying to persuade me to come and play for Newry United under-nineteen's for a month or so. They were the junior team of Newry Town and he felt certain I'd get a game, especially as their regular keeper was leaving Ireland to look for work. Once he got me there I trained with them on the Tuesday and Thursday nights and got picked for the team on the Saturday. My first game ended in a one-nil victory and went on to finish the season by winning the Irish Junior Cup, which three hundred teams had entered.

So where did Brian's advice lead you?

After a year I was promoted to Newry Town's first team, and near the end of that year the Chairman informed me that he was putting me forward for the Irish Youth side.

I had no idea of the implications. He told me that there would be trials, and if picked, I'd play in a North versus South of Ireland game to determine who goes through to represent Ireland at youth level. Of course, when I found out that the tournament was in England I didn't want to go because I'd never been away from home before.

Apparently, scouts from Ireland and England were queuing up to see me in light of reports that were circulating about my performances. I'd left school by now and was working with my father, John, at the local Haldane and Shiells timber firm.

So it turned out to be great advice?

Oh yes, it proved an excellent move going to Newry Town, and one of the highlights was winning an Irish Cup first round tie against Crusaders, two-nil. The Crusaders Chairman also sat on the youth football committee and came in to our changing room after I'd played out of my skin that day.

He told me that it'd be a pleasure having me in his youth team. Soon after I was picked to play against the Republic at Dalymount Park in Dublin in the first leg of The European Youth Championship preliminary round. We qualified for the final in England on an aggregate score of four-three.

Were any of your teammates with professional clubs at the time?

Yes, there were four of them. John Napier was with Bolton Wanderers, Tommy McKeown and Sammy Todd joined Burnley, and Dave Clements was with Wolves. John, Sammy, and Dave all went on to win full caps, with Dave becoming Manager of the Northern Ireland squad after his playing days.

And so to the tournament in England. What happened?

It was a case of Belfast to Bognor Regis. That's where all of the sixteen teams were based, although we travelled around for the games. The first match was in Eastbourne, where we beat Belgium two-one. We followed that with a win over Czechoslovakia at Woking, a three-all draw with Sweden at Bromley, and a one-one draw against a good Bulgarian side in the semi-finals. The luck of the Irish certainly prevailed as we won the right to a final place against England on the toss of a coin. That was my first ever visit to the great Wembley stadium.

Were you nervous?

I wasn't so much nervous as apprehensive. Some of the boys were carrying injuries from previous games and I guess the big occasion got to one or two of them. England had some strong lads that would go on to bigger and brighter things.

Ron Harris, Chelsea's tough old captain led their side out and they also had Tommy Smith, who of course starred with Liverpool, Jon Sammels, a big star later on with Arsenal, and John Sissons, the old West Ham and Chelsea star. We lost that final four-nil but I still felt I did myself enough justice to hold my head up high.

It was a great experience and there was a large crowd who supported enthusiastically. The game was also shown on the television and attended by many scouts from all over. If anything, it was that game where my name really came to the fore.

So the clubs were by now queuing up for your services?

Yes. It transpired that Watford wanted me, and within a day or so of returning home they put in a bid. Coincidentally, Jimmy Hill at Coventry had been tailing me too, but he couldn't get over in time. It was probably too late for Jim anyway as it looked like the Chairman had shaken hands on a deal with Watford already.

Was it an emotional move to leave your home in Ireland?

There were eleven of us in the family, I became the first to move away. Anyone who has ever left a close-knit family will understand how I felt. I remember Dad leaving me at the airport as I looked forward to my new career in England. Yes, it was an emotional time but it had simply not crossed my mind that I was good enough to be a pro-footballer, and probably more pertinently, that the opportunity was there for the likes of me. I just didn't know that the opportunity to turn professional was available, but once I got amongst the lads and started to learn, it suddenly dawned on me that I could do this and become a full-time pro.

The last salary I earned in Ireland was the princely sum of £4.18 shillings [£4.90] per week in the mines. Before that I worked in the timber mills, which was an enjoyable place to work and an atmospheric place to be. I still remember the horses dragging the timber to distribution points because they couldn't get heavy machinery up into the mountains in those days. I came along with an axe and cleaned up all the logs ready for dispatch. The horses used to drag the logs away after I'd cleaned them up.

Have you been back to visit that place very often since?

Yes, we shot a BBC documentary there before the 1982 World Cup. It brought back lots of happy memories of that time, especially with me and my Dad walking around the place we used to work at. In fact, I bought about fifteen acres of family land there some thirty years back. It overlooks the mountain where we worked and is steeped in sentimental value. If I close my eyes I can still picture the horses pulling the timber along.

So who was it who actually 'discovered' you?

The manager who brought me to Watford was the old Spurs hero Ron Burgess, but it was a man called Bill McCracken who'd recommended me to him. Bill was an Irish-born scout who only went along to the youth game at Bromley because he thought he might run into some old mates from home. According to Bill, I stuck out like a sore thumb and he felt that he had to get in his report double-quick before anyone else got hold of me.

Bill had enjoyed a good professional career himself. He'd played for Distillery in Ireland, then Newcastle United and Hull City as a full-back. He then moved into management with Hull, Millwall and Aldershot. In fact Bill was actually one of the men responsible for the introduction of the offside rule in 1925. I had the pleasure of thanking him personally when I received the PFA Player of the Year award in 1976.

The event was televised live from the Hilton Hotel in London and was an extremely proud moment in my life. It meant so much to have the opportunity to thank Bill publicly for the part he'd played in my career.

How did you settle to life at Watford initially?

There were four games left and Watford were hovering around the relegation zone. Once they'd secured safety, I was picked for the final two games, making my debut at the old White City Stadium against Queen's Park Rangers. I became an ever-present the following season and Watford had gone from strong prospects for the drop to the verge of promotion in one year. I was still floating along and loving my football and settling to my new career.

Was it consolation for you that Watford were able to make a nice profit out your sale?

To be honest, I was very happy at Watford and hadn't even thought about leaving them, and the fee wasn't my concern. That decision was down to the two clubs. Watford bought me for around £7,500, and sold me to Spurs for £27,500. The transfer was good for all parties involved and I got the chance to move up to the top flight to work with Bill and the lads.

Any lingering memories of Watford before joining Spurs?

Ronnie Burgess, the old Spurs Captain, was Watford's manager at the time. He made the first move to buy me and was almost immediately replaced by Bill McGarry once I arrived. Bill was a tough character who never forgot the little touches that mattered so much to some of us players.

Despite being as hard as nails, he would occasionally turn up with a ticket for me to go back to Ireland. Three or four times a year he'd do this. "There you are son" he'd say. "Go and have a few days away back home and be back in time for training on Friday." It was my first year away and he knew that I'd be missing home. It meant so much to me.

I was the only player in that situation and Bill was extremely thoughtful in his actions. Travel was much more difficult in those days but he'd never forget how important it was to see and be with your family. I'll never forget that. It was like getting a thousand pounds. He didn't have to do it but realised the value of rewarding us and keeping us happy. It was a great touch from a great character.

That clearly affected your view of youngsters, and how to help them settle?

I can't emphasize how important that extremely kind gesture was to me. Even now, when I see young kids coming to the club here at Tottenham, I always ask them if they've been home lately.

A good manager will always realise that kids coming away from home for the first time need a few days back with their friends and families.

Did you wobble in the early days and think about returning home?

No, not really. My first season over was really only for a month, which included four games, two of which I didn't play in. Then I had about six or seven weeks off, which was unbelievable. In many ways it was a perfect way of breaking me in and I knew that I'd be getting fairly regular tickets back home to re-acclimatise.

How much contact did you have with people back home then?

I was writing back every week to the family and sending money home.

Your dad must have been strutting around like a proud peacock?

I guess he was but I had a grandfather who was alive then. He lived on one of the main roads that dissected the town. Everybody spoke to everybody in those days; probably still do. Of course, me leaving the town as a footballer would have been one of the big news stories of the time.

My Grandfather simply couldn't get over the fact that somebody would pay you £25 a week to play football and his conversations were along the lines of, "D'ya believe it? £25 a week to kick a football around!" Everyone knew him so I guess he never had to buy a drink after I went [laughs].

And then on to the mighty Tottenham Hotspur. Weren't you just a little bit scared?

No, not really. I was still just floating along, and as they say, ignorance is bliss. The implications of joining such a big club as Spurs never really hit me, although once I'd joined we were always made well aware of the club history and what was expected of us. The 'Double' was only three years past and the club's expectancy was extremely high.

How did the move to White Hart Lane come about?

I'd returned to Newry for the close-season break and remember getting a call from Mr. McGarry to come back to the club for 'some extra training'. On the way back from the airport he asked me if I knew what I was there for.

I said no, and then he dropped it on me that Bill Nicholson was waiting back at Watford to see me. Bill Nicholson was already a legend by then. On being introduced, I put out a hand and said, "Pleased to see you Mr. Nicholson".

He replied "Forget the Mister, just call me Bill". I immediately felt at ease, and like Mr. McGarry, Bill had that personal touch and eye for detail that was so important.

In those days there was no such thing as goalkeeper coaching. McGarry had enjoyed an excellent football career but openly admitted that he didn't feel he could teach me anything about goalkeeping, we were there simply to save shots when outfield players trained. In fact it wasn't until I joined Arsenal that I had a dedicated goalkeeping coach in Bob Wilson. I don't know who was more embarrassed, him or me. But I really enjoyed those two days a week that we trained together. It was brilliant.

Did you learn much from him?

No, not really. I'd already been a pro for many years and had experienced everything I could in terms of my profession. There wasn't much left that I hadn't encountered already. I'd learned much through making my own mistakes, or from the experience of playing games. When you look at the young kids now they're tapping into our experience from the off. What had taken us twenty years to take on board, they're learning immediately. That's what we're putting back into the game now.

Life must be vastly different for budding goalies today?

The youngsters are now doing hour upon hour of ball work every day, practising the repetition of their skills. They now have good hands and good feet, and they're spending hours taking crosses. When I was learning, you'd sometimes go through periods of games where you might only touch the ball half a dozen times or make a handful of saves. If the team was successful you might only touch the ball a few times in a month. Most of them are getting at least a couple of hours every day learning the ropes whereas we had nobody to help us with the technical side of our game.

Do many of the current goalkeepers come back for extra training?

Oh yes, a lot of them come back now. I'm at the Spurs training ground twice a week whereas Hans Segers is often out there with a lot of the kids doing extra work day in, day out. The senior keepers often return for extra sessions, it's not just the juniors.

So you'd consider 'keeper's coaching to be more professional now?

It's all valuable experience, every time you pick the ball up, or simply handle it, nothing's wasted in goalkeeping coaching. I often say to the kids at Spurs that not all of them will go on to play for Tottenham, but it's like putting money in the bank. All of them are out there gaining their experience and none of that coaching or training goes to waste. One situation that's tough for them can be summed up by the case of Rob Birch.

He was on the bench after showing enormous promise, then the club had the opportunity to acquire Paul Robinson. All of a sudden Rob drops down one, but that's no reflection on him, it's just football and circumstances. Paul was available and was a great capture for the club.

With outfield players, maybe they can play in more than one position.

But 'keeping tends to be a more specialized art. The upside is that 'keepers tend to have much longer careers now, but you can't always sit around forever waiting for your chance.

Look at the situation with Ian Walker. He didn't want to sit behind Neil Sullivan in the pecking order; Sullivan didn't want to sit behind Keller; Keller didn't want to sit behind Robinson. That's not just the scenario at this club, it's the same everywhere. Once you've had the flavour of playing in the Premiership, you don't want to go back to the experience of playing in the reserves at Stevenage. That's the problem all along the line. From the club's perspective, they need back-up goalies; guys who can replace the senior 'keeper and still be able to do it at the top level.

So what was your first Spurs manager, Bill Nicholson, like?

Bill was a disciplinarian, a trait that seemed endemic with the era. Bill Nicholson was a hard taskmaster. If you completed nine objectives out of ten, he'd readily pick you up on the one you hadn't mastered, the one where you'd made half a mistake. He was a perfectionist, but that's not to say that he didn't praise you, but he did it in his own way.

When I look back over all the coaches, trainers, and managers I ever had, I never really learned anything that I hadn't heard originally from Bill. Even in training now, we go back to some of the old stuff that Bill originally put in place all those years ago.

Did you have the luxury of a fitness coach back in those early Tottenham days?

Yes, there was a chap called Bill Watson at Tottenham way back in 1964. Bill was an Army man who came in a couple of times a week and was one of the people to introduce weights to our training. He was a weightlifter himself and a very famous man in his own right.

With praise coming so rarely from Bill Nicholson, do any examples spring to mind?

There was a game against Grasshoppers in Zurich, where I'd basically kept us in it. Back in the dressing room, he opened with, "Well, you can all give your bonuses to the goalkeeper". It was a lovely compliment. Nobody argued and Bill had made his point extremely succinctly. The man's presence demanded respect, and when he entered the changing room all the banter stopped as he appeared at the door.

Bill never had to fine anyone for being late, such was the respect that ran through the whole squad for him, but I have to admit that the first year or so was tough for me. The 1961 team was breaking up with new faces filling the changing room. Alan Mullery had come in, with Terry Venables,

Alan Gilzean, Cyril Knowles and Mike England forming the nucleus of a new side. I'd had my teething problems too and initially shared the goalkeeping duties with Bill Brown. It was an era when Tottenham had to finish in the top four or five, and maybe pick up a cup to maintain their great reputation. Anything else was a disaster. Bill Nicholson had extremely high standards that had to be maintained.

Who were the main influences on your early Spurs career?

Of course Nick was the main one. In fact he was probably the main influence in life, let alone my career. He and Eddie Baily were a superb partnership. By reputation, Eddie had been the most skilful of the two during their playing careers. He had skill to burn and a desire to push every player to the limits, whereas Bill would kick anything that moved as a player; and if he couldn't kick someone he'd kick the grass. He simply hated losing. Both were tough in their own way, yet had different ways of putting it across.

When Eddie coached us you could see that he'd retained those skills. He used to put the ball down on the line and fire it in to the middle of the circle on the wall with pinpoint accuracy. "Right, that's your next exercise" he used to say.

[Laughs] He used to join in the five-a-side's with us, although at the time he was a big old lump. We were always trying to get a little dig in at him, maybe a little kick here and there, but by the time you got near him the ball had already gone. He was that skilful and must have been in his early forties at the time. Despite that, Bill was the one who really used to appreciate the skilful side of our game, yet in training it was completely the other way round. When Eddie took coaching he could still do things that some players only aspired to, yet was hard as nails and impossible to get off the ball.

And the goalkeeping training?

Established keepers at clubs rarely worked together, preferring to look on up-and-coming talent as a threat to their position.

Bill Brown was a decent fellow, and a very nice guy off the pitch, but he rarely passed on tips or tricks of the trade. It just wasn't like that in those days and no reflection on him as a person. You always felt that goalkeepers were only to be used for shooting practice for outfield players and was a vastly different art then.

What was your first task as a new Tottenham player?

Sadly, that was attending the funeral of the recently departed John White, who had been killed while out on a golf course. It was a strange experience. I didn't really know John and the atmosphere at Spurs was extremely low and sombre. Tottenham had clearly lost one of its favourite sons, which was a testament to the popularity of John as a player and as a man. It was a sad, sad way to lose someone who could have gone on to become one of the all-time great names.

Who else inspired you in the early days?

I must say that Jimmy Greaves was also a great help at the time. If I ever made a mistake in those early days Jim would be there to put a friendly arm around my shoulders. He was always telling me that I was the best. It really helped my confidence and to have a man of Jim's stature helping you through was really a great bonus.

What did he do?

Mainly it was little things. Sometimes I'd parry or block a ball instead of catching it; the things that you can't get away with in the top flight that maybe you weren't punished for in lower divisions. People like Jim pointed those weaknesses out and helped me to work on them. It was mainly about the learning process, and ironing out mistakes before they became ingrained. I feel that it was the naivety of not knowing what was required at the time. Help like that was invaluable.

It must have been daunting facing the crowd in your early days?

In those days the Tottenham roar was phenomenal. If you weren't thoroughly prepared for facing those huge, partisan crowds you'd be in trouble. The noise of the crowd used to send the hair on the back of your neck for a walk. You had to be physically and mentally prepared. I couldn't have wished for the backing of a better team of people and will never forget the help they all passed on.

You played in the first-ever all-London Cup Final. What memories remain from the match against Chelsea in 1966-67?

It was my first, big professional cup final, which was another very special event in my life, as the European Youth Final had been as a seventeen-year-old. The game itself wasn't too exciting, but I made three or four good saves early on which boosted my confidence. The atmosphere was fantastic and I wanted to savour every moment of that marvellous day.

If anything, I made a small mistake for the Chelsea goal. Bobby Tambling scored, but we ran out two-one winners in the end with goals from Jimmy Robertson and Frank Saul. There was a lot of pressure just knowing that your every mistake would be captured for all time on television. Overall, it was a brilliant day and a stepping stone to building a very, very good side. For many reasons that day remains very, very special to me.

What are your memories of those incredible European Nights?

They were so special for players and fans alike. In those days you didn't get the turnover of players that you have now. Sides were more settled without the ever-present threat of somebody new coming in to take your place, or squads being totally changed during or after the season.

Playing against new sides from Europe presented its own challenge, with their new styles and different ways of doing things compared to the weekly rituals of League football. I was lucky in that I'd experienced all of this at International level already.

Did team strategy change for those games?

We always wanted the away leg first in Europe. It allowed us the benefit of knowing exactly what was required back at home. With the passion of the White Hart Lane faithful right behind us we knew we had a great chance. On many occasions they simply intimidated away sides. We always knew that the fans would turn up in their droves and that they'd act like a twelfth man on the night. Wearing all white, the noise of the crowd, and enjoying some great results against world class opposition certainly made for some special nights at White Hart Lane.

Who were your most physical opponents in those days?

There were many. I'd been brought up on the rigours of Gaelic football so the physical side of soccer didn't really worry me that much. There were some real tough guys in that era; Alex Dawson of Preston, Wyn and Ron Davies, who were all big strong fellows. Derek Dougan, and latterly Joe Jordan spring to mind as tough opponents too.

In later years referees were instructed to cut out most of the physical side of the game. It wasn't really until the advent of Kinnear and Knowles that full-backs actually crossed the half-way line. Previously they were just expected to defend and stop wingers from doing their stuff. The game was changing, as was the role of the defence.

Wasn't it Derek Dougan who helped set up your Belfast Testimonial?

Yes it was. Derek was a Northern Ireland team-mate, he a Protestant, and me a Catholic. The pair of us linked up to head walks between Dublin and Belfast to promote a stronger link between youth communities in Ireland. There were many events staged, which raised a lot of money and prompted greater awareness. 'The Doog' and I became great mates, and although he could be an awkward customer on the pitch, he was never dirty. After all, at six-foot-four, he was a pretty big lad. As you say, Derek had kindly approached some business people at Co-operation Ireland with the idea of a Pat Jennings tribute match.

The game was put on by Co-operation North, a company based in both Dublin and Belfast, and dedicated to forging links between both Irish communities. They worked in liaison with Linfield Football Club and the list of players who turned up was truly amazing.

The game itself was between a Pat Jennings Select and an International XI and the two squads included so many household names. It was really warming to know that so many of those guys wanted to share my night.

Did you first meet Derek on Ireland duty?

No, strangely enough. I'd read and heard a lot about Doog and how he came from Ireland. I was playing for Watford at the time while Derek was with Peterborough. If you've ever been to Vicarage Road you'll know that the steps that go down to the pitch almost disappear into the ground. I'd been in to the changing room, then back outside to leave tickets for friends. When I looked back up the steps, this huge figure stared down at me. As I started to walk back up, stair by stair, Derek came wandering back down with a glint in his eye. We met half way and he said, "I'm going to put four past you this afternoon son". That was the first thing he ever said to me and was typical of his sense of fun.

And did he?

No he didn't [laughs.] In all those years we played against each other he never scored against me. Right through from our Third Division days, right up to Blackburn Rovers and Wolves in the top flight. There was one that he claimed, but it deflected off one of our players on the way, which was probably the closest he ever came to getting one past me.

Is it true that you lost your temper in one game?

I didn't really lose my temper, it was just that in those days I considered crosses to be mine. The Gaelic game had toughened me and nothing was going to get in the way of me taking the ball. We were playing Leeds away in an era when they really were a very tough team. Every time the ball was crossed over one of them jumped into me. I warned the ref in the second half what they'd been doing, but as I went to punch yet another cross, in came Mick Jones who bulldozed me to the ground.

As we fell in unison, we got a little tangled, and he started trying to hold me down. As I glared at him he must have thought I was going to hit him, so he chinned me first. I chased him for a few strides and kicked his backside. The linesman flagged, gave them a penalty, and I got booked. They'd bashed into me God knows how many times with little intention of getting the ball. It was all done to intimidate and to stop me catching it. This was clearly a tactic on their behalf to put me off my game. I can tell you, Bill was not happy!

Who were the best players you played with?

I hate being asked this question, simply because I don't want to insult anyone by forgetting them from the list. As far as goal scorers are concerned I have to mention Greavsie, he was a class act. And if you want to talk about captains, Dave Mackay was in a league of his own. The man led by example. Of course, there were many, many others including the brilliant George Best.

Are there any players that you'd single out since your playing days?

Yes, without doubt it would have to be Jurgen Klinsmann. The man was the consummate professional in every way; a brilliant signing who almost kept us up single-handed. It was an inspired piece of business on behalf of Alan Sugar. There's no doubt that the goals he got for us, nobody else would have scored them.

In past times there were always players you'd want to go and see, but Jurgen stood out alone in his time at the club. We show video footage of some of his goals in the hospitality lounges most games, and all eyes are transfixed whenever Jurgen's goals are on. There's one where he manages to volley the ball from behind his own body. Who knows where he got the ability to dig that one out? Jurgen was lightening quick and oozed class.

What was he like as a person?

I couldn't speak highly enough about the man. Sometimes at three o'clock on weekday afternoons there'd be a group of kids left at the training ground, and there was Jurgen sitting in the middle of them, when some, maybe lesser gifted players were already home with their families.

Nothing was too much trouble for him. Jurgen had won more or less everything in the game, yet still had time for people, or made time for them. I just can't emphasise enough what he meant to this club as a player, and as a man.

What games were most special to you during your Spurs career?

Outside of the cup wins, the one that really sticks in my mind is the home game with Leeds when we needed to stay up in 1974-75. Leeds were a top team then and we desperately needed the win to survive. I really didn't want to be part of the team that took the great Tottenham down to a lower division.

It was our last game of the season, there were nigh on 50,000 fans squeezed into White Hart Lane that night, and Leeds were packed with top internationals like Billy Bremner, Joe Jordan, Eddie Gray, Trevor Cherry and Paul Madeley. We won the match four-two, with two goals from Cyril Knowles, and one each from Alfie Conn and Martin Chivers. Martin had been out of the team for two months and it really looked like his Spurs career was coming to an end. I remember us bombarding their goal in the first half, and in reality, I had very little to do on the night personally.

Didn't Alfie Conn have a brainstorm that evening?

Well, just as it seemed we were cruising to victory, Alfie had his mad moment. He'd comfortably beaten a couple of Leeds players then sat on the ball taunting them to come and get it back. They were not pleased, while the rest of us had been eager not to rile them. I believe he apologised afterwards but it was a very untimely move on his behalf, especially enjoying such a fantastic game with those mazy runs of his.

That was a truly fantastic night where the home fans celebrated like they'd won the cup. They were still out there an hour and a half after the match had ended and it seemed that most of them spent the night on the High Road.

So that meant more than winning the cups?

It's fantastic winning silverware but avoiding relegation that year was a huge relief, although by then the writing was clearly on the wall for us. Unfortunately, the team was in decline and the drop just around the corner. Many players were coming to the end of illustrious careers when we were finally relegated at the end of 1976-77. What a relief it was to go back up at the first time of asking.

Do you remember much about scoring in the 1967 Charity Shield?

[Laughs] I remember thinking how lucky it was to have the game screened on television! Back in those days only a handful of games made it on to the small screen.

We'd been awarded a free kick on the edge of our area. I called to Dave Mackay to give it back to me, then I picked it up and aimed for Alan Gilzean. 'Gilly' was great at holding the ball up, fortunately it missed him and we all stood still as it bounced over Alex Stepney's head into the goal. I remember standing there and wondering what the ref would give. Ten seconds later I realised I'd scored a goal.

I also recall the late Kenneth Wolstenholme going into raptures about a Bobby Charlton goal in that same game. Truth was, it was my mistake, and I think I'd save that shot today given a second chance. It simply slipped off the ends of my fingers but the television people made a huge song and dance about it. Bobby later said on the television that it was one of the best shots he'd ever hit!

You played in some amazing games for Spurs, do you remember much about the eight-two defeat at Derby in 1976-77?

I'm not sure I want to remember it. I was mortified, but not surprised. Derby had a great squad in those days and we were going through an extremely tough time. We clearly didn't have the depth or quality of previous teams and things got worse before they got better.

That season the side let in five at both West Ham and Manchester City, four at Everton and West Brom, eventually suffering relegation to the old Second Division. We even lost at Cardiff in the Third Round of The Cup and went out of the old League Cup at home to Wrexham. Unfortunately, I missed nineteen League games with an ankle injury, so 1976-77 wasn't a brilliant season for me personally either.

If anything, that Derby County game was the one where I could've lost my temper for real. I remember looking up during a sustained period of Derby pressure and seeing outfield players with their hands on their hips while the defence were being run ragged. I can't tell you what was said afterwards!

With respect, you seemed an immovable object at Tottenham for many years. Do you think you got stale knowing that you had little competition for your place? *[Ask question, test reaction, scan room for door to run to...]*

I feel that I never got stale at Tottenham. I trained exceptionally hard, never took my position for granted, and worked to make the position my own. In fact, I always kept the thought in mind that, if I put in two or three dodgy performances, I'd be dropped. That applied to both club and country.

My overwhelming feeling was that I loved playing for the club, and the supporters, which made the whole job easier. Every time I played I felt I had a reputation to forge in the early days. Once established, nothing was going to stand in the way of making the position my own. Complacency simply never came in to it.

What do you regard as the pinnacle of your career?

Without doubt, picking up the Player's Player of the Year Award in 1976, although there were many that ran it close. It was the culmination of many years' hard work and the highest accolade that fellow players could bestow on me. That genuinely meant so much to me.

You won so much in your career Pat, you must have trouble remembering it all?

[Smiles] No not really. Each one has its own special place in my heart. Of course the cups and European nights were exceptional occasions, but there were other tributes that I received that meant as much in their own unique way. I was awarded the MBE in 1976, which was later upgraded to an OBE. Then I was given a KSG [Knight Saint Gregory] in 1999, which was presented by the Pope for my services to Charity. I was also given an Honorary Doctorate by The University of Ulster and voted Footballer of The Year in 1973.

Captaining the Rest of The World Team was also a very special occasion. That was just after the World Cup in 1986. The great Franz Beckenbauer managed that side, and I can honestly say that he managed like he played; with class running through everything he did. One minute I was wondering if I'd play in the team, the next he made me captain [Laughs]. Each and every award and accolade has made me a very proud man.

You played in dangerous times, did the terrace trouble ever affect your game, especially being the closest player to the action?

Not really, although over the years I've been hit with almost everything. At Tottenham the crowd were right on top of you, although as far as personal insults are concerned, you probably heard worse at reserve games because the sparse crowds made it easier to pick out individual insults.

I've been hit by door handles, snooker balls, ball bearings, and filed down coins. I remember once being bombarded with wire staples in a home game against West Ham. But the worst incident was when I was playing at Forest one year with Arsenal where a missile came flying out of the crowd. I didn't see it but suddenly felt a pain surge through my upper forearm. I glanced down to see a dart sticking in me. It had penetrated all the way up to the hilt.

What was your first reaction?

I remember pulling it out of my arm then placing it in the back of the net with my other belongings. I recall a policeman rummaging around trying to take it out but I didn't know whether he was checking the evidence or whether he was trying to hide it. The match was still in progress so I didn't have time to dwell on it there and then.

I wasn't going to report it to be honest, but then the thought passed through my mind that another 'keeper might have to suffer the same or worse at a later date. When I got back to the dressing room at half-time I didn't make a fuss and asked Fred Street for some spray. It was Fred who told Don Howe that I'd been darted.

What happened then?

Don immediately flew in to Cloughie's office asking him what kind of place Forest was for allowing that kind of behaviour. Brian reassured us that something would be done and responded by apologising in a personal letter the following week.

[Laughs] It was addressed to the "Big soft Irishman" and signed, "Love, Brian". The thrower actually got caught and served six months in jail, so Brian was true to his word.

Was that your only dealings with Brian Clough?

No, and to be fair to Brian, he helped me when I was short of players for my Testimonial in Ireland in 1986. The week leading up to the game I had three teams, then all of a sudden managers started pulling their players out and were dropping like flies for various reasons. Derek Dougan was in charge of organising the game and the pair of us came in to the office on the Sunday morning to work out a strategy.

I believe Derek was at loggerheads with Cloughie at the time, but he phoned the man anyway, asked him to speak to me, then I explained the situation to Brian. Amazingly, although he was taking his side to Hartlepool that week, he was still offering to send me players.

I asked for Neil Webb but he then offered me Carl Shutt and Steve Sutton as well. All three of them turned up on the night! That was the type of man Brian was and a tribute to his thoughtfulness and kindness. I'll never forget the way he helped me.

Were there any other on-field moments that come to mind?

I famously got snowballed in a game for Arsenal up at Sheffield United, and once got hit square in the back of the head with a Coca-Cola bottle whilst playing for Spurs at Goodison Park. It didn't break but left one hell of a bump. Everything has hit me bar the kitchen sink in my career.

One year I recall a shower of glass bottles smashing in my penalty area at White Hart Lane against Manchester United. The game was still in progress and I had visions of having to dive on the stuff. Luckily, Alan Mullery put in a saving tackle on Bobby Charlton who was bearing down on goal. Mullers then spotted the glass and disposed of most of it behind the goal. We got the game stopped and the Police ended up clearing the rest of it.

I've often wondered what would have happened had Alan not got that tackle in and spotted the glass.

Did the crowd trouble bother you much?

Overall the trouble didn't bother me personally. I'd never let it. Of course, you don't like to see it for a number of reasons. Amongst other things, you knew that you were in for negative headlines the next morning regardless of the football result. No team wants that.

To counter that question, do you remember many funny moments at Tottenham?

Oh yes, there were many, and some of them I couldn't repeat. We were in Mauritius one year on a club tour. I remember the team sitting around the pool waiting for a coach to return us to the airport. We were all suited and booted and the atmosphere had been great.

Terry Naylor had been swapping banter with a Mauritian waiter we'd befriended over the fortnight tour. Suddenly, Terry pushes the poor lad into the water. Everyone was laughing hysterically and the sight of the guy flapping around was so funny. Terry simply got up and in the guy went, straight into the deep end. One of the waiter's friends suddenly came running out of the hotel shouting, "He can't swim. He can't swim" at the top of his voice. Terry then had to plunge in to the water to save him fully suited.

Luckily, the chap took it in the way it was intended, but the sight of a bedraggled, fully-clothed player crawling out of the pool was absolutely hilarious, especially with the team coach approaching to take us all home.

What about any on-pitch moments?

On the pitch, one particular moment sticks in my mind. It was against Liverpool at Anfield in 1973. They'd been awarded a penalty and Kevin Keegan and Tommy Smith were wrangling over who should take it. It was typical of Liverpool during that era. They were hugely competitive and that was an extremely difficult place to get a result.

While the ball comically bobbed around between them, Kevin grabbed it and tucked it under his arm. Then they argued over who should take it and I could hear Tommy saying "No, give it to me." Keegan finally won the day, but their continued dispute sounded like two squabbling children in a playground. Kevin placed the ball on the spot, strode back, stared at both sides of the goal in an attempt at confusing me, then stepped forward to see me save it. Smith was extremely angry. I could hear him calling Kevin some choice names and asking why he didn't let him take it.

Later on in the game they were awarded another. Kevin hesitated for a moment as Tommy grabbed the ball and marched purposefully towards the spot. All he had to do was beat me to prove his point to his colleague, and probably win the game for them.

Up came Tommy with determination written all over his face. He struck the ball and gasped as I went to one side and saved again. The two Liverpool legends just stared at each other in disbelief and frustration.

Wasn't that a specially arranged morning game?

We played Liverpool in the morning that day as the whole world would converge on Aintree to watch the Grand National in the afternoon.

I remember Smithy being interviewed after the game. He claimed that I'd have probably won the National as well that day such was my form in the match. Luckily, I'd made four or five other saves which were as good, if not better than the penalties.

Liverpool were a great side, I used to love playing at Anfield in those days. Even though I'd kept out those penalties we still only managed a one-all draw, so I guess the last laugh was on us in some ways. To be honest, neither were good penalties, but despite the tension of the situation the moment had a humour of its own.

Tell me about the special affinity you enjoyed with the Spurs fans?

Just like my place in the side, I never took my relationship with the fans for granted either. They were absolutely fantastic to me and always gave us a boost when we needed one.

I'd built something of a reputation for myself and was probably more aware that I had to live up to that at away games. Of course it was a pleasure playing at home, where supporters see you every other week and know what you're about. That's not to take anything away from them, it's just that turning up at grounds where they don't see you regularly with a 'Footballer of the Year' tag is quite a standard to meet. It put added pressure on me and I just wanted to show them what I was made of.

Like I said, the first year or so was very iffy so the pressure was on from the start. Despite that I soon settled into a level of consistency that I felt compelled to maintain.

The Tottenham fans were fantastic to me over my career, even while I was playing down the road. I'll never forget them, or the way they treated me so fairly over the years. I can still hear the chants from The Shelf and remember particular games when they sang my name for what seemed forever. That's the kind of thing you remember for the rest of your life.

Away fans used to cheer you too, especially at Liverpool.

[Laughs] That's right, must have been all the Paddy's!

After years in the World Cup wilderness, Northern Ireland finally made it. What memories do you have of Spain 1982 and that incredible game against the hosts?

I'll never forget that game in the Luis Casanova stadium in Valencia. The crowd was just under 50,000 and extremely passionate and partisan, so we had to hold our nerve to win through. So much was going on around us that we had to concentrate just that little bit more than usual.

We scored through ex-Spur Gerry Armstrong just after half-time and then, just as we were looking quite strong, Mal Donaghy got sent off. That happened around the hour mark so the rest of us had to double our concentration for the remaining thirty minutes. The atmosphere was as frenetic as any I'd played in, and I'd noticed that Spain had been granted two dubious penalties in previous games. I kept a special eye on the referee as much as Spain. I didn't want him buckling under pressure and giving any dubious awards against us.

You must have been under tremendous pressure during that match?

There was a ball cleared off our line very early and they kept up considerable pressure right till the end. Juanite led their line well and I remember taking a couple of strong crosses away from his head. After that it was just a matter of holding what we had.

We weathered the storm well and everyone did their job totally professionally. We'd climbed mountains to get to Spain, then we had to climb another to take us in to the second phase. I thought I'd been around far too long to get emotional over the result of any match, but I've got to admit, I had a lump in my throat when the final whistle went.

Of course, I'd played in many better teams in my time, but I've never been as proud to be a member of any side than that moment. No words can really convey my feelings. It wasn't just national pride, it was a sense of belonging, of being part of something special against all the odds.

You returned four years later to play in Mexico at the age of forty-one. How did it feel to bow out at the top?

I felt good, both physically and mentally, but knew I wanted to wrap my career up. To be honest, I thought the chance had passed me by, but ended up playing against a great Brazil team. We may not have enjoyed the same success as four years earlier but it was still a superb experience. The guys played good tenacious football against some top sides, including Algeria, Spain again, then Brazil. That game was my 119th cap for Northern Ireland, and my last. Of course I was registered as a Spurs player again by the time Mexico came around.

And so to that most burning of questions - the move to Arsenal. How and why did it happen?

I can promise you it was not of my doing. I didn't want to leave and had no plans to go anywhere. Keith Burkinshaw, the then Spurs manager, decided that he had adequate cover in Barry Daines and Mark Kendall, and that maybe I was approaching the end of my career. Barry had filled in for me on a few occasions and Mark was an emerging Welsh under-21 international. Of course, time proved that he'd released me too quickly. The Press had a field day when the story broke and many Spurs fans have told me since that it was a nightmare decision for them. I can tell you that I wasn't exactly pleased with it myself. Yet the move was filled with irony in many ways. Bill Nicholson had himself been pushed out from the club, a habit sadly replicated with my situation, and a good few other players down the years if truth were told.

I genuinely didn't know if that was the way that you were supposed to leave a club or not - especially one that you were happy at and loved playing for. I'd played in all of Spurs' pre-season games up to then and was settling in for yet another happy and productive season. The thought of a move was the last thing on my mind.

Do you remember the circumstances leading up to finding out?

Keith had actually spoken about Bobby Robson's interest in taking me to Ipswich at the end of the close season, but the whole thing just seemed to die in the water. Nothing further was said all the way through pre-season so I just thought that was that. I was looking forward to helping the team back up to the old First Division.

I remember kicking a few footballs around with Gerry Armstrong when Keith came over and asked if he could have a word. He said, "They've decided you can go and the sooner we do it the better." He also explained that I was dropped for the tour of Sweden, because "I'd be an embarrassment to Barry Daines".

What was your immediate reaction?

I asked if he wanted me to apologise for being a good player all these years. That was my first reaction. He then informed me that Bobby Robson would be calling me at six o'clock and that he himself would ring me at half six to find out where I was going. He wanted to clear it up before the squad went on tour. I couldn't believe what I was hearing. After fourteen years with the club, I was being given half an hour to sort out a move that I didn't ask for in the first place!

So why Arsenal if Ipswich wanted you?

Keith's parting shot was the fact that Arsenal had also come in for me. He said it in a way that left no doubt where I should go because Ipswich were the better team at the time. It seemed that the deal was almost done for me to go to Portman Road, and to be honest, the last place I wanted to go was Arsenal because of the rivalry between the fans.

I then talked figures with Bobby Robson over the phone that night and he said he'd come back to me. Unfortunately, he didn't but called Bill Nicholson direct to say that Ipswich had to pull out of the deal. It transpired that Trevor Whymark had broken a leg in a practice game over in Holland, which had forced them in to buying another midfield player instead of a 'keeper. So that was it. I'd have to return to the club next morning knowing whatever happened I was leaving against my will.

Were there any late suitors throwing their caps into the ring?

Yes, and it wasn't as if I wasn't rated or wanted by anybody else. There were a lot of clubs in for me, including interest from Tommy Cavanagh at Manchester United and Aston Villa's Ron Saunders. Fulham were another who came in. Besty and Bobby Moore were there at the time and there were many other options to consider. My family was settled in the London area and didn't particularly want to uproot or move house.

Next morning I arrived at the club as the boys were about to go on tour. I knew that if I went in during the week there'd be nobody there to say goodbye to. It was then that the directors chose to totally blank me as they walked across the car park towards the departing coach. They must've known what was happening. Why else would they have walked past and ignored me en masse? If they'd been unaware of the situation surely they'd all have come and asked why I wasn't going on the trip?

I was devastated. Not a single director bothered to phone or speak to me, or to thank me for my input over all those years, yet Arsenal had been in touch a number of times offering a bigger contract and all that goes with it. All I got from the directors was the fact that they'd decided not to renew my Spurs contract and was free to leave.

What were the conditions of the contract?

It was pretty straightforward really. I signed for them on a four-year deal on £5,000 more than I was on before. That may not sound a lot now but I can assure you it was at the time. Jimmy Rimmer also left Highbury for Aston Villa and the rest, as they say, is history.

What was running through your mind at the time?

Had they stuck a knife in me it couldn't have hurt me as much. I lived for Tottenham and based my whole life around them. Bill was also like a father to me, as he was to all the others. Bill had instilled loyalty and an appreciation of how things should be done the Tottenham way in us all.

Spurs later replaced Milija Aleksic with the thirty-three-year-old Ray Clemence. Ironically I was only thirty-two when I left, which is quite a young age for a goalkeeper really which compounded my view that I needn't have gone. I often see Keith now. He's a friend and an extremely nice guy. I just wish that he hadn't made that decision.

On leaving Tottenham the one thing that kept burning a hole in my mind was how Bill Nicholson would view it. Fortunately, during a long chat, he revealed that he thoroughly understood me, having experienced similar treatment himself. I like to think that my successes after Spurs went a long way to proving me right. By winning further honours it proved that I'd been released far too early and that I had more to offer. A lot more!

Was it strange wearing their colours after years as a Spurs man?

I'll never knock Arsenal. They are a great club with a strong tradition. After all, it wasn't my decision to leave and Arsenal had offered me a vastly improved package without ever having kicked a ball for them. But it never was about the money.

I joined a great set of lads and had a fantastic time at the club mixing with their strong contingent of Irish boys. They treated me exceptionally well right from the off and I had some great times in my seven and a half years there. I'm Tottenham through and through but I still admire the way that Arsenal do things, and the way they do them with style.

I can understand the fans having their rivalry, it's is good thing. It makes the game what it is, but it shouldn't be taken to the extent of hatred.

Then, amazingly, you returned to White Hart Lane.

Being given the opportunity to return was fantastic and I'm very happy now, although it will never in my eyes make the original decision a correct one. At the end of the day I was a professional, discarded by one great club, taken on by another. They were happy days where my career was allowed to progress without moving my family or our base. After all those enjoyable years at Arsenal, I returned to Spurs just in time for the World Cup.

So what, or who, brought you back to White Hart Lane?

It was Peter Shreeves who got me back. Peter approached me with a view to bolstering the Spurs goal-keeping ranks, and I was offered the opportunity to train for the month leading up to the World Cup finals. To be honest I'd almost retired by then. Tony Parks had suffered an ankle injury and although Lawrie McMenemy had offered me a two-year contract at Sunderland, I simply didn't want to go that far north.

Were they a little closer to home I'd probably have considered the move but it meant unsettling my family and uprooting after so many happy years near London. I'd have gone for a few months to do Laurie a favour, but I didn't want to move to the other end of the country on a full time basis. Meanwhile, Laurie had phoned the then Irish manager Billy Bingham and told him of the offer. He asked Billy if I was in his team, would he still pick me for Ireland. "Of course, no problem. I'd pick him for the team" said Billy. I got to hear of the conversation and knew that it was Laurie who put my name back in the frame for the World Cup, but Laurie needed someone on a two-year contract so that was me out of the equation. Shreevesy phoned me the next week in Ireland knowing that I'd make the national team if I was back playing again.

Having literally done nothing since the previous pre-season, Peter wanted me to play in the reserves on the following Tuesday. I rang him back and confirmed I'd play. I put on a good performance in a nil-nil draw against Chelsea reserves in front of good crowd which kept Billy Bingham happy. He then picked me for the qualifying games, the last of which was against England at Wembley.

There were rumours of a contrived result in that game. What have you got to say about that?

You're joking. I wish somebody had told me that! There were players in both teams playing for a World Cup place. Who's going to turn down the chance of scoring at either end, or for either side, with that prize on offer? I remember making a few good saves from Glenn Hoddle and Kerry Dixon in that game, one in particular from Kerry.

Alan McDonald, our centre-half, was standing on the line and I was scared that he might handle the ball before I did. Luckily I scooped it over the bar to safety. Later in the game he went down on the ground clutching a head injury. I glanced over to the sideline to see Tony Woodcock warming up and went over to Kerry and shouted, "Quick, get up. Woody's warming up on the touch-line. They'll have you have off in a minute". Dixon shook himself down and I've never seen anyone get to his feet quicker, or felt so happy to see an opponent recover like that. I certainly didn't want to see Tony on the pitch at that time of the game. [Laughs loud]

Didn't you sign for Everton for a while?

[Laughs] Yes, and it must be one of the most-asked football pub quiz questions ever! I actually signed for them for two weekends and only to do them a favour because Neville Southall had injured himself in an international game in Dublin. Realising they were down to one goalkeeper, Bobby Mimms, who later came to Spurs, I went there simply as cover for two weekends for a Cup semi-final and Final, and with Pete's approval because we were out of the cup ourselves. I joined Everton just to help them out of a crisis and became their most highly capped player!

Do you have any regrets?

No, apart from the obvious one! Of course the money is better now than during my time but players before me thought that our generation were spoilt too. I don't begrudge the players what they're getting. It's a short life and you have to grab opportunities when they rise. The game has given me a great life. I've been all around the world, met some fantastic people, and played for some superb teams, and now I'm back at Spurs working at the place I call home.

It must be very rewarding passing on your experiences and knowledge to the Spurs goalies of the future?

Yes, I'm thoroughly enjoying myself. It's not like the old days where the senior 'keeper kept himself and his ideas a secret. We all work together for the common good here. The facilities at Spurs Lodge are first class and it's a pleasure being back. I work at the club on a match day and have a large collection of memorabilia on show in the Pat Jennings Lounge. It's not only great to have a lounge named after me, but to be able to share all my memories with the fans who supported me over the years.

So after all's said and done Pat, what will be your lasting memory of Tottenham Hotspur be when you eventually walk off into the sunset?

I don't think I'll ever walk away from them now. Tottenham Hotspur are in my blood. They'll always be my team and part of me.

Cliff
Jones

Era 1958 - 1968
Appearances 370 **Goals** 159

Make no mistake, Clifford William Jones was hard as nails. At five feet seven in stockinged feet, and of extremely slight build, Cliff was born to a family of winners. Despite their proud Welsh heritage, the Jones' were a very successful and famous football family.

Father Ivor had been a war-time international; brother Bryn represented Newport, Bournemouth, and home-town Swansea, while uncle Bryn attracted a then-British record fee when moving from Wolves to Arsenal.

Rugby didn't stand a chance in this particular branch of the Jones clan, and to be fair, it was the oval game's sad loss. To the local football coaches, the Jones family must have been truly heaven sent.

Spurs paid £35,000 to Swansea Town to secure the signature of the young Cliff Jones, and what fantastic value and foresight that turned out to be. The winger with the winning formulae was as dextrous as he was popular, covering both wings with speed and agility whilst displaying the athleticism of a stag. Jonesie's spectacular leaps are legendary; famed for his incredible heading ability, and excellent scoring record that reaped 159 goals in 378 first team appearances, eight as sub.

It still surprises me how such a slight man stood up to the physicalities of yesteryear, and still emerged comparatively unscathed - and always smiling. But that was Cliff. Everyone who knows the man will immediately remark on his famous sense of fun and humour, and how he was the life and soul of the party during the greatest years in Tottenham Hotspur history.

On meeting him, and other members of the famous 'Double' team, a pattern clearly emerges; of tough, hardened, and uncompromising characters who fought, lived, and died for one another. Not to mention the fantastic skills of the Jones' of this world.

Unfortunately, Cliff's Spurs career got off to the worst of starts when he cruelly fractured his leg in a pre-season training accident. On recovery, his debut was against 'that lot down the road', and was the catalyst for a long and successful career in a white shirt.

Despite this, and the fact that he won so much in an illustrious Spurs career, Cliff also enjoyed fifty-nine appearances in a red shirt when representing his beloved Wales. Cliff proudly played in the 1958 World Cup Finals, and clearly revels in the story of his second international match. This was against England, scoring the only goal of the game, which he will happily relate to you with a huge smile on his face. There you are. I knew there was something I never liked about that man...

Cliff Jones; Great player, great Welshman, genuinely great human being.

Cliff, you're a very proud Welshman. Tell me about the early days in The Valleys?

Well, they breed them hard down in Swansea y'know. [Laughs] There were some exceptionally tough boys down in the Rhonnda Valley then and some went on to succeed in other sports. I'll never forget the kids of Swansea in those days. Each part of the town had its own section of the bay to play on. They used to come down every day and map out their own territory and play their matches out there.

As far as my career went, what made me famous was scoring with a flying header against England and being carried shoulder high by the crowd. The pitch was a sea of people. It was a proud moment I can tell you. I got to work the following Monday and was told to get on with some 'proper work'. Talk about being bought back to reality!

As an ex-player, your father must have helped your development?

Yes, he became a steelworker after his playing days were over, but before that played inside-forward for Swansea and West Brom. He also represented Wales a dozen times. My Dad instilled a powerful work ethic in me, which I carried on throughout my career. For five years I had worked as a ship's plumber in the Prince of Wales dry dock. That always acted as a reality check if I ever got too full of myself.

What was it like early on at Swansea, were they happy days?

Oh, they certainly were. My favourite story from that time involved a big, tough character called Frank Barson who was our coaching back then. Six foot two, with a broken nose and profuse scar tissue. He wasn't a man to mess around with and had a way of fronting you in the most aggressive of ways. We were playing in a practice match when Devo Williams put the ball down and whacked it. The ball flew through the air, eventually finding the back of Frank's head with a loud 'thwack!'

The sheer momentum jettisoned Frank's head forward causing his false teeth to fly out in front of him. As he turned to confront Davo, he shouted, "Williams, you'll never make a player as long as you've got a hole in your arse..." We all collapsed with laughter; The venom of Frank's outburst trebled by the loss of his flying dentures.

Were you ever tempted by the pleasures of the oval ball?

I played most sports in those early days, but despite the image of Wales as a rugby nation it was always football for me as a youngster. Ironically, I did finish up playing for Saracens after my professional football career was over. I turned out for their sixth team at outside-half proving that every Welshman has at least some rugby in his blood! [Laughs]

What was life under Bill Nicholson like when you joined Spurs?

Bill managed the club from boot-room to the boardroom. He was a born leader, and gave us great values about the game of football and life in general. Winning wasn't enough, it had to be done with a certain style. Bill absolutely hated players confronting referees, and he'd tell us that they were only human. I'll never forget his words, "They're going to make mistakes, but won't make as many mistakes out there as you will!"

I think lots of today's players are disgraceful in the way they intimidate referees. Bring in modern technology. It's so much easier to spot things and to accept the ultimate decision. I'm going off track here a little but these are things that Bill used to instill in us so I feel it's an important point to make. He also used to hammer in to us that the most important people at any club were the supporters. They come through that turnstile, they do forty-hours plus per week and that we had a right to entertain and do them justice. If we didn't there'd be trouble. Bill got us to work hard at the game and think about it. Bill should never be forgotten, not only for what he gave to football but for what he gave to the club and its people - sixty years of his life.

What was he like outside of White Hart Lane?

I didn't really know him outside of work. He was very similar to Shankly in that he lived, died and loved football. I remember once, after the maximum wage was abolished, I was chatting with Greavesy and Dave Mackay. Between them they managed to wind me up about the money I was on. I was playing out of my skin at the time and the pair of them convinced me that I was the best winger in the world and deserved a rise. Off I went to Bill's office, banged on the door and demanded a pay rise.

"I'm the best winger in the world" I said. "That's a matter of opinion" he replied, and the conversation ended with a terse, "Shut the door behind you." I came back out a few seconds later with my tail between my legs and even more determined to prove the man wrong.

Bill had that sort of effect on players. You just wanted to prove that you were right and he was wrong. And he was no different on the subject of praise, preferring to point out and work on our faults. We once passed each other after a game: a game that I'd played particularly well in. "Well done", he said. When I looked back, he finished off with, "Remember Cliff, a slap on the back is only a yard away from a kick up the arse!"

Great man, great manager... The best.

And of all those great players you met, who impressed you most?

Dave Mackay was the greatest I ever played with, and I'd shared a pitch with John Charles and Ivor Allchurch, so that's saying something. Dave had a great influence on the team and was a marvellous competitor. People talk about his toughness but he was also very, very skilful. He was our engine room. I remember him coming down from Hearts in 1959, when we immediately jetted off to a game in Russia. I roomed with Dave for that trip and eventually went off to ask Billy Nick for an interpreter.

He said "What a Russian one?" I said, "No, a Scottish one. I can't understand a bloody word the guy is saying!" Superb character and the greatest player I ever knew.

Dave could put himself around a little too, eh?

Yes, especially in that match against Feyenoord in the 1961-62 European Cup run. We beat 'em three-one on their own patch but Bill still wasn't very happy with us. In fact, he was extremely annoyed. People kept gate crashing the dressing room while he was talking to us and kept throwing them all out. He wasn't satisfied with the way we played and wanted to let us know as much. That's what made him such a great manager. He was a perfectionist and the changing room was his domain.

Did you play any part in helping Mike England come to Tottenham?

I like to think that the Welsh boys helped each other in their careers, and knew that Bill Nicholson was looking at him. Yes I knew Mike and like to think I was instrumental in his arrival at Spurs.

Bill clearly couldn't ring him at Blackburn, so I made the call and told him what it was like down at Spurs. Mike was the final piece in a newly revamped side. He was an excellent player and only had one real weakness - which was his temper. The opposition would often wind up Mike, and woe betide anyone who tried it on. I don't think we ever replaced Big Mike in the team at Spurs, or with Wales.

What about the other stand-out players in the game from your era?

Oh, there were many. Obviously the great Pele comes immediately to mind. I've already mentioned Ivor Allchurch, but there was also John Charles my Wales team-mate, plus of course Danny Blanchflower from my Tottenham days. Not forgetting one of the most incredible players I ever saw, the late, great, Stanley Matthews.

I was invited up to play in his testimonial game. He was about fifty then and coming to the end of an illustrious and amazingly lengthy career. On reaching the ground, Stan was already running around in his kit with these huge heavy boots on, jumping up and down like a man possessed. The rest of us were still suited and watched in amazement as he went through a punishing warm up routine wearing what can only be described as deep sea diver's boots.

Wembley 1961: Cliff making history on the way to clinching the famous 'Double'

We went and changed, returning to the pitch just before kick-off. It was then when we spotted Stan changing into a lightweight, cut-back pair of boots that had been handmade from calf's leather. Stan was already as quick as Olympic Sprinter Jesse Owens over a short sprint and must've felt like a two-year old without those big heavy ones on. Stan was a chap who took his fitness seriously. He was into vitamins, detoxes and fruit juices long before the advent of modern football. One drop of those shoulders and off he'd go. The man was a true legend and a fantastic role model for any sportsman in any era.

How does the modern game compare with your heyday?

After being bought up on a diet of Bill's philosophies it gave us a good set of morals and principles. I hate the way that indiscipline rules modern players sometimes. Then there's the old argument of how players from my generation or before would settle to today's modern game.

Personally, I think it should be asked the other way round. How would the present ones like the pitches we had to play on? How would they like heading a rock of a football and going home on a bus or train with the crowd? How would they cope with the travelling amenities that we had in those days when a match in the north could take up to two days to get home from? And they wouldn't be over impressed with the wages either!

Yes the game has changed drastically, but I honestly feel that the main thing that mattered back then was the football.

It certainly did seem more of a man's game in those days. Where were the toughest places to visit as a Spurs player?

Going to Bolton Wanderers in the late fifties and early sixties was a little precarious. They had a big reputation for putting it around in those days. In fact, Lancashire in particular bred some tough men and Burnley and Blackburn Rovers both had their fair share of abrasive characters, especially if you'd travelled up from the south. [Smiles]

Southern teams used to return with an affliction politely referred to as 'gravel rash' from those games, but we could dish it out as well. European games could get a bit excitable too. One tie where the 'nastys' spilt over from the first leg was against the French side Olympic Lyonnais in the Second Round of the 1967 European Cup Winners' Cup. One or two side issues certainly got sorted out then for sure.

You had another toughie against Gornik Zabrez in 1961. Do you remember much about it?

Yes, the away leg was a nightmare, scary. We got off to a terrible start. Spurs were four down to a very, very tough side and never really got going.

At four-nil we got a bit anxious. There were quite a lot of tackles flying in and the Press murdered us for it. We managed to pull back a couple of goals, which to be fair, didn't really reflect how poorly we had played. Bill wasn't happy about it. With newspapers universally giving us bundles of stick, Bill gave us even more, which got us massively pumped up for the second leg. We came out on to the White Hart Lane pitch for the second game to a continual roar for ninety minutes.

Can you describe that atmosphere?

We didn't have seated ends in those days. It was just a huge wall of noise with thousands of shouting Spurs fans willing us on to victory. The crowd was awesome. When the teams came out it wasn't like the continental scene. We didn't have a running track between the fans and pitch, ours were bearing right down on top of the opposition.

I guess they bottled it to a certain extent. The atmosphere was amazing and the Poles seemed very, very unhappy right from the off. We broke away from the kick off with Bobby Smith immediately smacking their crossbar. We were off, that was it. Unstoppable! I think we would have beaten any team that was, or ever has been, or ever will be, that night.

It was simply the best night's football I ever played in. You have to remember that Gornik were a top class European Club at the time and we thrashed them eight-one with yours truly wading in with a very tidy little hat trick. I think it was the first European match played under floodlights.

What are you doing Saturday Cliff?

I've gone past that now. I can talk about it, but I can't actually do it anymore. [Smiles] I can remember 1959, I just can't remember what happened last week!

This was in an era before foreign imports and the Spurs team was made up of regionally diverse British players wasn't it?

Yes, but the Welsh lads were the best! [Laughs] There were quite a few London lads in Les Allen, Peter Baker and Ron Henry. In fact they made up the base of the team. Of course there was Blanchflower from Ireland, and Smithy and Bill Nick were Yorkshire, but teams in those days were always driven by at least one major Scottish player.

In that department we were well looked after with Dave Mackay, John White, and Bill Brown. It always made me wonder why Scotland didn't have a world beating team. Too many conflicting personalities I guess. [Smiles]

What are your memories of playing with Jimmy Greaves?

Jim was simply the greatest goal-scorer I've ever seen in my life. He

was my roommate for six years, and along with John White, my best mate. Jimmy was one of those guys who lived hard and played hard and had a great sense of humour. It's strange how things turned out because we were never aware of any excessive drinking. It simply seemed like a social thing. As far as the game is concerned, I strongly believe that he packed in too early. A great guy, a funny guy, and a fantastic finisher. You only get one Jimmy Greaves in a lifetime!

You played in Spurs record win; a thirteen-two drubbing of Crewe Alexandra in February 1960. Do you remember much about it?

Quite frankly, we were lucky to get the chance to take them back to White Hart Lane! It was two-all last knockings at Gresty Road when one of their's broke away and should have made it three-two. We were on top form in the replay and were ten up at half-time. In the second half they scored two but we added another three.

We played to true form that night, which we hadn't matched in the first game. I think they must've been a bit overawed by the White Hart Lane 'welcome'. Tommy Harmer scored, Bobby Smith got four, Les Allen got five, and I got three myself. [Laughs] John White reckoned he made them all!

How close were Spurs to winning the European Cup in 1962? What do you recall of that great semi-final against Benfica?

To be honest, we should have won the first leg in Portugal. We played exceptionally well but just didn't get much luck. Greavesy had one disallowed, as did Bobby Smith in the last few moments. With two Benfica defenders standing on the line I was amazed when the ref blew for offside. In the second leg, which we won two-one, again, we just couldn't get the breaks.

But that's taking nothing away from what was one very good side. Their 'keeper, Costa Pereira, had made a collection of great saves, and their centre-half had stood up to Bobby Smith where others had failed miserably. Bobby had intimidated teams and defenders all around the world. He was our own special weapon.

Benfica were more or less the Portugal national side with names like Torres, Coluna, Eusebio and the rest, those players formed the backbone of the 1966 World Cup side that played England in the semi-final. Spurs versus Portugal in fact.

Did any other clubs ever come in for you Cliff?

Yes, in June 1963. Juventus came in very strongly. John Charles, my Welsh team-mate, was playing for them at the time. He put my name forward and they had me watched a few times. I was probably playing the best football of my career about then and Signor Bonapuerte, and the club president Signor Agnelli, were told in no uncertain terms that I simply wasn't for sale. To be honest, my family had settled around London. I was amazingly happy at Tottenham, but I still wonder sometimes what it would have been like to play in Italy and to experience a different culture and way of thinking.

I believe I would have loved the experience of playing and living there. Either way, I had a fantastic career and never regretted my decision to stay at Spurs. It was a privilege and a pleasure to be part of that great Tottenham set-up at the time.

How did it all end at Spurs for you Cliff?

It was October 1968, when I was thirty-four. Bill Nicholson had given me his word that I could transfer to Fulham, but had already picked me to play my last game against Manchester United.

On the Saturday, I scored against United and played exceptionally well. I'm sure he wanted me to stay after that but Nick's word is his word, and off I went to Craven Cottage the very next day.

What happened after Fulham?

After Fulham I had spells with Kings Lynn, Wealdstone, Bedford Town, and Cambridge City, before becoming player-coach at Wingate, who were in the Athenian League. I retired from football in 1977 and went on to run a butchers shop. I then worked in a Sports Leisure Complex, followed by twenty-three years as a sports teacher at, would you believe, Highbury Grove School.

So after all those years, you went back to school?

I really enjoyed those days at Highbury Grove and got myself involved in football, cricket, badminton, weights and a number of other activities.

My philosophy being that I wouldn't ask the kids to do anything I couldn't do myself, although I must say, [laughs] none of them went on to become Welsh internationals.

Steve
Perryman

Era 1967 - 1986
Appearances 862 **Goals** 39

S trewn across my office carpet lay a dozen crumpled pieces of paper; each having missed their target by a matter of inches; each a vain attempt at describing a very special man. In reality, my abject failure is an admission that there are simply no words to express what he meant to two generations of Spurs fans.

During the compilation of this book, many kind people made special contributions - one clearly stood out above all others. A tireless worker who went out of his way to help and advise; a spirited leader, who rallied players, coaches, and managers alike; a loyal and ever-present rock, bearing a degree of loyalty sadly missing in today's disposable life.

The man was the same off the pitch as he was on it. He never let us down. In Steve Perryman's world that is normality; to help, to cajole, to prompt and probe, to nurture the best from his proteges, and to add his enormous experience to those lucky enough to be within earshot.

In Paolo Hewitt's "The Fashion of Football – From Best to Beckham", the writer's words succinctly encapsulate the enormity of Steve's presence, and I quote, "In June 1979, I had my first music review published in a national newspaper. Since then, I have interviewed a considerable number of major musicians, including [he said not a little proudly] Marvin Gaye, Smokey Robinson, Stevie Wonder, and Nina Simone. Through my job, I have travelled the world, met hundreds of interesting and funny and charming and inspirational and extremely obnoxious people. I've had some amazing experiences. I have written eleven books, been on TV countless times, same with radio, but when Steve Perryman came through the door of our City Wine Bar, I was rendered speechless... It was... Steve Perryman".

Through our similar lifetime passions for music, football, and to a larger extent, Tottenham Hotspur, I'll admit that I also shared Paolo's momentary flirtation with lockjaw. Steve Perryman was more than just a player, epitomizing many traits sadly lacking in the modern football cauldron. To quote figures is easy. To tell you that he played more games in a white, first-team Spurs shirt has been done to death, anyway, as Eddie Baily told me, "The first thousand are always the hardest".

I will always remember Steve Perryman as a fighter, a warrior, and a man who never knew when to give in. His personality never waivers; his honesty remains long and true. I'll remember him in many, many other ways. As a player sadly by-passed by his country for lesser mortals, as a man who always spoke his mind as well as the truth, and quite simply, as the greatest ambassador Tottenham Hotspur ever had. Steve Perryman hated losing, and loathed letting people down. In fact, he dedicated many years to repaying the faith that certain believers had placed in him from an early age. But most of all, I'll remember him the way that his ex-colleagues still do to this day, quite simply as "Skipper." – Fingers crossed, thirteenth time lucky!

Take us back to the early days. Who did you support?

I grew up on a Northolt council estate with two elder brothers. One week we went to Brentford on the bus, the next we travelled to QPR. We basically grew up watching old Third Division football.

Wasn't there a rivalry between those two then?

Strangely enough, the rivalry between the two clubs didn't enter our heads then, but if anything, I favoured QPR as we seemed to find ourselves sampling the pleasures of Southend, Bournemouth and the like at Rangers away games. I felt like I belonged at Rangers having put myself out to travel away. That's why I've had the deep-rooted feeling all through my career that I knew what the fan felt and what they wanted to see.

At home, you were just another face in the crowd, whereas away you were part of a smaller collective, battling to be heard above the dominant home crowd. We felt like we'd earned the right to go and see them in times of adversity, and that our support mattered. In fact, I had a chance to join Rangers, but my elder brother, and mentor, told me not to go there as he felt I'd be better off with the superior facilities at one of the larger clubs. It would have been easy to join QPR, but I listened to Ted, and decided to choose one of the brighter lights. It was such a shame though. Rangers were finally starting to hit the headlines with the likes of Rodney Marsh in the team. I guess every schoolboy wants to join his childhood team.

When did you finally make up your mind about which club to join?

Decision time came when Spurs played Chelsea in the 1967 FA Cup Final. I'd been training with Spurs all year and they were trying their best to get me to sign. Despite this, and what all the clubs were saying to me and my parents, there was nothing written down to say that I must sign for the team I was training with. My brother and I wanted to show Spurs that we had done our homework. It took the pressure off to a certain extent but the scouts were still all over me from various northern and southern clubs, including the two Manchester sides, but leaving London was never really an option.

Were the scouts pushy in those days?

It was madness really. I remember one particular day when we had scouts from all over the country in different rooms at our house and it was proving a job to keep them all apart. My mum saw me as the runt of the litter and actually sat with one trying to talk him out of taking me on. It was nothing malicious on her part, just that I'd earlier been diagnosed with a heart murmur and both of my brothers were physically bigger. She always thought of me as the little one and therefore not strong enough to be a pro. Still, it didn't put any of them off and we carried on being inundated with calls and visits from club scouts.

So what was the defining moment that swung it Spurs' way?

Tommy Docherty was Chelsea's manager at the time. He had written to my brothers offering us five Cup Final tickets and the chance to meet the players, plus an invitation to the after-match celebrations. All of that and not a single mention of signing for them! Bill Nicholson was a lot more direct. "Are you going to join us lad" he said. "Because if not, you aren't going to get any Cup Final tickets." My family and I responded more to that kind of prompting and that would remain the story all through my career, with Bill always just a thought away from my actions. Without doubt, he was the single most influential person in my career. I signed shortly after and never looked back.

Did you always think you'd make it in the game?

I was influenced by some great thinkers on my way to becoming a pro. As a small lad I lived in a cul-de-sac and spent most of my childhood playing football with the older lads. I always had a ball at my feet and was chosen to attend the School of Excellence at Brentford. It was there that I actually heard a coach asking lads if they knew the implications of attending.

That man had an amazing insight in to the world of a small boy. On hearing his question, and then having the time to mull it over, it was clear that most of the lads had no idea why they were there. Most just followed the system, playing school and representative games and never quite thinking about the end result. Of course, that trainer knew that some of us might end up playing at Wembley, although to us, it was just another game of football to play in at the time.

We'd assumed that success was only going to happen to other kids. I guess that was down to our humble upbringing and lack of expectation. My brothers and I always analysed my performances in the car on the way home from matches. Not just whether I'd had a good or bad game, but a much wider view of what was happening. It was from those chats that the realisation sank in that I could become a professional, although something still told me that it wouldn't happen to me.

In truth, I never really rated myself that highly. What I'd failed to take on board was that I was always playing against older and stronger lads than myself, so when I was pitted against my own age group I stood out.

What were the early days at Spurs like for you?

Tottenham set their stall out as soon as you become attached to them. This was the Bill Nicholson influence on the club and the way he did his business. The man is a legend in my eyes, and in some ways I became a sort of disciple to him. He was extremely sparing with praise, preferring to criticise rather than give you a swollen head. He was totally honest, straight and clean cut, although later in my career I felt that, maybe sometimes he had overpowered me with the weight of his personality - and I don't mean that in a derisory way.

Who else helped you?

My first youth team coach was Johnny Wallis, who spent fifty years at the club and managed the old Metropolitan League team. Johnny was more of a trainer than anything else. From the very first morning I walked in, he let me know in no uncertain terms that Spurs expected me to play it quick, fast and accurate. That's the way Tottenham did things.

Fortunately, that was right down my street so Johnny became a big influence on my career. Sadly, he passed away not so long ago, but I'll never forget what he did for me.

It seemed that the old Tottenham was a tough place. Is that true?

Much of the talk then centred around players who 'bottled'. Football life is tough and I always remember thinking that I'd never give them reason to talk about me like that. I was no coward and went out to prove that to the whole of the football world.

Although Tottenham provided a fantastic football environment, I vividly remember those early conversations about guts and steel, and how to stay strong in adversity. We had an emerging talent on the books at the time called Brian Scrimshaw - what a player. He certainly seemed to have a huge future, but found himself being replaced by lads who were physically stronger. Remember; boys are heavily influenced by what they hear. Brian must have believed his publicity but couldn't cope with the physical side of the game.

Eddie Baily was a great coach and judge. He had a particular style about him and was the perfect foil to Bill Nicholson. Talk about a man who could change a game with half-time tactics. Bill was direct enough but Eddie was the manipulator and instigator, and did a passable octopus impersonation at the break. His arms and fingers directing all around the changing room letting players know what he expected of them. He was a massive influence on me. He also made me think about the game and the way it should be played, which helped to form my character.

If you didn't have Baily's work ethic you were labelled a 'fancy Dan', or worse, at a time when inside-forwards like me suddenly became midfielders. Of course, if you had a very special talent, like Greavesie, Bill would never ask you to go around smashing into people, but the game definitely changed there and then forever.

How did you view your own style?

I'm sure that the vast majority of Spurs fans would disagree with me, but I never considered myself to be the midfield dynamo type. My brothers, who only wanted the best for my career, had told me to go to West Ham. They believed that I would then not have to compromise my style for the good of the team. Both were only looking out for me so that I could play my natural game and enjoy myself.

When I broke into the first team Spurs were struggling. I'd only played six reserve games, but suddenly felt the huge influence that permeated from the crowd. The more I ran and broke up play, the more they got behind me. It wasn't really my style to play that way, but that crowd reaction meant that, if I compromised I'd please them more. I'd always thought of myself as more of a controller and a passer; a footballer in the true sense. Unfortunately, as far as I was concerned, they never really saw the real me.

Do you remember much about your debut?

You could say it was a triumph of nerves over naivety. It was a home game against Sunderland, on a very hot and sunny afternoon. My very first pass went astray and very nearly gave a goal away. Spurs had already lost a couple of home games, which was almost unheard of in those days. You could say the fans were unhappy with the team at the time.

Gordon Harris, the Sunderland midfielder, showed me a lot of the ball so I nipped in and intercepted him, and the crowd immediately reacted to my decisiveness. I remember being shattered at the end of that game. The heat drained me of every last drop of energy.

Sunderland beat us in both fixtures that year and then went on to be relegated. It was a strange time for me appearing with guys that I didn't really know, but to play alongside Jennings, England, Knowles, and Greaves was truly unbelievable.

What was your initial contact with the first team?

That was at the old Baseball Ground, Derby. It was Dave Mackay's first game against us and everything went wrong. John Pratt got injured, we got beat five-nil. Even Willie Carlin scored from a header - and he was about five foot nothing!

Bill said it was between Dennis Bond and me for a place in the next home game the following week. Dennis had been a regular in the reserves, Bill felt that changes needed to be made, but he didn't know how many. Bill arrived at one-thirty on the Saturday and immediately pulled me aside to tell me I was playing. If the enormity of what he had said had sunk in there and then I'm sure I'd have wet myself. At seventeen, I was a boy in a man's world and thank God I was.

Did you suffer much criticism from crowds, and how did you react?

I used to love criticism from away crowds. When they were having a go at me it was because I'd either played well, or I was having an effect on the fortunes of their team. I always had to find an edge from somewhere, and away criticism always gave it to me. If I heard things like, "I hate you Perryman, you little bastard", it would really inspire me. Sometimes an opponent would kick out and I'd think to myself, 'Okay, we'll see about that". I was really motivated knowing that the opposition knew we were there and competing.

What about criticism at White Hart Lane?

Home crowds were different. As I've said, I never wanted to let anybody down, and criticism from the White Hart Lane faithful could really get to me. I desperately wanted to entertain and please them, although I must admit, I rarely got many negatives from our home crowds. There was one occasion, against Birmingham, when I got exceptionally angry at one particular shout from the crowd. I ran to the sideline and leapt on top of the perimeter fencing to sort the guy out. I can still remember him peering back at me like it was yesterday. As I looked down it just turned into a sea of faces. Fortunately the crowd was so big that I just got pushed back again.

God only knows what I thought I was going to do. I guess I just reacted in the heat of the moment. You should have seen the look of surprise on the Birmingham players' faces. [Laughs] Yep, I nearly had a Cantona moment while Eric was still in nappies!

Were you superstitious as a player?

Not in the way that other players were. Steve Archibald always had to put the ball in the net before kick-off, while Phil Beal, then later Graham Roberts, used to insist on being last out on the pitch. The big thing for me was not to let anyone down! I always wanted the crowd to go away thinking that I'd given maximum effort and that I hadn't hidden. I always wanted to give them full value for money.

Although I'd often argued with my brothers about changing styles for the team, my true ability began to surface when I reached my late twenties. I started to play more with my brain than with my legs. Glenn Hoddle always said that I was a much better player than people gave me credit for. If we ever had skill competitions, I was always up amongst the top three, but if you said that to the crowd at various stages of my career they'd never have believed it

Three Spurs managers had a massive effect on your career, tell us about Nicholson, Burkinshaw and Shreeves?

Billy Nick was a hard, dour, but honest-as-the-day-is-long Yorkshiremen. With no freedom of contract then it was up to the clubs how much they wanted to pay you. I was eighteen when I made the first team and wanted a rise to over £20 per week, which Bill characteristically contested. I decided to stand firm and went to see Alan Gilzean, who told me that he was on £95 per week.

I know I shouldn't have done it but I told Bill that I knew what other players were earning and there was no way that Gilly was four times better than me. Bill stared back across the table and asked me how many of the crowd came to see me. To be honest, he knocked the wind out of my sails. I sat back, couldn't think of what to say and quietly crept away to rethink. Bill always had a strong hold on us; an influence that I never, ever, quite felt with anybody else in the game.

I understand he was stingy with praise too?

He was very hard when it came to praise. In fact, he'd rather praise the opposition, as he did after our first UEFA Cup win against Wolves in 1972. We'd won, and won well at Molineux, although the home game was very different. Our opponents really bossed that game and got themselves a well-deserved draw. Back in the dressing room, Bill told us we weren't at the races. Our consolation was holding up the UEFA Cup, but Bill was a purist in every sense of the word.

Don't get me wrong, I loved the man and the influence he'd wielded over the club, but when he left it was probably a good thing for my career. A day or so before he went, I was very much lined up for a move to Coventry. The club wanted to bring in Jimmy Holmes and Mick McGuire and Coventry had asked for me to go the other way. I needed to break out and to become my own man. Bill had done his job getting me where I was, now I needed to see if I could fly. Fortunately, I stayed, and the rest is yesterday's news.

What was your relationship with Keith Burkinshaw like?

I didn't get on very well with Keith Burkinshaw at first. He came in as Terry Neill's coach and was very blunt and forthright. Despite that, he obviously cared about what he was doing.

Relegation had been looming up on the club for a long time before Keith joined, he'd inherited a team on the way down. Amazingly, after relegation, the club kept faith in him, and what an excellent decision that turned out to be. Maybe that should go out as a message to all chairmen? Things are sometimes not quite as dark as they may seem.

I'll never, ever forget the day we went down. It seemed like the whole crowd had swarmed on to the pitch. It looked like a shingle beach and there were people who had climbed up to the Director's Box in the main stand singing their hearts out. I was later told that the crowd had been shouting for us to make an appearance. To be honest, we didn't come out because we thought we had nothing to celebrate. We were embarrassed at our failure and just wanted to hide.

The fans were amazing that day weren't they?

The true passion of Tottenham Hotspur fans came to the fore that afternoon. I remember them chanting, "We'll be back again next year", which seemed to go on forever after the game. That kind of heart-warming show deserved a response from the players the following season. There was no way I could leave Spurs then.

Sometimes fans commented that we didn't wave to them at the end of particular games. What they don't understand is that, in players like me, there's a shame in some performances. All you want to do is get off the pitch, get cleaned up, then put some distance between a horrible performance and yourself. Now, after hearing the fan's opinions, I'd make absolutely sure that my players went back out to say thanks for their support and loyalty.

Somehow, we just knew that we'd go down that season, but to give him all due credit, Keith was already planning for our return. It wasn't like nowadays where you'd lose most of your best players on demotion. In fact, in a reshuffle, I moved in to the defence and we were encouraged to play the ball out more skilfully. We got out of the division by the skin of our teeth the next year but at least we'd entertained everyone and played it the Tottenham way.

You really seemed to enjoy yourself that season?

Without doubt, that was my best footballing season. Previously, I'd been involved in the hurley-burly of midfield, so it was an absolute pleasure to be encouraged to play from the back and deliver the ball to the likes of Neil McNab and Glenn Hoddle.

Tell us a bit more about that proposed move to Coventry?

Apparently, whilst in a discussion in one of the offices one day, somebody told Charlie Faulkner, who had signed me as a schoolboy, that he thought I was jaded and coming to the end of my career. Charlie was furious on hearing this and threw his tea cup in the air. "I'll show you how finished he is" he said. "I'll show you how much money people will offer for him". Charlie then phoned to inform me that Bill Nicholson would call me in to his office the next day.

He shouldn't have done that, but wanted to prove a point. Bill said "I've never thought about selling you, but we want to bring in two new players.

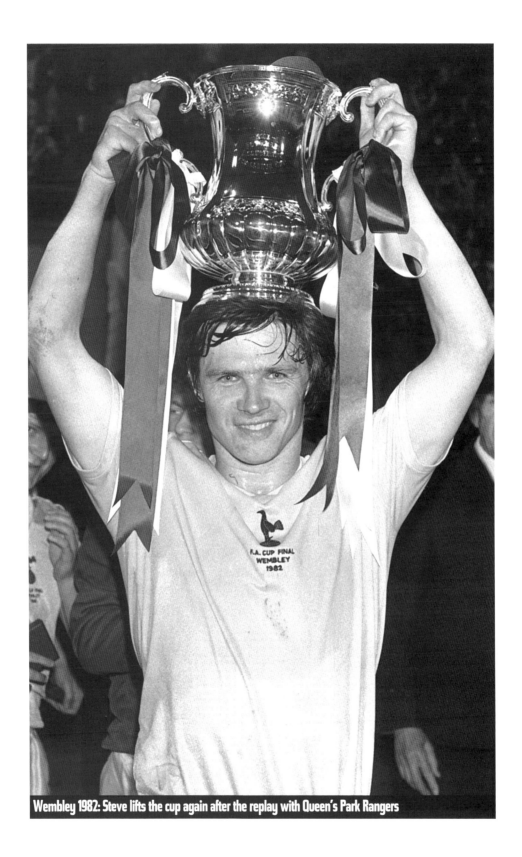

Wembley 1982: Steve lifts the cup again after the replay with Queen's Park Rangers

Have you ever thought about leaving?" Armed by Charlie's information, I answered very quickly, "Yes, of course I have". Bill refused to tell me which club was after me, although I'd also been privy to that news too.

Sounds like a poker match?

Yes it was. I said that I didn't want to go too far from home. The north was not an option but I'd consider something a little closer due to family and business commitments. Bill said I was to go home, talk to my family, and think my answer through. I came back next day and he'd resigned!

Terry came in soon after and immediately told me I was staying. He helped and released my game, even to the extent that I managed to score seven goals at the end of one season, although I guess some of it was from being freed from the shackles of Bill.

Not everybody thought the same way of Terry, but for me he was certainly a breath of fresh air. At the very least, he was responsible for bringing in Keith, so he wasn't all that bad in my eyes.

Talking about Keith's departure, it was a very sad moment for the fans, did the players view it the same way?

Unfortunately, Keith was never going to be right for Irving Scholar, who was greatly influenced by everything going on in Europe. After defeating Austria Vienna once, Irving called Keith over to meet their coach. "Thanks" said Keith, "But I've already met him. We met before the game!"

Irving then told Keith that he wanted him to come over to watch the guy coach. Irving strongly believed that foreign coaches were the best and that we had a lot to learn from them, despite the fact that Keith's team had just beaten the Austrians!

The grass was always greener as far as Irving was concerned. Keith once received thirty-six phone calls from Irving in one day. Mainly along the lines of "Have you done this, have you done that?"

Unfortunately, it led to Keith's resignation. As much as Keith liked things done properly, he wasn't prepared to work under those circumstances, hence his infamous quote as he walked away.

And lastly Peter Shreeves?

Peter was bought in as one of Keith's assistants and was one of the reasons why it all went so smoothly. He was Keith's foil in the dressing room.

The squad was packed with young cockney kids and Peter immediately picked up on their problems and needs, whereas Keith was more 'John Blunt' with them. The balance of those two was terrific. I respected both of them greatly and later employed Pete as my assistant at Watford. He's always been a great coach, a sociable, affable man, and a very close friend.

What made Peter Shreeves different?

I remember us getting turned over at Highbury one year. I assure you, the drive home from there is awful if you've lost, so I just wanted to get in the car and get away from the area. Keith immediately invited us all back to his office, which was a great way of getting it all out of the system. Pete regularly instigated that kind of thinking and it always helped to take the bad times away. Both had their own unique style, and each have influenced my own managerial career.

Even when I'd won nine on the spin in Japan, the philosophies of Keith and Peter were never far away from my mind. I often used to wonder how everything had fitted into place so well, but soon realised that it was down to the total confidence they'd instilled into the squad.

You can't tell me that Alex Ferguson does absolutely everything right. That's not to denigrate the man's achievements, just that he must have people in place who pick up or elaborate on his short-comings. And so it is with every good or great side, a complete team effort. Peter played a big part in making it work so well.

Apart from Coventry, were there any other potential suitors?

Over the years I heard that a number of clubs had tried to buy me, but I was so happy at Spurs I simply didn't want to leave. I'd been called slow; that I wasn't as skilful as some, but I always knew I was doing a job for my team. I know that Leeds came in for me when they were a top, top side, and I know that Terry Neil wanted to take me to Arsenal.

In those days Liverpool were top dogs. They had a philosophy of taking the meat off the bones of lesser carcasses, especially ones that were going down. That way they could take the engine rooms out of clubs. I know they wanted me on a couple of occasions, but again, I wanted to stay south and I wanted to stay at Spurs.

I never saw you happier than when picking up the FA Cup in 1981?

I'd had great early success with Tottenham in the shape of two League cups and two UEFA Finals. I'd joined a magnificent club with all that tradition, ambition and desire going on. Then we tasted failure.

I was distraught. We'd failed to replicate the success of previous Tottenham teams, we'd also failed because we were relegated, and worse still, we'd failed all the fans. At a lot of other clubs they'd have been baying for our heads. In fact, I often wondered why they didn't and was sometimes asked why I didn't leave.

There was a simple answer as far as I was concerned. I joined a club at the top, and wasn't going to leave them after relegation. I wanted to do the right thing by them. That was my legacy to a club that had helped me establish myself and to the thousands of fans who deserved better than they were getting. Then what happens? We win the FA Cup Final. Maybe not in the way that previous Spurs teams had done, but football had moved on a lot from those days.

Then, just as I'm basking in the ecstasy of the evening, somebody mentioned that it was time to go and lift the cup. I truly wasn't being thick. It just hadn't occurred to me that one of the best days in my life would be crowned by personally picking up the cup. Life just doesn't get much better than that.

How did the emotions hit you?

Everything was there, elation, excitement, happiness, plus personal and professional glory. It also returned the club to the forefront of British football. It's all well and good saying that we were a good team, but one, we had to prove it, and two, it's great looking back on honours lists knowing that we actually won something. I'd sadly led the team to relegation and then enjoyed the sweet taste of success under Keith.

Suddenly we had less to prove to people. I'd been part of something great – and we'd done it in style. Our collective spirit told us to go out and do it again; to underline our ability. Personally, I don't think we ever fulfilled that potential. We should have gone out and won the League the following year but we were battling on too many fronts.

Believe it or not, I once approached Keith with the idea of playing more in the Arsenal way. Harder to beat, more resilient, more able to win the League by how we set our stall out. He just shook his head and said, "It'll never happen here. Not in my time anyway!"

Tell me about the European nights. Were they as special to you as other players say?

They were from a different world. It was a very clever move wearing all white in European matches. It made them so special, and separate from the bread and butter fare of the League. There was an incredible buzz of excitement around the place. I'll never forget travelling to Newcastle with the first team squad when I was just fifteen years old. Bill Nicholson demanded I wore a suit for the day although I'd be pushing the skips that held the kit for the team. I sat on the bench entranced by a Mackay-inspired victory over the Geordies. The buzz from that crowd was mesmerizing, as it was with European nights at White Hart Lane.

What was the best of them for you?

The best team effort was when we beat Ajax. Johann Cruyff had been making derogatory comments about us and how much better Dutch football was than our's. Despite Ajax dragging it back to four-two, it was the closest I'd seen to perfection from eleven men. The best for me, personally, was when we beat AC Milan at home two-one in the semi-final of the 1972 UEFA Cup. I scored twice and often remind cocky, upstart strikers that I could actually do it at the business end of the pitch too!

Those goals really stood out for me. To go one down against Italians at that time was asking for a recovery of miraculous proportions. They had some of the cream of Europe playing that night; Romeo Benetti, German international full-back Karl Schnellinger, and their great captain, Gianni Rivera, who did me with the greatest piece of skill I've ever fallen victim to.

I also watched him do John Pratt with a marvellous trick. He dug his foot into the ball, it span back and around John like he wasn't there. I'd never seen anything like it at the time.

In highlighting Europe, how much did crowd trouble in Feyenoord on the day of the Final affect the players in 1974?

Bill didn't come in at half-time so Eddie Baily did his team talk. I'd never known that before so we got wind that something was going on. Rumours were circulating that some trouble had broken out and my Dad was in the crowd that day, as was Bill's daughter. I was worried about their safety and hoped that the trouble would subside.

It was a hard and disappointing match for us. We'd cut through Europe like a knife through butter that year but came up against an exceptional Feyenoord side who could dish it out as well as take it. After the game, the stadium was smashed to pieces, with seats strewn across down the terraces. It was a very sad occasion in an otherwise great European campaign.

You were involved in some very physical battles during your career. How do you look back on the Wimbledon saga, when Gary Mabbutt had his skull broken and the infamous 'Butchers of Barcelona' fiasco?

To be honest, the physical games didn't bother me. I could look after myself and in some cases actually thrived on them. Like I said, it was where I got that edge to make me a winner. Most of those situations were about the team and how we coped with a physical threat.

Barcelona were exceptionally tough, and yes, they acted like animals on the night. Realistically, it was up to each one of us to stand up and be strong, especially with so much at stake.

The one match that really sticks in my mind, and throat, was the cowardly attack on Gary Mabbutt that caused his fractured skull. I detested that loathsome attack with a passion, and the signal it sent out to any children watching the game, or thinking about becoming professionals. Yet strangely, there was no real big uproar about it. Now, over ten years later, we've got the leading lights in football demanding that they want some-thing done about the elbow and that it should be banned.

Well, if it wasn't clamped down on after that occasion, it never will be. To be honest, I really didn't like the way that football covered up the enor-mity and seriousness of that incident.

As club captain, and on the medical advice of the club doctor, I had to announce that Gary had 'fractured his skull'. Apparently if two of the four sides of the eye-socket are broken it constitutes a fracture. I then received a very interesting phone call from the then Wimbledon chairman ranting on that in some way I was 'trying to build myself up', that I was 'a cheat', and obviously an 'enemy of Wimbledon Football Club'.

After hearing how he was friends with our then chairman, and how he was going to get me sacked, I told him in no uncertain terms to go to hell. He accused me of lying and cheating, and trying my best to inflame the situation. I further informed him that if my chairman sacked me for tell-ing the truth I'd happily go anyway and that if that's the way the game of football was going, he could stick it where the sun doesn't shine!

I don't mind tough games, but that was nothing more than a mugging. By the way, it was you who bought up the subject of Wimbledon, not me.

Hypothetically, how much would you pay for Steve Perryman in the current transfer market?

Well, I guess the yardstick now is the £29m Rio Ferdinand transfer, which, in my opinion, was totally ludicrous. I'd say £5m or thereabouts, especially when you consider how long I lasted. I tried my best to be loyal, a good leader, and somebody that the players could always turn to.

Were wages ever an issue for you?

I once had a big barney with Keith Burkinshaw over the duration of an impending contract. He wanted to offer me a yearly extension but I wanted three. I feel that I proved him very wrong in the long run by lasting more than the three years and going on to win some trophies.

I understand you once took umbrage to a negative newspaper article about you?

Yes, definitely. One of the broadsheet reporters once wrote the fol-lowing about me. "Perryman never smiles. 'Death Mask' is a reasonable player but it's just a job to him". Thing is, I'd never ever met the guy. He didn't know me, had never met my family and he certainly didn't have an insight in to what I was about, as a man or a human being. I must admit, it made me analyse myself and how the rest of the world saw me.

What conclusions did you come to?

After much soul-searching, it occurred to me that, despite what this stranger had written, this was a serious business. It was easy sitting in the comparative safety of a Press box, but come down here and put yourself at the sharp end. Try and cope with fit, agile and aggressive footballers trying to take you on. Put up with all the brickbats thrown by crowds and critics. Then see how much you want to write about it 'just being a job'.

Yes, it was a touch hurtful but I thought the game was serious enough to treat it as such. You can't go around smiling at referees and players anymore. I couldn't be like, say Gazza, and get away with it. My personality wouldn't let me do that, especially being club captain.

What do you consider to be the strong and weak points of your personality?

I'd say I'm very consistent. I tend to stick with my original thought and that ethic has got me through over the years. My ex-chairman at Watford believed passionately in checklists. He kept hundreds of files pertaining to his professional business life and regularly called me at three on a Friday afternoon. Once he told me that I was 'one consistent bastard', and proceeded to ask me what I'd do with an imaginary half a million quid.

I told him I'd split it to buy several players from various clubs. When that money eventually filtered through, I'd have to have a damn good reason for not going with my original thoughts. In essence, I was as consistent a player as I've been in my managerial life. I know what I like and don't like, and harbour few traits or surprises that could be seen as weak. After all, some of our strengths are also seen as weaknesses.

I also believe strongly in the ethic of giving value for money. I want to leave people with a good feeling about Steve Perryman. I guess if my first wife reads this she'll contest the part about me wanting to stay loyal, but that's life.

What do you consider to be your biggest weaknesses?

My main weakness is that I take criticism to heart more than most. That's probably why I liked Japan so much. If they were criticising, I sure as hell couldn't understand it. In England, it was easy getting my point across to the players, while out there I sometimes had to do it via an interpreter and would then have to test the player to see if he'd understood.

In Japan, they are also more willing to give you the time to get things right, which obviously worked for me judging by my track record. Sometimes it's too easy in England to say that somebody is not good enough. In Japan you're given a lot more time to nurture and improve players. In England it's thrust upon us to buy, sell, use, and get rid of players a lot quicker.

Players are more disposable here, while Japan opened up my mind. I believe I prospered, both as a man and as a manager out there. I certainly became more patient.

How did it change you as a person?

I was very much an Englishman before, steak and chips and all that, I was very regimented in my ways. Out there I tried many new things and believe it made me more adventurous, a bit more outgoing and willing to try new concepts. It really was such a great experience. They listen to your every word in an attempt to improve as players and human beings.

They're brought up on a mission to increase their knowledge and understanding of things, always seeking out improvements and how to achieve success. Everything was also so bright, clean and alive. How many times had I sat in traffic on the North Circular, hating the routine of it all and desperate for something to enliven and enrich my understanding? Mind you, if they say something is 'difficult' in Japan, what they really mean is it's impossible, but that's all part of the learning process.

As a management pairing, how close do you think that you and Ossie Ardilles were to getting it right at Spurs in 1994?

From the outset we were never given a set time to get it right. There was no directive, and certainly no sign from the top that this was a team effort and that we were all pulling in the same direction. That message should have come down loud and clear from the top. A good team on the field should be backed up by a good team off it! To win a championship, or indeed to build a successful side, a club needs leadership from the top.

What some people don't realise is that Ossie has one of the most impressive, astute football brains around, and has always been an absolute joy to work with.

So how did you take it when the end came?

To be honest, that time remains a constant disappointment in my life, especially as it was Tottenham, the club we both love.

What was it like working there after the successes of your playing career?

You could say it was a case of 'right place, wrong time', or what Ossie has dubbed, 'The Impossible Job'. That went for then, not now. At that moment in time, we were both seduced by the aura of the place. We tried to instill a feeling of harmony; to bring back the flowing, flamboyant football that had been lacking. We wanted to resurrect the football that modern day Spurs fans had been crying out for.

We didn't just want players and officials of the club to turn up on match days, or any other working day, and just go through the motions. We genuinely wanted to rebuild that Tottenham spirit which I'd experienced under Bill Nicholson and that both of us had tasted with Keith.

Do you think Ossie regrets taking the Spurs job so soon in his managerial career?

I can't talk for Ossie, but, as I said, he always called it "The impossible job" under the circumstances that prevailed at that time.

Personally, I would just love to see him back there in some capacity. He genuinely loves the club, and feels much the same as I do about its allure and the way we were dismissed.

He's an incredible man, Ossie. He allows players to work on their own intuition, but is never far away to offer a lending hand.

What was your working relationship like?

We've always shared an excellent partnership and understanding. We're 90% the same, with only that odd 10% that differs on various issues. I'd love to see him back where he belongs, although I feel that he became a victim of typical Press pigeon-holing. They will forever look on our attacking formation as something that should be marked against him.

It's the same with Kevin Keegan. He'd win ten on the trot, then as soon as he lost the eleventh, the Press would slaughter him for his so-called 'tactical ineptitude'. So how did he win the first ten, guesswork?

The guy can't win with the Press, whatever he does. In the same way, we'll always be lambasted for that era, although in Japan I had a more successful period than even Arsene Wenger. To date, I've not yet seen the Press mention that!

Ardilles was very brave as a player. What's he like as a man?

I'd put Ossie in the same category as Glenn when it comes to the bravery stakes. Despite his disappointment at his dismissal from White Hart Lane he still had the guts and dignity to face a Press conference on the day. Few men would have had the courage to have faced that ordeal.

If Spurs rang you tomorrow to take over the club, what would be your reaction?

I'd be there like a bullet from a gun. I'm Tottenham through and through and would love to return to the club one day in some capacity, especially now that the circumstances are so different. Again, if things had been different the first time round, events could have turned out so much better. Glenn Hoddle loved the club in the same way.

How did you view Hoddle as a player?

One point that I feel is never made about Glenn was his considerable bravery on the pitch. Whereas I was a head down and functional kind of player, Glenn was seen to be the extravagant, skilful one. But his bravery on the ball took a lot of pressure off the rest of the team.

If any of us got into trouble with the ball, even if Glenn had four players around him, we knew that he'd still accept it and probably play himself out of trouble. That to me was the height of bravery and he should have been praised for it more often. There are different levels of bravery on a football pitch. Hardness and steel are two; accepting the ball in difficult situations, with three or four tough defenders bearing down you, certainly has it's place up there with the rest.

I always said that Glenn had a set of golf clubs in his feet. He could chip, shoot, or putt, and I used to warm up before a game with him in the hope that I could feed off some of his confidence and skill. Styles have to compliment each other. I hope my positive approach also affected him too.

Do you think that somebody with a Tottenham Hotspur history should always be asked to take over; somebody who knows the traditional Spurs way of doing things?

Yes, but as long as that person has the right credentials for the job at that given time. It's not as simplistic as calling yourself a manager and sitting in a chair. The job is diverse and a background knowledge of your club should always be an advantage. Under Nicholson and Burkinshaw the club was financially in good hands, with neither willing to waste a penny. Both were deep thinkers about the game and first class at keeping young, precocious, talented young men in their place.

I remember discussing a twelve pounds a week pay rise with Bill. "I can't buy a pair of shoes for twelve quid Bill" I told him. "You can where I shop" he quickly replied. That's not living in the past, or refusing to spend our cash. It's clear that money can buy you a place at the top table but why waste what you have?

Rival fans love to tell us that we're 'not a big club anymore'. What's your take on this?

Of course as a Tottenham man I'm biased. But how can you possibly ignore the past or the many achievements of the club? It's a history based on values such as style, passion, great names, and fantastic loyal crowds who know what they want and how they want to see it. Spurs have always enjoyed huge support, whereas other teams have not been followed so loyally during the leaner times. Spurs were the first team to win the FA Cup as amateurs. They were the first British team to win a European trophy and the first British team to win two different ones. They were the first club to float on the Stock Exchange, the first modern club to win 'the Double', and until Manchester United's recent run, enjoyed the most FA Cup Final wins. Small club eh?

It seems to me that some of these press people like to take it out on Spurs because of the way they've been treated under previous regimes. It's ludicrous to suggest that we are no longer a big club. If that was the case why are away grounds packed out wherever we go? Why is White Hart Lane normally packed to the rafters every home match?

It's easy to jump on the bandwagon during lean times. I wonder if they'll be so scathing when the club's on the way back again?

What are your biggest disappointments in football?

Apart from the obvious big disasters like Heysel and Bradford, and deaths of colleagues, on a personal level, having to leave Tottenham twice in such disappointing circumstances.

I still feel that I never said a proper goodbye to Tottenham Hotspur, and that sticks in my throat at times. I feel that I've been denied my chance to part on the best of terms. That's not to say that we parted on bad ones. I'd just like to say my piece to the relevant individuals, including saying a big thank you to all the fans who backed me for so many years.

To be fair, I often visit White Hart Lane these days and even played in a benefit game for the late great Danny Blanchflower. That was a match arranged to help Danny's family after he passed away. A match played out for one of the Tottenham 'family'.

And regrets on the playing front?

On the playing front, my biggest disappointment was sitting on that coach back from Manchester in the relegation year of 1976-77. We'd been hammered five-nil at City and knew we were going down. I was distraught. I remember that all through my career I'd been a ball winner. The guy who wins the ball to pass it on to the Glenn Hoddle's of this world. In that game I was so frustrated at the lack of spirit that I purposefully held on to the ball longer than usual out of sheer anger and frustration.

How much did it mean to captain the club?

I don't think there are words to describe how proud I felt, it's a special and great honour to captain Tottenham Hotspur. I was amazed when Bill originally made me vice-captain as all through my early career I'd never worn an armband. It was Phil Holder who captained the FA Youth Cup Final win and later on I had to learn how to become a good skipper. Picking your captain is an important decision in the building of a strong side. Firstly, he must be a regular player in the team. It's no good picking inconsistent individuals who miss a lot of games.

Then he must be consistent in his own play. If the captain's constantly having trouble with his own form, it tends to knock on to the other players. They need somebody to look up to, somebody who will be there when the team needs new spirit. Dave Mackay was the ultimate captain on the pitch.

How do you regard the relationship between skipper and manager?

It's imperative to have a good working relationship with the manager, somebody to carry the influence of the bosses ideas on to the pitch, then carry them out. In the 1981 FA Cup Final against Manchester City, Ricky Villa had experienced a nightmare. He just couldn't get in to the game and was eventually subbed. I was very annoyed at the way he dejectedly trudged away from the pitch.

I felt that he should have gone to the bench to add his support to the team, so I advised Keith Burkinshaw to drop him for the Thursday replay. To me, he hadn't shown a team spirit, and should have paid for it with his place. Keith listened, then ignored me. Shows how much I know eh!

And how about your relationship with the supporters?

In truth, I'm in awe of the way our supporters are loyal to the club and the way they want it to succeed. I can feel it through every newspaper, every radio phone-in, and the way they react in the ground. I've met Spurs supporters all around the world and they're all a similar breed.

They may be of many different nationalities but are similar in that they all want the same success bought back to Tottenham, and are one-minded as to what they want for the club. Some of the best moments in my career have been while out in public. I've wandered through the West End on the way to meetings and cabbies have pulled up, jumped out and thanked me for everything I've put in to the club. That's a wonderful feeling. You walk away ten feet tall and proud to have served such wonderful fans. It's a feeling of being in unison with all those people and being responsible, as the captain of an era, to carry on those standards and traditions.

Your return seems a big regret to you?

Not a regret really. It just all felt so wrong. Under that regime it wasn't about pulling together, it was about looking after yourself. There was a constant air of mistrust. I told Alan Sugar once that the place I once knew no longer existed. I know it sounds silly, but I felt that every phone call was tapped, that everywhere I went there was a security camera on me. I had no proof or evidence that it was true, but it was just a vibe, a gut feeling that said that we'd never be allowed to see this job through without being

watched. That's not an atmosphere conducive to people producing their best. It was so different to the way things had been before.

So you regret taking the offer?

If ever there was a wrong time to take a job, that was it. There's no doubt about that. I believe they'd offered the job to Glenn Hoddle at the time and that he'd wisely turned it down. Then they offered it to Ossie, who had enjoyed success elsewhere, and he rightly took it.

He's not a fool by any means but just wanted to be back at the club that he loved, which is why I joined him myself. I walked out on a managers' job, a good job, just to get back to White Hart Lane.

Returning to one of your questions, I feel that lack of ego is also one of my great strengths. I don't have to be the number one man. I've been a captain, I've been a leader, but I don't need to be the number one, hence my decision to join Ossie and subsequently the reason why I went to Japan with him. After that he won a trophy on his own, so did I. Maybe that's the clue, maybe we should have been separated [laughs loud].

Did the financial situation in football dictate the rules the second time around?

Most definitely. By then the rules had changed and business was every-thing. We had the Stock Market flotation, the money troubles, the Vena-bles-Scholar situation, and latterly the spat between Venables and Sugar. Suddenly there was a new breed of man on the block, yet for all Scholar's faults, at least he understood the traditions of Tottenham Hotspur.

Yes, he knew facts and figures, but he also had a feeling for the club as a fan. Then of course the new man came in and he had little, if any, feeling for the club at all. I saw many good people lose their jobs because of the path that the club followed. That was heartbreaking.

So did you and Ossie feel powerless in your roles?

As long time skipper, I felt I had the power to look after people, but now that power was taken away and the whole situation just didn't seem right. On hearing the crowd chanting for our heads, I was delighted to get away from what it had become. It just wasn't a place to succeed and I never felt happy that we'd be given the time to get things right.

A manager has to be the top man, only under that regime he wasn't, so I had periods where I fell in and out of love with the club. But whoever owns it, the fans will always remain loyal to their image of what Tottenham is.

When you first met Ossie Ardilles was there any sign of how strong a bond you'd have?

I feel I've always been a communicator and like to feel that I tapped in to the man immediately. It wasn't always easy to understand him at first, but the bond grew immediately and we're still great friends to this day.

Is the rumour correct that you almost joined Arsenal?

[Very long pause] Bertie Mee told my Dad, and if you knew my Dad you'd never speak to him like this, that he wasn't sure about me. Apparently, ten Arsenal scouts had watched me, but they couldn't make their minds up. I already had a long choice of clubs after my signature but wanted to make sure in my own mind that I was joining the right one.

Bertie told Dad that if he was "looking for a drink" he was not going to get it here. Dad was extremely unimpressed and told him he wasn't after a 'drink' and that I'd sign for whoever we felt comfortable with, not because of any outside influences or inducements. He replied that if ten scouts can't make their minds up then it was clearly the wrong decision.

It came across as a kind of superiority, and although I trained there for a few evenings, it just never felt right. Spurs and Arsenal were similar levels at the time but I just felt a coldness that said something was missing. That was compounded by Dad's conversation, and he'd only gone there because Islington were playing Ealing schoolboys at the time.

How do you feel about them now?

Over time I've gained some sort of respect for them, but bearing in mind my character, I suppose I wasn't a true Tottenham flair player anyway. I have to admit that I really liked their 1970 'Double' team. Although it lacked the Tottenham style, it had a consistency that I liked.

Over the years I heard lots of stories about Arsenal, especially how they did things with a bit of style. As a Spurs man I didn't want to believe that they did things more stylishly than us but I don't think they'd ever have allowed a Sugar situation to manifest itself.

There was something at Highbury that would never allow that financial scenario to occur, and for that reason I've learned to respect the people at Arsenal. Chelsea are somewhat different though.

I often had the feeling they'd rip me limb from limb given the chance. I've felt very frightened in a couple of situations there, where the Arsenal people have always shown me a lot of respect. I'm not as anti them as some would expect. Even so, I'm glad I took my time and joined the right club.

Looking around your beautiful home, Japanese culture has clearly had a major effect on your life. Can you tell us about your time there?

We came back from Japan in October 2002. My wife returned more or less speaking, reading and writing the language fluently. We originally went out there with our six month-old daughter but returned a family of four. Obviously our lives were based around the school and what it could provide for the kids. I didn't learn as much as Kim linguistically, but came back with a reasonable understanding and insight. Just enough to let my players know how they were doing [laughs].

It's great to learn about foreign cultures and lives, but sometimes learning a new language can be a bit much, especially when trying to run a football club. Our eldest daughter picked up Japanese almost immediately. They are so much more receptive at that age. The country had a good overall feeling about it. Everything was new, fresh and interesting to us. We learned a lot and will never forget the experience.

So what are you doing now that you're back?

I still manage the Steve Perryman Sport Travel business, which transports Scandinavian people around the world on sports packages. We often take them to Italy and Spain to visit two or three of the top football teams. I've also been helping out down at Exeter City in an advisory capacity as Director of Football. Things were in a bit of a mess down there but it's been a pleasure to help out and keep my hand in. To be honest, I'd love to manage or coach at the highest level again. The game is in my blood.

So what do you think the future holds for Steve Perryman?

Who knows? I've had a great career. I've lived in Norway and Japan, and now I'm pouring myself back into football in the best way I can down at Exeter City. Of course, Spurs are my club and always will be. Who knows what the future holds? I'll just keep battling and hope that more success comes my way.

Ron
Henry

Era 1953 - 1968
Appearances 287 **Goals** 1

Ronald Patrick Henry joined Tottenham Hotspur as an amateur way back in January 1955, and neither his immense love for the club, nor his dedication to the cause has waned in all those years. As the front door opened on the large, white, Hertfordshire house, I was soon to be given another lesson in loyalty - a word further diluted by every passing day in modern life and even more so in modern day football.

Henry had to wait over five years for his big first team break at Spurs yet remained strong and confident. Then, when his chance finally came, Ron grabbed it with both hands and never looked back. But little did he realise that his grasp on the left-back position would be such a permanent one.

He and Peter Baker formed the back line of the famous 'Double' team. They were a side filled with star names, yet built on strong, home-constructed foundations - Ron and Peter being the only locally born players in the team. The Mackay's, Blanchflower's, and Smith's of this world would sleep a whole lot easier knowing such rocks were always there to defend them. And to this day, over half a century after joining the club, the name Ron Henry still defends the great name of Tottenham Hotspur.

Were you always a Spurs man Ron?

Most definitely. My Uncle Sid first took me to White Hart Lane when I was a very small, wide-eyed lad. He lived down at Stamford Hill, and I remember my first match was against Chesterfield. I couldn't believe my eyes. I just hadn't realised that football grounds were that big, and with such huge, swaying crowds.

Having passed through the old iron turnstiles, we made our way out on to the vast terracing. It wasn't all seated like it is now, and both ends of the ground were massive banks housing thousands of fans. As soon as we arrived behind the goal I smelt the atmosphere and knew that I wanted to play for them.

After that I used to travel from Redbourn with mates and regularly stayed in my aunt's place in the old Guinness Trust Buildings at Stamford Hill just so that we didn't miss a game. Spurs have always been my team. Always have been, always will be.

So where does the Ron Henry football story start?

My twin brother and I were evacuated from London during the War. They took us to Redbourn in Hertfordshire, where we were taken in by a grand old lady called Mrs. Pacey. But as far as football is concerned it all started out for me on the green in the village. I'd always mixed and played against older lads, and at the age of about fourteen got picked for Redbourn village men's team. I was never fazed or daunted by the size of my opponents, in fact I revelled in being able to get stuck in and use my strength against them. But it wasn't until I joined the Army that I really started to learn my trade.

The Forces were packed with top players and internationals in those days. People like Albert Quixall of Sheffield Wednesday, Derek Healey of Orient and Freddy Cooper from West Ham. They were just some of the names I played with and against. What a perfect breeding ground for what was to follow!

What were the Army years like?

I joined up at eighteen and vividly remember standing in the mess with all the other new recruits. When asked who could play football, my arm shot up, and because I told them that I'd played for Luton in the Midweek League, I was immediately drafted to Woolwich Barracks. I was told that I'd be permanently stationed there and that's where I teamed up with Terry Dyson. We've been mates ever since.

So how did the move to Spurs come about?

While washing the mud off our legs after a game for the Army, a man approached us and asked if we'd like to play for Spurs. "What do we have to do?" I said naively. "Sign these forms" he said.

We had no phone at home in those days but were given permission by the people down at the village shop to use theirs. I called the number that the scout had given us and called through to the club. The voice at the other end was Arthur Rowe, the then manager. I told him what I'd been doing and he told me that I was to come and join them.

"There's three week's money waiting for you down here" he said. "Where do I have to go?" I replied. No second thoughts, no questions about travelling or conditions, and certainly no agents involved.

Money must have been really tight back then?

We got paid twenty-five shillings a week in the Army, and out of that we had to pay for everything; boots, dubbing, laces, blades, toiletries, and boot repairs. We also had to put thirteen studs into each boot then! Travelling to so many games proved extremely expensive, but none of us seemed to care at the time. On being accepted at Spurs, Sergeant Major Anson from Woolwich pulled me aside and said, "If you don't become a pro I'll have you back in the Army in double time Henry!" - I was off to Spurs for a fortnight's trial and couldn't get there quick enough.

And so you signed for the mighty Tottenham Hotspur?

I certainly did. The journey to Tottenham was a shocker in those days, though, but I was so wrapped up in playing that it didn't really bother me. I used to get the 6.50am bus to St. Albans, then I'd run down London Road to get the 7.20am train. That would get me in to Kings Cross by 7.50am, where I'd pick up the underground to Manor House. The Victoria line hadn't been thought of at that time so the last leg of the journey involved a trolley-bus ride to Tottenham, which got me in at around 9.00am. Then I had to do it again in reverse on the way home!

You did this for every training session and match?

Yes, even in my first team days I used to do that journey all the way to White Hart Lane, travel with the boys up to Manchester or Newcastle, then because I'd missed the last bus, had to walk the last five miles back from St. Albans. All this after playing a full League game remember. On some match-days I'd be on the move for the best part of twenty-four hours!

Do you remember your first day at White Hart Lane?

Of course, I'll never forget it. Just beyond the main front gate there used to be a doorway that I managed to confuse with the club entrance. I remember walking in there and asking if I could see Mr. Rowe. "No, you can't" said the old gentleman behind the desk. "But I need to see him. I'm starting here today and he told me to be early" I protested. "But you can't see him" said the man. "Why not?" I replied indignantly. "Because this is an Undertakers" he replied. I turned in my embarrassment and fled as quickly as I could.

Did it take long to settle after you found the right way in?

After two weeks of getting in early, and always being there to help organize the kit, Arthur Rowe turned to Cecil Poynton and asked, "What's this young Henry boy like?" Cecil replied, "If enthusiasm makes a player, I'll sign him as a pro!" I'd made it. From those early years standing behind the goal with Uncle Sid, to being taken on full time by Spurs.

Not long afterwards I was told to go down to a little local tailors in Tottenham and sort myself out a blazer with club badge. I was the proudest lad in the world and wore that blazer around Redbourn whenever I could. In fact, I doubt if the village locals ever saw me out of it.

You waited five years before forcing your way into the first team. What was the experience like?

I made my full debut at Huddersfield on Easter Monday, April 1955. We needed a point to stay in Division One so you could say I was thrown into the cauldron for that one. Mel Hopkins had broken his nose in an international against Scotland and Arthur Rowe told me that I was going to be twelfth man. There were no substitutes in those days remember.

"Don't worry son" he said, "You won't be playing". But Harry Clarke then managed to hurt his leg on a train door and Arthur came back to tell me that I was in. "Thanks Mr. Rowe" I said. "Don't call me Mr. Rowe" he replied. "Call me Arthur now".

Were you always confident of getting your chance?

Yes, I always knew my chance would come, although I loved playing in the reserves, and realistically I was still learning my trade. It was a huge jump going up to the first team with all those well-seasoned professionals. Still, I'd worked hard and deserved my chance, especially after all the extra training I'd put in.

Nerves effect different players in different ways. I was normally cool as a cucumber, but even I got nervous as Cecil handed me my playing kit. "Who's number one?" I asked him. "Ted Ditchburn" he replied. Oh my God I thought. "And who's that peg belong to?" I went on. "Oh, don't touch that one" he replied. "That's Alf Ramsey's". We got our point to stay up, then I went back to the reserves for the next game.

What was life like as a young Spurs player in that post-War era?

They were great times, a real mixture to be honest. By then, wife Edna and I had moved to Green Street, so I'd walk down to the ground every morning to clear my mind and prepare for the day.

Sometimes she'd get bored if the club went on tour or if I was away for a match somewhere, so I decided to buy her a television set that I'd seen while walking to work one morning. I had to buy it on H.P. though, as I couldn't afford to buy it outright at the time. Believe it or not I used to work on a local chicken farm earning £6 a week to supplement my close-season pay.

In my day we didn't do all that warm-up lark. It just wasn't thought of then. You'd do a few exercises in the training room and that was that. There's so much more to consider now, especially with the younger players. Some kids still need an arm of reassurance round their shoulder; some simply need a boot up the backside.

Back then we all used to wash our own kits. Each player would head home with a full kit which had to be returned the next game. Alfie Stokes had washed his so many times that his socks had no bottoms to them, but the times dictated that we kept them until they disintegrated.

Sometimes a few of us would sneak back into the five-a-side court at the ground. The last one in would lock the door behind him so Cecil Poynton couldn't get back in. We were big kids really who just loved our football and regularly returned for extra training or just to have a kick-about match between ourselves.

When did you first realise that your Spurs team was going to be something really special?

It was in the Lenin Stadium in Moscow. The venue was massive and a very, very special place to play. We knew that we must put on a big performance there. I soon realised that 'somebody up there' put that team together!

What was it like playing in Spurs' most famous side?

Very special. There were no prima donna's in that side. We were all one. There were no individuals and very much a team effort. It was also just as much a pleasure being out there on the pitch with them as it was off it. From the moment I met Terry Dyson as a youth, to the moment the team started to go their own ways, there were never any cliques.

We had a fabulous team spirit and I spent every day mixing with a great bunch of friends. Each one had his own job on the pitch, and every one knew what that job was.

Mine was to defend and rarely was I encouraged to go over the half-way line, [laughs] hence my historic goal haul. You could have put two young-sters in that side and it still wouldn't have changed things. Everyone had his job to do and it ticked over like a well-oiled engine. In fact, it almost got to the stage where it was a pleasure to lose! It brought us back down to earth again and made us realise why we were all put together.

Winning the 'Double' was unheard of in those days, can you explain the experience?

It's like most other things in life, the first is always the best. It's like a book, the first copy is always the most valuable. We sometimes used to discuss doing the 'Double' in the changing rooms amongst ourselves, but never breathed a word outside or to the Press. We just used to keep our feet on the ground and got on with the next game.

You got the man-of-the-match award in the 1961 FA Cup Final. What do you remember of the match?

I'd studied Howard Riley, the Leicester City winger, for weeks leading up to the great day; what he did, what he liked and didn't like. He was certainly one of the best outside-right's in the game at the time. I really think my preparation helped me gain my man of the match award. It helped me pre-empt most of Howard's moves before he made them and watered down any threat from a wide position.

Were you calm on the day, or did nerves take over?

I couldn't wait to get to Wembley quick enough that day. That was a time where we just knew we'd win every game and that included the final. Really, it was just a matter of how many goals we'd score. We also played with one of those old heavy footballs, and to be honest Spurs didn't play well, certainly not as well as the rest of the season. I remember coming off the pitch at the end to see Bill Nicholson's face staring back at me. "We owe you a lot for today" he said. "In twenty years time you'll know exactly what you've achieved today". He was right.

After talking about the 1961 Cup Final, how could I leave out a question about Europe and the famous 'Lilywhites'?

It was an inspired moment in history making Spurs wear all white in European matches, and went a long, long way towards making them such special and unique occasions. There were many great moments of course. Night's I'll never forget as long as I live.

Which one sticks in your mind the most?

Gornik Zabrze of Poland were a good side. At one stage they had us four-nil down in the first leg with our backs against the wall, until Cliff Jones and Terry Dyson rescued us to take a two-goal deficit back to White Hart Lane the following week.

We went on to beat them eight-one at Tottenham in the second leg but I don't think they'd ever encountered a crowd like our's before. They just froze on the night as we smashed in goal after goal. We were awesome in that game. Our supporters really lifted us too and even had the sense of fairness to applaud a tremendous goal from Pohl of Gornik.

Are there any other games that stick in your mind from Europe?

Feyenoord were another top side that we played in the European Cup. They were extremely tough to break down at the time, and remember there were only real Champions in the competition then. But probably the best of them all was the great Portuguese side, Benfica. They had Mario Coluna, Simoes, Captain Jose Aguas, and the man known then as the 'Black Panther', the great Eusebio. In reality they were very, very lucky to get past us in the semi-final.

They were the basis for the great Portuguese side that lost to England in the World Cup semi-final, and later the Benfica team beaten by Manchester United in 1968. I remember playing against the great Jose Torres later in my career. I didn't half f...ing kick him. He told me that they would beat Spurs. "You won't without any legs" I told him!

In travelling the world with Spurs you must have had some great times with the lads?

Yes, as I've said, they were a tremendous bunch to be with, both on and off the pitch. In my playing days we visited many places, including Poland, Portugal, Czechoslovakia and Spain. We also did two tours of Canada and two to the United States. Long-haul journeys like those usually lasted between six and ten weeks, so it was very, very tough on wives and girlfriends who were left behind. I remember travelling over on the 'Empress of England' on one trip when I got a telegram to say that Edna and my son Steve were doing well – I'd missed out on both his birth and the first six weeks of his life due to being on tour with Spurs.

Going to Moscow really was one of the big experiences of my life with the lads, although, if he were still here to tell the tale, John White wouldn't have exactly agreed with me. We were standing in Red Square, which was choc-a-bloc with pigeons, when John suddenly clapped his hands loudly and all the birds swirled upwards to the sky. Of course, he was only messing around and all the lads started to laugh. Next thing, a group of Russian police officers hauled him off to the station. Naturally, they let him go once they found out who he was, but it was nip and tuck at one time.

We were the first English side to visit Moscow and what a story the press would have made of that had they kept him in. But of all the places I visited with Tottenham, the best was definitely Israel. It's a beautiful location and even now I always think of it with warm affection.

I remember sitting around the pool with the players looking out to sea one day when we spotted a film crew and a small collection of people had gathered. We later found out that they were filming a feature called "The Longboats". Anyway, all of a sudden a man came over and asked if he could sit with us. "By all means, take a seat" I said. He then went on to explain that he knew who I was, and that I probably wouldn't know him. The man was Richard Widmark, a famous Hollywood actor at the time.

Three years later, I was standing in Grand Central Station in New York when Widmark walked up to me and said hello. I asked him how he was, and what he was doing there. He replied that he was waiting for a friend. While we talked I remarked on how impressive his overcoat was, so he reached inside his pocket and gave me the contact details for his tailor. "He'll make you one" he said. We shook hands again and off he went to meet his friend. So, with a little time on our hands, me and a few of the players wandered off to the tailor's to have our coats made up.

I really loved that mac. It's a shame it got ruined by a marker pen while signing autographs.

What was your relationship with the Spurs fans?
Generally, I loved my relationship with the fans at Tottenham, but being a naturally shy kind of character it was nice to get back to Redbourn where people treated me normally rather than as a personality. I know that there

were a few criticisms of me but every player suffers that at some time in their career, especially if they stay in one place for a long time.

How did you cope with the criticism and intrusion?

Important factors of the job involved conditioning yourself for being either criticised or recognised in public places. I never minded signing things for people, but there were times when the family and I just wanted a nice quiet day at the seaside wearing jeans and sweaters, and eating fish and chips out of a newspaper without being bothered.

Then somebody would recognise me and I'd just want to go and hide. Not because I didn't appreciate their attention, more because we were on a family day out and just wanted to be treated normally. I've never been one for hogging the limelight.

Who were the characters and tough opponents that you faced then?

Lancashire was a very searching place to go in those days. Places like Bolton and Blackburn had their very own way of welcoming you then. They played hard, and dished out as much as we gave them. Nobody complained though; it was all accepted as part of the game. As you probably know, I was no shrinking violet myself.

One player who stuck in my mind as a very difficult person to mark was John Connelly, the old Burnley, Manchester United and England winger. He was very fast, exceptionally tricky, and always gave me a good, tough game. I had a lot of respect for John.

Dave Mackay was a rugged old so-and-so, and there were many, many others who plied their trade in what were tough times. George Best? I kicked him a few times and he went off... [laughs]

At the beginning of the 1960-61 season, we went on a run of eleven consecutive wins. We were away at Wolves and had just thrashed them four-nil. Wanderers were no mugs in those days. We'd finished third the season before but they managed to finish a place and a point above us.

I'll never forget the great Billy Wright coming into our changing room after the game. He climbed up on to the table and said, "If there's a team that can beat you lads, I'd love to be there to see it". He didn't have to do that but Billy was a true football man and a superb ambassador for the game. He was a great, great captain and how much do you think that meant to all the lads sitting in the changing room witnessing that sight?

What was Stanley Matthews like?

The first time I played against him I had an exceptionally good day. Cliff Jones and I had got our heads together and planned a way to block his runs. I also managed to push it past him a few times and got a few tackles in while Jonesy and I played together as a partnership. Stan rarely got a sniff in that game, and as he wandered past me at the end, he stopped me and told me that I'll be a very good player with a little more experience. I thanked him, but told him not to forget my partner in crime, Cliff Jones. Matthews laughed and wandered back to the changing rooms, but again, it was an accolade from yet another great pro that meant so much to me.

You scored one goal in two hundred and eighty seven Spurs appearances, I bet you were a nightmare on the coach home that night?

Thought you might bring that one up [laughs]. We were playing Manchester United at home in February 1965, not that I remember much about it you know! As I said earlier, we weren't exactly encouraged to cross the half-way line in those days as full-backs, but I remember the ball being cleared and seeing it bouncing directly in front of me about a foot high.

It sat up beautifully. I just swung a boot at it and watched it fly into their goal. No one was more surprised than me to see it hit the back of the net. Couldn't have been so bad though, it won us the game. I was king of the jungle after that.

Bill Nicholson made you Captain post-Blanchflower, how proud a moment was that?

After Dave Mackay broke his leg there hadn't been much talk of captaincies and the like. I remember lining up to go on to the pitch for a game when Nick casually handed me the match ball. The full implications of what he'd done didn't hit home for a few seconds, but when it did, I was so proud. It's something that nobody can ever take away from me, and as a Spurs fan myself, well, simple words can't explain how I felt.

You were also picked to play for England, what do you remember of the game against France?

I played for England once, in a European Championship Qualifier in February 1963. We lost five-two in Paris on a terrible pitch and I never got a look in again.

Who had the biggest influence on your career?

I'm sure you're expecting me to trot out a number of names from the back-room staff, maybe Bill himself, or some obscure teacher from my past. The truth is, all of those helped me in no small way to become a better player, but the real hero in my life is Edna, my wife.

She's an incredibly hard worker who has backed me in everything I ever wanted to do. She had to contend with some extraordinarily long periods where I was travelling and playing, and always stuck by me whatever the circumstances. Edna's simply the best wife I could ever have wished for, and without her, my career would never have been so successful or enjoyable.

Knowing that you have the full support of your immediate family is an exceptionally warming feeling. In fact, to pre-empt your next question, yes, I'd do it all the same way again, or should I say, *we'd* do it all the same way again.

So, after almost half a century at Spurs, you're still coaching there?
They're my team, my club. It would be impossible to even contemplate being anywhere else. In fact, I think I'm the longest serving player in Spurs history as I went back to play in the reserves right up until 1968!

You must have witnessed massive changes at the club in that time?
Yes, I've seen things change drastically; from the austere, spartan places that football clubs were in the mid-fifties, to the high-tech, modern institutions that they've become.

Why has your relationship with the club always been so strong
I've been associated with Spurs for over half a century now, they've never cheated me, and I certainly don't think I've ever short-changed them. Everyone knows that players from my era never earned a great deal out of the game in financial terms, but Spurs were generally very good to me. In fact, I bought my first-ever home from them and offered to pay back a sizeable chunk of any profits, not that I was looking to make a profit out of it.

They turned it down and told me to keep it. How can I ever say a bad word about a club that looks after you like that, and after so many happy years? They're not only in my blood but in my dreams too. Some nights I still wake up literally in a sweat. I have to go downstairs and dry myself down.

Edna says, "Where have you been?" I always say, "Playing football". "Did you win?" she'd say. "No, we lost" I reply. Would you believe I still even have nightmares about forgetting my boots or kit, as if modern clubs wouldn't be stocked to the roof with spares!

Did you ever consider going elsewhere during your career Ron?
Like I said, Spurs are my team. Even as a player I never considered anyone else. I was supposed to travel to Wolverhampton Wanderers while I was playing for the village team, but the trial got cancelled due to snow. I simply never, ever went back there, and certainly didn't want to move that far away in any case. There were also rumours at one time that Blackburn Rovers wanted me but the same rules applied. It was

always in my mind that Spurs were my team, and that's where I always wanted to play and stay.

Do you know many of the current first team?

No, not really. I coached Ledley King when he was a thirteen-year old. It was clear to all that he was going to make it. I spend most of my time with the under-eighteens now and have more contact with the junior sides than the first team squad.

Finally Ron, who's that little chap smiling out of that photograph on the mantlepiece?

[Pause for answer] Oh, that's my nephew Clive. A bonnier, more cheerful lad you couldn't wish to meet and a complete and utter Spurs fanatic. In fact, when he was alive, he sat on the bench a few times at home first team games. He was twenty-three when he passed on and only lived across the way, opposite our house in Redbourn.

There's not a day that goes past that we don't think about him or mention his name. When he died, Spurs sent us a special club tracksuit to bury him in. He'd have loved that. So many people turned up to celebrate Clive's life. That will stay with me forever. It was a fantastic gesture from a great football club and great people. The warmth they showed to Clive and his family will never be forgotten.

He was a wonderful lad who was always teasing that he was going to take my England badge away from me. In the days that I played in, they used to give you a large badge with the three lions on to pin on to your kit. I was so proud of that badge, and Clive knew it. With that cheeky grin of his, he'd find lots of little ways of trying to talk me in to giving it to him. Well, he's got it forever now, and I couldn't think of a better place for it to be.

Phil
Beal

Era 1960 - 1975
Appearances 417 **Goals** 1

Laurie McMenemy once outlined a theory that the UK was made up of several 'hotbeds of football'. When it came to unearthing young football talent, his suggested areas were familiar ones, with most of our larger cities nominated. According to the former Southampton manager, a quiet, leafy suburb in Surrey was the last place you'd search for an emerging star, that is, until Phillip Beal put little Godstone on the map.

In reality, Phil received scant encouragement in fulfilling his early dreams, yet was driven by a steely determination that soon drew the attention of other professional clubs. Their loss was Spurs' gain and for many years his name became ensconced in a defence that virtually chose itself. In fact, history writers fall over themselves to praise the Highbury back five of the late eighties and early nineties, but unfortunately, they fail dismally to acknowledge the White Hart Lane half-dozen from the previous decade.

Jennings, Kinnear, Knowles, Mullery, England, Beal; names that formed the bedrock of a new era in Spurs history, and icons who warmed the hearts of those lucky enough to have seen them play.

Whatever the challenge, Phil met it head-on, throughout a lengthy career. Spurs fans saw this attitude demonstrated when Beal made his debut to replace none other than the late, great Danny Blanchflower. What an act to follow, but Phil rose manfully to the challenge.

With many of Tottenham's great 'Double' team coming to the end of their careers, a new dawn was breaking; one based around the solid rocks that were England and Beal. With excellent timing in the tackle, a quiet, authoritative, dominance, plus a distinguished touch of class. Phil retained a reliability of nature that made him one of Nicholson's stalwarts, Beal's game reminded me of an early-day Gary Mabbutt, unheralded by some, relied upon by many, and at times, the only uncapped player at a club used to buying the cream of the crop.

To those of his era, Phil Beal represented many things; reliability, honesty and integrity. While others blew hot and cold, this was one blonde that stayed calm no matter the circumstances. The public persona of Phil was of steely-nerved efficiency carried out behind a mask of stone. Where others oozed personality, Phil would rarely show on-field emotion. Behind that facade, though, lived a practical joker par excellence. For a man labelled 'The Quiet One' in his testimonial programme, Phil Beal's great sense of fun and humour stands out to this day. It just goes to prove that appearances are not always what they seem. – All four hundred and seventeen of them.

Where did the football adventure start for you Phil?
I came from an unconventional background as far as footballers go. Having stepped up from Reigate Borough to the county side, I was spotted

by Spurs' Assistant Manager, Harry Evans. Not long after that game a letter arrived from Tottenham Hotspur inviting me for a trial. It was more or less end of season by then, and in those days the Spurs pitch wasn't the best. I recall just a sprinkling of grass down the wings while the rest was suffering from the ravages of a busy season. After the game they asked me if I'd enjoyed myself and then invited me back to Cheshunt for a second trial.

So being a Surrey lad you must've been a Manchester United fan?

[Laughs] No, believe it or not I was a Wolves fan as a kid. At the time Wolves had some great players and were appearing in the old European Fairs Cup. People like Bert Williams in goal, Billy Wright, Johnny Hancocks, and Ron Flowers. I really admired all of them, and how ironic that we'd go on to meet them in later years in the UEFA Cup Final. Wolves had a superb stadium then, with great crowds. The one game that really sticks in my mind is that famous tie they played against Honved.

Were you always a defender?

Yes, even as a lad, then all through my professional career.

How many others were plucked from those trials?

I was the sole survivor from thirty-six boys who took them but was joined by another lad called Alan Dennis, who the club decided to sign without a trial. Spurs had been after the England schoolboy for some time and were extremely happy to have signed him. Unfortunately he only made the reserves, but was considered the hottest full-back around at the time.

Were you always totally confident that you'd make it?

I had to be in many ways. My parents weren't really football people and I hadn't exactly been born in a footballing area. In fact, my parents didn't want me to join Spurs at all to concentrate on my education. They felt it was all too risky and worried that I'd reach seventeen or eighteen on the scrap heap having missed out on my schooling. Eventually, after much discussion, they gave me their blessing to join Spurs. Once there, all I wanted was to become a full-time pro and force myself into the first team.

What were your career options other than football?

As far as sports were concerned it was always football for me, but before Spurs came in I'd had notions of joining the Merchant Navy. I really couldn't tell you why, maybe I was swayed by my parents view that I should be forging a more solid career. As a young man I wanted to travel and see the world but Mum and Dad found me a job in an electrical company. Then the Spurs offer followed.

Were there many clubs in for you when Spurs came into the mix?
Fulham and Crystal Palace had both had me watched and were considering moves, with one or two others keeping tabs. Once Spurs threw their hat in the ring that was that. There was only one place I wanted to go.

How were you accepted at Tottenham?
Right from the beginning it was a great place to be. I joined at fifteen and from the onset they started to help and develop me. The lads used to call me 'Little 'un' due to my small stature and the club quickly sent me to the club's weights trainer, Bill Watson.

Before Spurs, I hadn't realized just how slight I was, so after normal training I used to go back for extra sessions. Sometimes there'd just be the two of us there but I was so determined to develop my size and strength that I felt every session was valuable.

When did you become full-time?
I was seventeen. Bill Nicholson called me in to say I'd made it. I can't tell you how I felt but it made me even more determined to make that first team. In fact, I made my debut in an away game at Aston Villa at eighteen-years-old. My first task was to replace Danny Blanchflower in a Monday night game. Most of that side was made up from the old 'Double' team.

Do you still have memories of the day?
Bill Nicholson phoned me on the Sunday to tell me I'd be travelling, then pulled me aside on the day to tell me I was playing. I guess he didn't want me worrying, or getting on edge, or even losing sleep over the matter. My ever-lasting memories were of a humid night with 42,000 noisy fans.

I still don't know to this day whether it was anxiety or just nerves, but when I ran out on to the pitch I felt drained of energy. The whole scenario of the big crowd and the hot, humid conditions really had me struggling.

Were you generally a nervous character?
Of course we all suffer from nerves of varying degrees, but even as a young man they died after the first few moments of a match. Even now, when I play in charity matches, there's a slight presence of nerves, but I still tend to burn that off very quickly.

Were the legends of the past a help or a hindrance to you?
They were fantastic. Nobody in the team thought they were too big to talk to the junior players and the older players were always on hand to help. There wasn't a single player who wouldn't put himself out for any lad who

needed a word of guidance or opinion. And that was consistent from the junior sides all the way up to the first team.

Did you immediately mix socially with the regular players?

Yes, especially after away games. I remember playing at Sheffield Wednesday in the early days. We travelled up on the Friday morning, and to be honest, I felt a little lost not knowing what the procedure was for games. Jimmy Greaves and Terry Dyson must've sensed this and asked if I fancied going to the pictures with them.

When we arrived there was a great big queue down one side, and another giant one the other, so I just stood looking at the pair of them thinking we had no chance. Greavsie didn't say a word but walked into the cinema and asked for the Manager. When they came out he looked at us and said, "Oh Jimmy. No need to worry, I've got three seats up in the circle if you'd like to come this way." Jim then turned round to me and said, "Stick with me Beally son. You'll make the grade".

I couldn't believe what I'd seen and had to give him ten out of ten for sheer cheek. Those boys made me feel welcome from the start. They were always great fun, always there to help, and despite the rumours, drinking was only ever at a social level.

Apart from Jimmy Greaves, who were the characters at the club?

The one that will always stick in my mind is Dave Mackay. In those days the senior squad used to train first and the youth side would go out last. Most afternoons were spent in the gym where we'd do special ball skills like chipping against targets on the wall. Invariably, the gym door would open and Dave would come back for extra training with the youths.

Status didn't bother Dave. He was quite happy joining in with the juniors and would even play in our five-a-sides. And mark my words, Dave hated losing. If you were on his side you had to play to win. He'd go through brick walls to get a result, youth players or not!

Were you in awe of him, scared of him, or both?

No, my way of bedding in was to treat everyone the same. In fact I looked on Dave as being just another player and probably treated him the way he treated me.

The man made no distinction between youth and senior. I think that was a really good way to be. Of course, there were a couple of sad occasions where Dave was concerned, none more so than when he broke his leg against Glasgow Rangers.

It was typical of the man to fight his way back into the first team and the tenacity he showed in achieving it was amazing.

So you had huge respect for him as a man as well as a player?

I think we all did. He was a fighter, and wasn't that captured for all time in that famous photograph of him and Billy Bremner? I believe that was in his comeback game and felt inspired by the man to stand up for myself. Dave's inspiration certainly rubbed off on everyone at the club. He was a great leader and a pleasure to know.

What of Danny Blanchflower, the man you replaced on your debut?

Danny was extremely eloquent and very, very deep. He generally kept himself to himself yet was extremely close to Bill. I always felt that team tactics were a mixture of both men's ideas. Danny was a real thinker.

The terrace image of Phil Beal was of the cool, unassuming stalwart. Were you aware of this or a persona you had to live up to?

No, to me I simply had a job to do, and nothing was going to get in the way of that.

You were focused, but I've heard you were very superstitious too?

Well, I had a match pattern that I had to stick to. Call it a ritual, call it superstition, call it what you like, but I had to be the last person out of the dressing room. To achieve this I'd always go out two or three minutes after everyone else.

Once, I got half-way up the tunnel and sensed somebody behind me, so I literally turned around and went back. When I got there, I checked the treatment room, the washrooms, and even the toilets. Once I'd done all that I was happy in my mind that I'd be the last one out, even though I'd already asked the trainer if anyone else was left behind.

This also applied at half-time. In one game I was last out for the second half when Bill stopped me to pass on some final instructions to the other players. I nodded and said I would, but as I approached the pitch I noticed the game had already restarted. When I finally got on none of the officials said a word but some of my team-mates seem bemused.

I don't know why I put myself through that ritual every week. Some put shirts or shorts on last, or whatever made them feel at ease. I just had to be the last player to run out on to the pitch, simple as that.

Did the others say anything to you or think your routine was weird?

They may have thought it but other players appreciate each other's routines. Alan Gilzean used to be ready in two minutes flat and would sit there staring. He'd be totally kitted out, and was probably wondering what the hell I was doing considering some of the oddities I went through. My way was to get in the dressing room around half past one and go through a list that made me feel comfortable. Others like Mike England would be outside talking with anyone and everyone until two forty, then stroll in and get changed. Everyone was different and we all had our own way of dealing with nerves. You have to go out there happy and settled.

There were rumours that Gilly and Greavsie trained on pints of Guinness, were any of these terrace myths true?
I never saw Greavsie drink Guinness for a start, and I was personally shocked when I heard that he had a problem. Truth was he was a social drinker like all the others.

Alan Gilzean was a real character. I remember hearing him let go an extremely loud belch in the changing room once. "Pardon me" says Gilly. "It must've been the sausage, bacon and egg I had earlier." Jim used to have a swift half in the White Hart pub, now and again, I think I'm right in saying that his problems started after he left Tottenham.

Were you a good trainer yourself?
To be honest, I never really enjoyed training, especially the long distance running. I work in the Oak Room at Tottenham on match days now and when Martin Chivers introduces us to the guests he normally begins with these words... "Welcome to Tottenham Hotspur. There's a friend of mine at the back there. Bill Nicholson always used to say that he'd pencil him in on the team sheet first – if he wasn't on the treatment bench!"

A lot of the time I suffered from calf muscle trouble and often had injections for it. This rather strangely used to occur at training time [laughs]. Invariably the lads used to ask me on Friday if I thought I'd pass my late fitness test. I'd simply shrug and smile. "Oh I wonder what the outcome will be?" they'd all laugh. I loathed long distance running but the irony was that I probably covered a similar distance in five-a-side training.

How did Bill Nicholson view this behaviour?
Bill was fine as long as you put in maximum effort and did it in the five-a-sides and gym training. If you didn't, he'd have you outside running around the track or power-walking. Once, I remember Bill up front leading the run when some of the lads hitched a lift on the back of a milk float – and Greavsie was the ringleader [Laughs loud]. Bill just stood there wondering how they'd managed to get back before him.

What effect did Bill Nicholson and his assistant Eddie Baily have on your development?
Eddie was more of a trainer than Bill. He put us through our paces and kept us fit and motivated. Bill was the tactician, always concentrating on

what we were going to do, and how to apply it. He also analysed what we'd done wrong in last weeks' game, win, lose or draw, and how we were going to improve in the next.

Eddie was superb at writing reports on the opposition. He compiled extensive dossiers, which we read on his return. They were superb. He'd report on individual players and team tactics. For example, if a winger was all left foot and tried to beat you down the line, Joe Kinnear and Cyril Knowles would be well primed. His reports informed us whether a player was good or weak in the air, or had a strong right foot, etc. Everything was covered and helped immensely in our build up to big games.

Did you or the other players take them seriously?

Oh yes, they were invaluable. Everyone read and digested them because they were helping us to win games. Of course, everyone had a laugh and joke about them, but if you were to read one you'd appreciate just how good a judge Eddie was.

He'd even have chapter and verse on the 'keepers, and whether they kicked with their left or right and how good they were at taking crosses. Those dossiers won us dozens of matches, so how could anyone knock them?

Were there any other tacticians in the team?

Not really; players didn't really talk tactics then. Of course Mike England and I had to have a good understanding because we were the central defensive pairing. We always wanted Mike to stay in a central position. It was pointless him moving to the right or to the left. We wanted him to stay in the middle to make it difficult for the opposition to pass. Mike was fantastic in the air and I don't believe the club ever replaced him.

The defence almost picked itself in those days. Would you have ever changed it?

No, because we were successful. Of course there was pressure from the reserves. They had players who'd walk into most other senior sides. I remember Pete Collins replacing Mike in the Aston Villa League Cup Final. Mike was injured at the time and I like to feel that I helped Peter through the game. He was due to face Andy Lochead, a tough, physical, and ungainly character at the best of times.

What did you say to him?

First of all I emphasised that he had to win his headers. Andy was a big strong guy and a formidable opponent in the air. I told Pete what he could expect and that he was to use his physical presence whenever necessary.

Pete was a good player and went on to have a marvellous game that day. He richly deserved his medal.

How did you prepare for the big Cup Finals?

Everyone did their own thing in preparing mentally but sometimes we'd do the simplest things as a team. I remember one year we strolled out of the hotel and just went for a short walk down Oxford Street. We looked in a few shops, wandered around, and then went back to leave for Wembley. Of course, a few people recognized us and shouted things out, but in the main people were pretty good. As far as mental preparation is concerned, I used to get ready for games the same way, whether they were Cup Finals or everyday League games against regular opposition.

Do you have many memories of the two League Cup Finals?

My overriding memory is coming down the Wembley tunnel to the roar of 100,000 voices. I've played in front of 125,000 in the Aztec Stadium for Spurs against the Mexican national side, but nothing comes remotely close to the Wembley experience. That was on tour just before the Mexicans came to London for the 1966 World Cup and I'll never forget the moat around the pitch or the armed soldiers protecting it.

Wasn't that in place to protect the crowd from the players?

[Laughs] I wouldn't be surprised, but they kicked off at midday just to give them an advantage. The place had everything. They even had guys standing around with oxygen because of the altitude. I remember asking Gilly if he fancied a slug, "Naaah" he said. "Just get me a cold beer".

You missed the 1967 Cup Final with an injury. How did that occur?

It happened against Manchester City at home. I remember running back towards our goal when a player clipped or pushed me from behind. I fell forward with my arm underneath me and heard it snap. During the operation they had to manipulate the bone back to its normal position, and as you can see, I'm left with this six-inch scar.

The following Monday's paper carried the caption, "This is the moment that Phil Beal broke his arm." The picture was of me, with City's Mike Doyle in the background. Later, I ran into Mike in an hotel whilst on holiday. He'd wanted to approach me before but thought I might be bitter at what had happened. To that day he'd always believed he was responsible, but to be honest, I couldn't tell you who did it. We subsequently became good friends and I even attended his wedding. I went to the Cup Final, and the banquet afterwards, but to be honest it made me feel worse. I never found it a comfortable experience just sitting and spectating.

Did you keep your medals?

I kept most of my memorabilia, although my daughters sent my 1971 League Cup winning shirt to the dustman in a spring clean. Anyway, I'll probably have to sell the rest when the pair of them get married [laughs].

What do you remember of the great European nights?

We loved playing at home in those games, and wearing all white. There was something special about that kit. Sometimes, you'd get into a tussle with a player at an away game and we'd remind them that they still had to come back to our place. They hated that. As tough as some of them were, they hated the close proximity of our fans to the pitch, and the fact that our's were so vociferous.

I've something of a mental block where the UEFA Cup Final at Wolves is concerned though. I can't tell you how I played, or much about the game, but I can remember the goals. In fact, if it wasn't for the goals I'd have questioned being there. [Smiles]

Who were the toughest side you encountered?

Without doubt that honour goes to Dynamo Bucharest. Bill Nicholson said he'd never seen a game, or a place like it in his life, with those huge perimeter fences to keep the crowd away. Jimmy Pearce came on as a substitute and was sent off after five minutes, and when Martin Peters tried to take his penalty, the 'keeper stood only five yards away from him. Of course, from that range he stopped it, and the referee dubiously allowed them to play on. When we got back, there were seven players on the table waiting for treatment. That game was so violent that they wouldn't let the film out of the country!

What's the funniest European story you remember?

A couple of days before the Vitorio Setubal game in Portugal, a few of us popped out for a meal. Just as my fish arrived, a call came through from Morris Keston so I left the table and went outside to speak to him. As I returned, the lads were finishing their first course. "Beally, the waiters have kept your fish hot for you mate" they said. When I lifted the lid off, I saw a fish head, a tail, and a long bone connecting the two. Everyone started to laugh, and this had clearly been prompted by Messrs. Knowles and Jennings, although the whole group were in fits of laughter.

Next day I was walking around the harbour when I spotted a local man selling fish heads. I asked him to put four into a plastic bag for me and took them back to the hotel. On arrival, I asked for the key to Cyril and Pat's room, and placed the heads in their pillows. They slept in that room all night, in between searching high and low for the revolting smell that filled the air. The next morning it absolutely reeked and they had to leave the room smelling like Billingsgate Market, with the fish heads still in the pillows. All the lads couldn't believe how bad it was and it didn't take them long to guess who'd got his own back, although they still struggled to find out where it was coming from. [Laughs] That might be where the phrase 'done up like a kipper' came from.

So you were the instigator of most of the practical jokes?

Yes, I was normally nominated to 'welcome' new players by pretending to be the Press. I'd disappear into my room at away games, wait for all the lads to turn up, then phone up the new boy with plenty of probing questions. I even did it with established guys like Martin Peters and regularly used to visit joke shops to find new ways of having fun.

I once got Pat Jennings with the old mustard pot trick. As he innocently opened the jar at lunch, a snake flew up in his face. OK, you had to be there! [laughs]

Do any other pranks spring to mind?

Barry Daines had only just arrived in the squad and we were all seated around a swimming pool on tour in Tokyo. I spotted a group of Japanese photographers, who all spoke good English, so I asked them if they'd mind taking a few snaps of Dainesy.

As he entered the room, I told him to put his swimming trunks on because they wanted some action shots of him diving. I also told him that there was cash in it for him and with this he went off to change. When he returned, he noticed that we hadn't got a football to do the scenes with. I told him not to worry and to pass me his flip-flops. Next thing you know, we're throwing them at Barry and he's diving off the board to catch them. The photographers were in on it and none of their cameras had any film.

Next day, I phoned Barry in my most convincing Press voice. I told him that the photos were excellent and that we'd leave them at the hotel reception with the money inside.

He seemed very happy so I went and got some A4 paper on which I drew a goal, a matchstick man, and a caption of Barry Daines saving shots for Tottenham. The rest of the lads were hiding around the corner when he picked up his envelope. On opening it, he glanced round and saw us all laughing our heads off. I can't tell you what he called us.

Who do you consider your toughest opponents back then?

When you came off a pitch having faced Denis Law, you knew you'd been in a tussle. Fortunately, Pat Jennings knew his game inside out. Denis was the eternal predator. Even now, at the Spurs training ground, Pat urges forwards to follow up free kicks and shots and encourages 'keepers to catch safely or suffer the Denis Law trick of nipping in and tucking in the rebound. I used to have some toughies against Bobby Gould too. When he was at Wolves he'd invariably play up front with Derek Dougan. I'd find myself marking Bobby.

He knew every trick in the book and dished out little digs and pushes all over the place. When the ref wasn't looking I used to dig him back just to even the score. Derek and Mike England were real enemies on the pitch but nowhere near as bad as Mike and Peter Osgood.

When I run into Ossie these days he sometimes blames me for some of those kicks, but those two really had their own little war going on – on and off the pitch.

Mike England was a tough guy who could really look after himself. Do you remember any particular moments of madness with him?

Yes, two come to mind and both against Manchester clubs. We were playing United once when their central defender, Jim Holton, popped up in our area. It was Mike's job to cover Jim so I turned round to find my own man to mark. Next thing, I've noticed the pair of them tangled on the floor and Mike with his fist clenched.

With that, Mike hit Jim square on the jaw. The ref missed the incident and Jim simply rose to his feet shouting, "That's one to you Mike." I couldn't believe it. Jim just accepted the punch as part of the game!

The second time was on leaving Maine Road by coach and returning to our hotel. The coach stopped, and for some unknown reason, two chaps across the road decided to taunt Mike. It seemed he was the sole target of their abuse and Mike sat listening to it without saying a word. Suddenly, he stood up and asked me if I'd take his bag for him. I asked him where he was going but ominously he remained silent.

Mike casually climbed off the coach, strolled over, confronting the one who had been swearing at him, before punching him on the chin. The coach pulled away in total silence.

There was another 'Big Mike Incident' up at Newcastle which I can remember like it happened yesterday. They had gone unbeaten for something like twenty-two matches at home and we'd just broken their record, two-one. We climbed down from the coach and tried to enter the train station, while the Geordie fans were mob-handed and being held back by the Police. It was scary to be honest, not to mention very dangerous.

As we were walking towards the train, one fan threw hot chocolate all over Mike England's suit. Once again we witnessed the old 'Welsh hammer' in action as a flying right hook caught the guy on the chin. That was a signal for us to leg it on to the train.

Come on, you must have a few more Mike England stories up your sleeve than just those?

[Laughs] Yes, there are many. I remember travelling up to Liverpool one year and rooming with Mike in The Post House hotel. At two in the morning there was an almighty noise going on so I called room service who told me that there was a fire alarm due to a bomb scare. I nudged Mike and told him we all had to evacuate the building and that everyone was assembling outside. Eventually he got up.

The next thing I knew, Mike was in the bathroom having a shave. I shouted at him to hurry, but he was undeterred, Mike had sauntered back into the bathroom and was putting on a collar and tie. And then, to top it all off, he strolled outside and called the lift!

Of course, eventually, we had to use the fire escape. As we clambered down we could see everyone from the hotel gathered in the forecourt in dressing gowns, jeans, or pyjamas. As they looked up, out came Big Mike looking a million dollars. None of us could believe it. It was one of the funniest things I'd ever seen.

Leeds and Liverpool were particularly tough sides in that era, what do you remember of the clashes with Tottenham?

Bill was meticulous about certain players' traits, but we'd played against them so many times we had first-hand knowledge of what we were dealing with. Even so, Bill would still remind us what we were up against. I usually found myself marking John Toshack and Kevin Keegan in that era and still remember our games against them. Leeds were probably physically tougher with guys like Bremner, Charlton, Madeley and Clarke in their ranks.

I remember in one of Steve Perryman's first games, after a few minutes he crashed into Johnny Giles. It was a fifty-fifty ball but Steve powered in leaving them in no doubt that he had no fear of reputations. Giles remained on the floor and I remember Martin Chivers turning round and saying, [laughs] "Oh no! Now Jackie Charlton is going to give me some real stick!" Leeds, in my memory, were the first team to line up on the half-way line to applaud the crowd and I'll never forget those little tassles that they had in their socks at the time.

Did you have good relationships with the Leeds players though?

Strange you should ask that as I was invited back about three years ago by Paul Reaney, which was strange really, because in all those years of playing against them we had never mixed socially. Of course, we knew their individual games but when matches ended we never got the chance to mix. That was the first time I'd ever had the chance to stand and chat with the guys we'd played against. There was a lot of banter flying around about who kicked who and it made a nice change to be able to stand and chat without the threat of a coach coming to whisk us away.

You had quite a good disciplinary record. Were there any misty moments?

I got sent off against Burnley once, after a tackle on their Welsh international winger, Leighton James. I didn't even look back to see the ref issue the card. I already knew that I was going for a walk.

Then there was the UEFA Cup semi-final against AC Milan. I went in to a tackle with Romeo Benetti, their Italian international, and as we stood up, he spat in my face. I stuck out an involuntary fist in his direction, which made his lip bleed.

Mike England came running over shouting "Beally, go down, go down." I ended up rolling around holding my ankle but the ref had missed it all. He obviously sensed a problem because Benetti had blood on his face and I was still doing my dying swan routine.

It was then that he booked us - but put the wrong numbers down! He booked the number six of Milan, and Spurs' number eight, Stevie Perryman. In the Press the next day the ref got slaughtered. It was even funnier when you think that I had a mop of blond hair and Stevie's dark. [Laughs].

Do you remember those half-time dog displays at White Hart Lane?

No I don't recall them, I was in the dressing room remember! [Laughs] But I do remember Cliff Jones completing one at Nottingham Forest one year! Suited and booted, we all walked across the pitch before the game. Bill was there. It must've been just before two o'clock because the crowd were just starting to trickle in. One of the lads asked Cliff if he fancied the obstacles himself. Of course, he was joking, but after we'd all chipped in a quid each, off he went around the dog display course in his suit. He was jumping fences, crawling through the tarpaulins, acting just like a dog. The crowd applauded and everyone was laughing like mad at his antics. And no, he didn't cock his leg half-way through, before you ask!

I understand you had a very good relationship with the flamboyant Spurs fan Morris Keston. Can you tell me about him?

I first met Morris via Terry Venables while we were players at Spurs. Morris has been a true and valued friend ever since. I don't believe that modern players have much time for people on the periphery of the game anymore. When we were playing, most players had friends outside of the sport. I don't believe that's true anymore, and Morris has certainly done a lot for all the players he came into contact with. Morris was a man with a big heart who never forgot his friends, and was always inviting my wife and

I to the Hilton or the Grosvenor for various functions, particularly when Spurs had won something big.

He was friends with everyone in that era and I always remember seeing him at parties with his great friend, Bobby Moore. In fact, through Morris, Bobby also became a friend of mine.

When Bob was Manager at Oxford City I was playing for Chelmsford to keep myself fit, so he invited me over to Oxford to play for them. I think Bobby only got me there because he wanted a drinking partner [Laughs].

It's ironic that you became friends with Bobby, especially as many believed it was he who cost you a hat-full of caps. Would you agree?

Yes, I'd love to agree, but we never thought about things that way then. Bobby was simply respected by everyone, especially me. In those days it was normally Bobby, Morris, Geoff Hurst and myself who'd share a table at functions. At one particular do, Bobby wasn't on our table. Everybody had got up to dance or whatever and Bob was sitting there on this own. It looked odd because he was normally surrounded by crowds of people so I wandered over to see how he was.

"You okay mate?" I asked; and as I glanced down, I noticed he had a large ice bucket on one side and a crate of lager on the other [laughs]. "Yeah, no problem Phil. I'm fine" said Bobby. He wasn't rushing it, just enjoying his own company and probably a rare moment of peace from everybody.

Was it apparent to you that he was very ill?

I knew at the time he was really struggling with his cancer and I tried talking to him about it before the 1991 Final against Forest. We met at the Hilton Hotel in Kensington, parked our cars, then headed off to the stadium. On the way in to Wembley I asked Bobby how he was coping with it all. It was only six weeks or so after his operation. "I'm not too bad" he said. "I just take one day at a time."

You know when somebody says that it doesn't augur well. Bobby was never one to say how he really was. If you ever asked him how he was he'd always say, "I'm fine, how are you?" Then he'd progress to ask how your family and acquaintants were, always deflecting the subject away from himself.

Football lost an icon when he died, and of course, you lost a very good friend.

I really think Bobby should have been given an Ambassadors job at the end of his career. I don't think the game looked after him as it should have. Bobby could have done a lot for British football in the same way that Bobby Charlton has. We really lost somebody special when he died.

Your own Spurs Testimonial went wrong. Can you tell me the story?

Spurs asked me what I wanted, a local club or a big European one. It was my choice. Somebody at the club had a connection with Bayern Munich, who were a great side at the time, so I chose them.

As well as the great Franz Beckenbauer, they had Georg Schwarzenbeck, Paul Breitner, Gerd Muller, and Uli Hoeness. Morris Keston headed my testimonial committee and there were a number of other high profile characters working with him. People like Phil Isaacs, Jimmy Tarbuck, Jimmy Hill, plus journalists Ken Jones and Jeff Powell. We were told that Bayern would cost in the region of £14,000 for the night. Of course, arrangements were all made well in advance. Unfortunately events weren't kind, a rail strike was called for the same night and petrol rationing was in force. I'd hired a generator to keep the floodlights going because power-cuts were frequent at the time. We couldn't change dates because Bayern had already arrived. I think the gate was around 25,000 in the end, which was a fabulous turn out considering the circumstances.

After that, everybody learned. People then decided to go for local opposition like Arsenal or Chelsea to negate future financial disasters. That kept expenses down but I just had to put mine down to unfortunate circumstances. I lost about £1000 on the night.

Did your benefit match lose its lustre because of those events?

If I'm honest, yes it did. I should have been enjoying sharing a pitch with some of the greatest players in the world, yet all I could do was keep checking out the crowd to see how many were in. I don't think it really allowed me to enjoy the evening, or to take in the enormity of what was happening to me at the time. There was a lot of expense on the night, like Police and turnstiles, although Tottenham kindly let me use the ground for nothing. Still, I had a lot on my mind when we took to the pitch.

You don't seem to have an ounce of bitterness. Were you very disappointed?

To be honest, it was a miracle that so many turned out on such an evening with so much going wrong, and I'll never forget the Spurs fans for it. I can't really be bitter because I chose such exalted opposition myself. The rest of the things that conspired against us on the evening were totally out of my hands, what with the strikes and the petrol rationing. Despite everything, it was a superb crowd in the end.

Thinking back, I got a lot of publicity for the evening. On the Sunday, Brian Moore had interviewed Uli Hoeness and Franz Beckenbauer on 'The Big Match' about how they'd travelled over for my game. I couldn't complain really. It was just one of those freak occasions when outside influences did their worst.

It seems that the fans were determined to see you off in style, no matter what?

Yes, I think the fans knew that I always gave one hundred per cent and that, despite one or two momentary lapses in form, which happens to everyone, I never hid. Overall, I had a very good relationship with our supporters. Even now, when I work up in the Corporate Lounges, they react very well to me. I think the older ones remember what those times were like and that I put everything in.

How did the influence of Nicholson, Baily, Poynton, Wallis and company affect you?

From the first moment I arrived at Tottenham the discipline was always strong. Even at fifteen, it was the high standards that got you on track. We had to clean the dressing rooms, make the tea, clean the boots, sweep the gymnasium and treatment rooms – and it had to be done thoroughly. To me, this is where it all comes from. It's the discipline of being a youngster and knowing that things had to be done, and done to a high standard. It was no good just doing it. You had to do it properly, or else.

For the first two years I was an apprentice and did everything I was told to. If I failed, Johnny Wallis wouldn't let me go home until it was done to the required standard. Tottenham's attitude was that they wanted things done properly and that you'd carry that principal through your whole career, and probably your life.

So you don't think Ledley cleans the toilets then?

Laughs. No of course not, but you did those things until you became a professional and had that discipline instilled in you when you ran out on to the pitch. It was Bill's way.

There were a number of handy looking lads who played one or two first team games then disappeared. Why?

It's because you have to be able to do it week in, week out. It's no good coming in to the team and having one good game. It's about consistency and doing things properly.

So Bill Nicholson could be quite ruthless?

Oh, most definitely. Bill had principles, but one included the fact that he'd always give you a chance to get back into the team when you were fit again. He felt that if you'd been a regular player, you had a right to return when regaining fitness.

If you had three or more bad games, he'd always give you the impression that he was thinking about dropping you. He was firm, but always fair.

How did the fame affect your immediate family?

My wife was never really a football fan and rarely came to League games. That suited me to a certain extent because I liked to keep a simple routine on match-days, which I hated to break. I preferred to stay fully focused. Knowing that I had to entertain guests would have broken that pattern.

In many ways my wife simply shunned the limelight. This suited me too because I liked to travel the same way, arrive at the ground at the same time and finish my chats with people a good two hours before the game otherwise I'd break my chain of thought.

I remember my wife coming to one League game up at Manchester City though, we were off to Mike Doyle's wedding later that weekend. I'll never forget it. We were approaching the ground when she spotted an old corner shop confectioners and asked me if I'd get out and buy some peanuts for her. I just couldn't do it. The place was swarming with supporters and I found it impossible to break with tradition. Luckily she understood, although it probably seems strange to most people, but I just couldn't break the routine. I guess I carried on with the rituals wherever I played in some form.

What was the fall-out after that notorious Rotterdam game?

Spirits were very, very low. To be honest, the talk consisted wholly of the crowd trouble. After the match nobody really discussed the football or even wanted to mention it. It seemed that trouble had never been far away all day. As we arrived at the ground there were a number of Spurs fans who'd gathered to see us off the coach.

I'll always remember one lad coming forward and asking me if I was alright. I replied positively. "I've already been in a fight" he boasted, and seemed quite proud of himself. He already looked a state and the game hadn't even started yet!

Was that your lowest point at the club?

Oh I think so, yes. The trouble that ensued that evening affected all of us. From the pitch you could see all the seats being thrown and huge gaps appearing in the terraces. I think that was when our concentration went and was certainly the turning point of the day.

Even lower than when missing the FA Cup Final in 1967?

Yes, without a doubt. I'd never known anything like it and had never heard of a manager missing his half-time team talk to speak on a tannoy to calm a crowd. After the game, defeat wasn't even mentioned. To tell you the truth, I can't even remember getting our medals, where we went to get them, where we stood, or who presented them to us. It was a major final yet I couldn't tell you much about the events after the trouble started.

Should the game have been stopped?

From what I've heard from fans since, yes, they could have stopped it. I later heard that our supporters had been provoked on ferries, and had run the gauntlet from various local villains on arrival. I don't think we've ever really heard the full extent of what happened during the lead up. It was simply the day from hell.

Were you ever personally intimidated or provoked by a crowd?

I remember running down the tunnel at the San Siro back in 1972 and picking up an iron bar, which had been left lying on the ground. We didn't really want to make a fuss to be honest so we placed it to the side and carried on down to the pitch. Getting back on the coach that evening was a nightmare. The Milan fans surrounded our coach and began rocking us from side to side. Bill told the driver to put his foot down and off we sped before the situation got any worse. That was extremely scary, especially as we'd just knocked them out of the UEFA Cup semi-final and were clearly fired up.

Do you remember the day Bill Nicholson stepped down?

I'll never forget sitting in the dressing room listening to his announcement that he was going. Bill felt that he'd lost the respect of some of the team, and although he'd managed some amazing players, he felt it was time to go. Martin Peters and I were then chosen to try and change his mind, but when Bill was set on something that's the way it was. We just had to accept his decision and respect it.

And then you left yourself, as part of Terry Neill's clear-out just after he arrived?

Yes, Terry came in and tried to stamp his own authority on the job and the team, but I feel that he got rid of too many players too quickly. I was told that I was being replaced by Don McAllister from Bolton. Unfortunately, the team hit an immediate bad patch and suddenly I was brought back again. That bad streak turned into wins and fortunes were looking up. Of course, when Don joined, Terry told me I could go, but changed his mind when the team started winning again.

The season had finished with that famous Leeds game when we needed a win to stay up. What a game that was. I'll certainly never forget Alfie Conn sitting on the ball and taunting the Leeds players. That certainly put the cat amongst the pigeons that night. It was later suggested in the dressing room that he should go and apologize. The whole team put pressure on him to go in and say sorry. Leeds were the top team of the time, and I remember Billy Bremner saying that he didn't want to see Tottenham go down. He'd rather we stayed up and see Leeds play in front of a 40,000 sell-out White

Hart Lane rather than visit one of the lesser lights each year. The man couldn't have been more honest, and sadly, that turned out to be my last ever game for Tottenham Hotspur.

Terry told me to join the lads on a squad holiday to Spain and to see how I felt about things. Sadly, his initial thoughts and comments had already made my mind up, and he crowned it all by asking me to stay until he'd found a couple more players. I found that truly amazing. To be honest, I didn't want to leave Spurs but by then I felt the situation had been handled less than tastefully. On principle I asked for a free transfer, which was granted by the board the following Wednesday. I literally fetched my boots and off I went after fourteen years at the club.

Where did you go after Spurs?

I went to Brighton, which turned out to be a huge mistake, especially having been accustomed to all those great Tottenham philosophies, principles and facilities. The move proved a complete disaster and everything seemed so amateurish. Neither Peter Taylor, Cloughie's old sidekick, who was manager at the time, nor his assistant, Brian Daykin, took training. They had a guy on the sidelines barking instructions, which he read from a book!

My first training session was a real eye-opener. We got changed, left the stadium, walked for a while, turned right at the traffic lights, and carried on walking. All along, I just kept wondering where this was leading. When I asked what was going on they simply told me to wait and see. Eventually, we ended up at a local park. I couldn't believe it when they told me this was our training ground!

There were members of the public walking past as we were training, dog owners out walking their pets, and of course, there were the remains of what the dogs left behind. There was absolutely no sign of Daykin or Taylor, until half an hour or so went by, when I saw two figures in the distance walking along the path with a dog in tow. As they got closer it turned out to be Brian and Peter, and suddenly they started shouting instructions at the boys. Twenty minutes later they disappeared.

I turned to another player and asked where they were going. His answer summed it all up in a nutshell. "Brian plays bowls for Worthing, so he's probably got a match this afternoon, and Peter will be in the office picking out his runners and riders on the nags". That was day one and it really bought home to me how special Spurs were.

So your bubble was burst on the first day?

Yes, but the other players thought it was normal. It left me regretting the fact that I'd declined an offer of a move to Washington in the States, and a possible move to Crystal Palace under Terry Venables, especially as Terry and

I were friends from our playing days. Unfortunately, this was typical of Peter Taylor's methods. I can't knock it too much because they were successful at the time, but I wasn't allowed to speak in team meetings either. If I tried to add something to a meeting he'd simply shout me down.

He wouldn't give me the opportunity to air my views on anything. In one meeting I was sitting with my arms folded listening to our orders when Taylor boomed out to Harry Wilson, our full-back, "See that 'Arry. See that over there, that's the Tottenham pose. That's how the players at Spurs sit. When you get up in to that sort of position that's how you sit."

What was going through your mind?

To be honest, I couldn't believe what I was hearing. Taylor seemed obsessed with belittling people, including embarrassing poor Harry about his shoes. In front of the rest of the squad he told Harry to go shopping with his wife to buy a new pair, because his were "disgusting".

After that initial spat I picked up a bad ankle injury in a game against Port Vale. This would mean missing the coming Wednesday game with Crystal Palace, but Peter kept bullying me to play although there was no way my ankle would hold out. He believed I was feigning injury and accused me of dropping down a division for an easy ride. We continued to argue about my motives for playing for the club.

I was furious. I'd always given 100% whoever I played for and I wasn't going to change now. You could say that I never really hit it off there, or with Peter Taylor. In fact, I had to have an Achilles operation because they kept making me play with cortisone injections to numb the feelings. This was basically down to Taylor's belief that I'd gone down to Brighton for an easy ride.

It later transpired that I'd detached a small piece of bone in my ankle, which was moving around and making any form of exercise painful. He eventually accepted the medical evidence and told me that once I'd had the operation, and got myself fit again, I could move on to another club.

Taylor let you go because he thought you were a Big Time Charlie?

Ironically, Taylor left at the end of the season and was replaced by Alan Mullery. Alan accepted the fact that I wanted to get away from the club, and when I received an offer from America again, he granted my move.

I didn't expect it to be another Tottenham, but I certainly thought it might be a little bit more professional. I hadn't realised that there were clubs training in local parks with people and their dogs wandering around. I couldn't believe that the manager and his assistant only watched twenty minutes of training, then disappeared to bowls matches and to pick out the days' horses. I was a professional who merely wanted the basics to keep my playing career going.

Supposing some local kids were in the goals first. Did you have to ask them for the pitch back?

Luckily, I didn't experience that one, but it makes you think. If only you could have seen the trainer running around with a book in his hand! [laughs]. In pre-season training we had to do a particular run in so many minutes. I told Ken, our 'trainer' that it was impossible, and that no matter how quick he thought the lads were, they were physically incapable of those times. "Oh, but that's what it says in my book here" he replied.

What was the American experience like?

I loved it in America. I loved the lifestyle and the people, and they made it so comfortable for us all. Everything was so much more relaxed there and built around the family.

Did you play with any Brits out there?

Besty, Charlie Cooke, Terry Mancini and Ron Davies.

Was football considered an alien sport there at the time?

We'd kick off at three o'clock on a Sunday in front of 5,000 while next door Los Angeles Dodgers would be playing baseball in front of 55,000. The biggest crowd we got was when we played New York Cosmos, mainly because of Pele, Franz Beckenbauer and Carlos Alberto. Mind you, the return in the later stages of the play-offs also attracted 55,000. Pele was still a class act then.

George Best, legend or waste of space?

I always said he was the best player in the world, although having seen Pele first hand I now think they both did things that were unique. I got on really well with George, but even out there he'd sometimes hit the destruct button. Sometimes he'd return from a bender a couple of days late and couldn't even remember where he'd been.

I've got to say I liked him immensely. We're always hearing of the negativity of George but there was another side to him. He'd regularly ask a 'keeper and a forward to stay back after training. George would then put in extra work to practice shooting and all those things he felt he needed to improve on.

What happened after you packed in football?

On returning from America, my children started to go to a small private school in Godstone, but the sports facilities were very poor, so I got myself involved there. The school had a small five-a-side pitch but the grass was long and hadn't been used for ages. I ended up mowing the grass, marking out a pitch, making some goalposts and volunteering to take the kids for football and P.E. Meanwhile, my wife was working for a local car-hire company, and with few kids attending the school, I eventually joined her company on a full-time basis. I now work for Flybe in Exeter and split my week by working there all week, and at Spurs on match-days in the corporate lounges.

Do you still get recognised after all this time?

Yes, quite often somebody recognises me, or one of the boys gets talking football with a customer who supports Spurs and tells them I work there.

I understand you nearly became a super model. Can you explain?

[Laughs] While at Spurs, a chap wrote to me asking if I'd consider modelling assignments. Having seen my picture in the newspaper we agreed to meet in Bournemouth the following week, as coincidentally, he was there on a business trip while we were on holiday with Martin Peters, Mike Doyle and the families.

I remember telling my wife that it seemed okay, and that I'd be modelling casual clothes. When I phoned him he agreed to meet me at my hotel, not inside, but outside in the car. I thought this sounded a little strange but still decided to go. While sitting in his car he asked me if I was okay with this idea and suggested that we visited the beach in the morning. Then he produced a thong, which he expected me to wear for the shoot. Then, he told me that I was expected to dive through the air for beach balls while he took pictures.

Well, by now the alarm bells were ringing, and to compound my worries he produced an extremely dodgy looking magazine. He then went on to explain that the raunchier the contents the more we'd sell, and therefore the more money we'd earn. Of course I declined, and Martin and Mike couldn't stop laughing when I told them. That incident did give me the idea for the Barry Daines wind-up a few years later though, so I had the last laugh!

Where do you see your future Phil, if no modelling?

I'd love to coach kids again. Like Stevie Perryman, I was a home-grown player and fully understand the strength behind developing youth players. Apart from that I find the whole experience extremely rewarding. We were reared as youngsters listening to old pro's, and learning how to go about becoming one. What's better than an ex-player passing on his expertise to kids? Anyone can get a coaching badge, but very few have first-hand knowledge of playing at the very highest level and winning trophies.

Passing a coaching course doesn't mean that you'll be any more adept at articulating that message to kids. The fact that you've succeeded in the professional game demands a respect of its own I think. There are many of us out here. Old pro's with much to offer, with the contacts to make the process work.

Gary
Stevens

Era 1983 - 1988
Appearances 187 **Goals** 9

How embarrassing can some kids be, and how often has "Why didn't you play for Spurs Dad?" been trotted out in front of friends and family? Truth is, I simply wasn't good enough, nor were the legions of 'trialists', and 'if onlys' who also 'nearly made it'. To become a top flight pro takes a special kind of person; the best in school, the best in the district, the best in the county finally earning that all-important shot at the big time. I remind myself whenever instinct gets the better of me, rising to berate the latest Spurs mistake, only to sit back down again once logic has overwhelmed emotion. No matter how badly that player was performing, he'd served his time on the roughest, toughest of playing fields, emerging as a fully-fledged professional player - something that millions can only aspire to.

As Spurs fans we set our standards high; some would say too high. Supporters of all ages can rattle off lists that generally start with a Hoddle or a Jones, and end in a Gascoigne, Mackay, or Greaves or three. Personally, I've always admired those who beat adversity to fulfil a boyhood dream; the quiet man who simply gets on with the job, leaving stardom to the blatantly more expressive.

In truth, their lives are intertwined, both depending on skills the other cannot supply. Furthermore, I also admire the guts, spirit, and determination of players who turn adversity into success, especially when it is achieved with intelligence or modest manner.

Gary Stevens emerged as one of the stars of Brighton's 1983 Cup Final team. That season he formed a famous partnership with the memorably head-banded Steve "Fozzie" Foster - while Steve took the accolades with a publicly more flamboyant style, Gary's quiet efficiency attracted the notice of Tottenham Hotspur.

By his own admission, his early Spurs days were not the best, but never did Gary's inner confidence or self-belief ever wane. As fans, on taking our seats for another roller-coaster ride, we do it from the safety of the stand. Now imagine yourself in the tunnel. You're approaching the hallowed turf, with the names of your team-mates being blasted across the tannoy. Then, as the cheers ring out loud and long, your own name is booed to the rafters, while the opposition supporters join in. How would you feel, with nowhere to hide, and thirty-six thousand pairs of eyes analysing your every move?

Gary, to his eternal credit, never hid, and when injury was crucifying his body, he never lost faith in his schoolboy dream. He not only fought back heroically but went on to represent his country. Now tell me that you'd have stayed the course. Guts, strength, integrity and steel, all topped off by a mixture of mental power and passion that set him apart. Whatever your first reaction on reading the name 'Gary Stevens', I hope this chapter leaves you agreeing that he is a very special person.

You initially came through the apprentice ranks at Brighton & Hove Albion. Were you always confident that you'd make it in the game?

Yes, even as a four or five year old I constantly told everyone that, one day, I'd play for Chelsea and England. Our home was in West Drayton in those days and The Blues were our family team. It was always football first and foremost in my mind. That was always the only option, even from that tender age.

How did you surface at Ipswich Town?

Around the age of eleven we moved up to Bury St. Edmunds in Suffolk. Many, including my Dad, felt that I had the ability to move to a professional club so he had a chat with a friend called Ken Craggs. Ken was a friend of Bobby Robson, the then Ipswich manager. Charlie Woods was their Youth Team coach at the time and ran a Thursday session for local kids. I joined in there, settled, and went on to sign schoolboy forms at the age of fourteen.

By sixteen, a number of boys had caught me up and gone past me in terms of ability and achievement, so Bobby released me. The squad was full of lads who'd go on to much better things; people like Terry Butcher, Russell Osman, George Burley, Mick Mills, and Alan Hunter; good, young, and strong lads who eventually fulfilled their early promise.

How did you feel when Bobby told you it was over?

Initially very sad as I'd grown to enjoy my time there. Overall, it was the making of me, as I was such a determined lad that I wasn't going to let this knock-back beat me. I rolled up my sleeves and tripled my determination.

Were your parents always behind you, or did your release cause them to have second thoughts about a career?

Thankfully, I received endless and total backing from them. Dad was a semi-pro goalkeeper who once had the chance to join Leeds and West Ham. Unfortunately for him, his father recommended he got a trade. Dad moved away from the game and ultimately regrets that decision. I guess, in some ways, he lived out his missed opportunity through me and my career.

When we lived in Suffolk, Dad ran the local team that I played for, Bury North End, acting as joint manager with a chap called Pete Thearle. Both of Pete's sons played and the whole atmosphere was that of a large happy family. Us kids used to mark the pitch and carry the posts and nets out, while Mum's duties were to cut the oranges and wash the shirts. Her input and dedication were immense, lovingly embroidering our club initials to shirts that, ironically, were Arsenal colours.

B.N.E. was almost like a community business, helped by the kindness of other parents, with everyone playing their part for the common good.

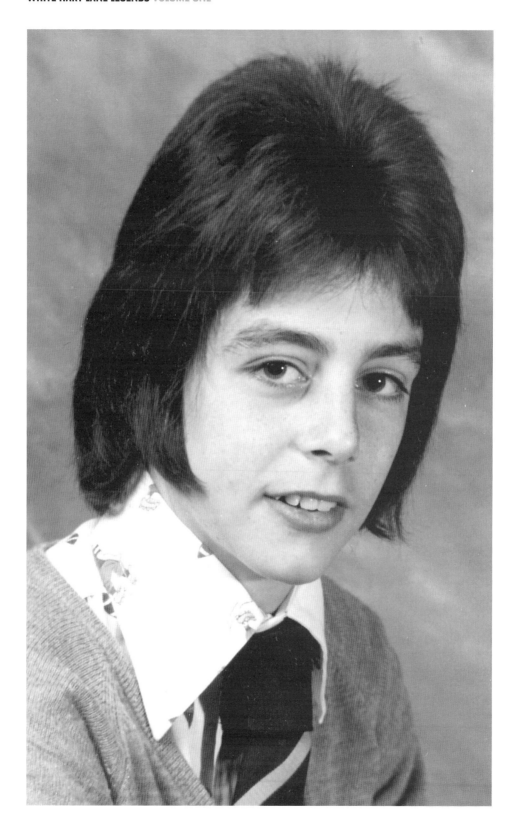

Mum and Dad also acted as an excellent taxi service [laughs]. At Brighton, they were even voted 'Supporters of the Year' for their loyal support. Their attendance record was superb, turning up whenever or wherever I played. They made me feel extremely proud.

Brighton proved an excellent move for you.

What a time to join them! The whole club was thriving from youth to first team. Alan Mullery was Manager at the time and had signed me as a trainee. There were some very recognisable faces playing for the club at the time, including, Mark Lawrenson, Brian Horton, Peter Ward and the Welsh Internationals, Peter Sayer and Peter O'Sullivan. Michael Robinson swelled the ranks at a later date. Mark then became their most expensive outgoing player when he moved on to Liverpool, with Andy Ritchie, from Manchester United, becoming the most expensive arrival.

That famous cup run, culminating in the final against Manchester United, was the Brighton highlight. Do you recall much of the lead up to the great day?

Unfortunately, as happened most seasons, there had been a dispute over bonuses. That wasn't just a Brighton thing, it happens at most clubs from time to time. From the minute the dispute was sorted, and those bonus sheets were signed, it seemed like we were destined to reach the final.

We were matched against a Kevin Keegan inspired Newcastle in the Third round at home, which we drew. The following Wednesday, Newcastle totally murdered us up at St. James's Park, but we beat them one-nil. From there we just went on a roll.

How nerve-wracking did you find big games, especially the Final?

I don't think nerves actually effected me, but I am a nervous person to the extent that I have on many occasions been physically sick before a match. There were certain games where I'd be in and out of the loo from the moment I woke up, to the moment I left the dressing room.

That never carried itself on to the pitch with me, but I believe that it does you good to be nervous in that it keeps you on your toes and alert. If anything held me back I think it was the fear of failure, I was determined to succeed.

How did you feel in the tunnel at Wembley that day?

Invincible, I felt eight feet tall. Nothing or no player was going to beat me. That type of scenario was made for me. The bigger the game, the better or more important the occasion, the better I seemed to play. Unlike golf, where I'd be nervous on the first tee not knowing where the ball may end up. With football, I'd always go on to that pitch knowing I was capable and that I had the ability to do myself justice. Of course, it didn't always turn out that way, especially at the beginning with Spurs, but that confidence was always central to my game.

When that Cup Final ended, and you'd won national recognition, how quickly did things develop with Spurs?

Not particularly quickly. There had been a lot of local speculation that I'd be sold off to the highest bidder. People put two and two together due to my strong performance in the Cup Final and Brighton's disappointing relegation. But I honestly loved my five years at the club and had no intention or desire to go anywhere really. In fact, I was in the throes of selling my first property at the time. I'd lived there since my nineteenth birthday and was looking to buy a very nice house in Hove Park. Even the people I was going to buy from asked the question about an imminent move.

I reassured them by saying that I was staying, that I was happy at the club and wasn't looking for a move. Unfortunately I eventually had to break my word to them and pulled out, but at the time of asking had no reason to be anything else but adamant that I'd be staying.

With respect, although your intentions were honourable, don't you think that may have been a bit naïve?

Yes. But at the age of twenty-one I was naïve. But having said that, it transpired that Spurs had been trying to buy me for most of that season. Every time they rang up for me, Brighton insisted on keeping hold until the cup run was over. The move was only stalled because we kept going, and going, and going... Had Newcastle knocked us out four months previously, then Spurs would have got their man for considerably less than £300,000, and I'd have been offered a much smaller contract.

How did the negotiations go?

I'd travelled up to Suffolk to see my parents when Jimmy Melia rang. He said that the club had agreed to sell me to Spurs and did I want to go?

Like anybody else who has to leave a job they like, I had mixed feelings, but I was excited that such a big club had come in for me. I guess I also let him know that I wasn't particularly enamoured that he didn't seem to want me. At this, Jimmy tried to pacify me by revealing that, when asked about my salary at Brighton, he'd doubled the actual figure! Again, I wasn't pleased with what he'd done and proceeded to tell him so.

Didn't he realize that your P45 would ultimately prove him a liar?

[Laughs] Well there's a bit of a clue there, isn't there?

And so to White Hart Lane?

Yes, Jimmy informed me that Peter Shreeves, Spurs' Assistant Manager, was interested and I should phone him. I did so, and arranged to meet at the ground.

With Pete's cabbing experience on 'the knowledge', his directions were spot on. I'd only ever been to White Hart Lane in the team coach before, but by now was willing to walk there to sign for them. We had our initial meeting in one of the club's offices. Peter told me of their plans for the team, and for Spurs as a club. We then discussed my best position and how to get the best out of me considering what he already knew.

He then mentioned that I should avoid lunching upstairs in the club canteen, in favour of the 'Chanticleer', which is now called 'Whites'. He said I'd be recognised up there, which was odd as I'd come through the main gate and had waited for him in reception. But first he wanted me to meet Bill Nicholson.

Did the butterflies return?

No, not at all, but I was fully aware of the stature of the man and what he'd achieved in the game. Bill told me that we could visit the training ground before lunch and we proceeded to get into what was, with respect, a very modest car and headed out of the ground.

He put me at ease immediately by chatting about the club's facilities and told me to scribble down the route because he was going to show me the quick way. This would help us from running into heavy traffic and save me time after I'd signed. It was easy to understand how Bill had become so acclaimed. He didn't miss a detail, which made me feel totally relaxed.

A million miles from Brighton eh?

Yes, the facilities were excellent, far in excess of what I'd grown used to. Funny how things stick in your mind though; I'll never forget Bill staring across the pitches while passing on some of that incredible experience of his. As we took in the scenery, looking out across the lush green turf of the training ground, he said, "I can't understand it. All the players at this club do long warm-ups, loads and loaaaaads of stretches - but they're always pulling muscles! In my days we didn't do stretches, and we didn't pull so many muscles either". His observations had a sound logic.

My first meeting with the man made me realize that things should be kept simple. After a wander around the grounds, he then showed me another traffic-beating way back to the ground whilst selling the club and stressing what a great opportunity this was for me. Sold to the man in the white shirt!

Bury North End proudly display their new badges, courtesy of Gary's Mum

Only Fools and Seagulls: Brian Horton and Gary test drive the club coach

Did signing for Spurs compromise your schoolboy club allegiance or doesn't that cross your mind when joining another professional side?

No, it doesn't work that way. I'd been making a living from football from the age of sixteen, I was now twenty-one. Reality dictates that you have to go where you're wanted, that was how I earned my living. Of course, the move wasn't just about cash.

One thing that Peter made a point of was asking me to keep our meeting confidential. He didn't want the Press getting hold of the story, and more importantly, didn't want to get involved in an auction. There had been talk of other clubs being interested, including Liverpool and Manchester United after my Cup Final performances. Being the character I am, I reassured him that it would remain private and that's the way it stayed.

So there were no agents lurking in the background?

Certainly not! That was back in 1983, but the modern way seems to be to feed the news to the Press, or involve an agent to force the ante up. I'm not saying that's right or wrong, but it certainly seems to be the way of the world now. The principals I grew up with meant that I should respect the club's wishes in keeping my move under wraps.

Spurs signed you as a central defender, but things didn't work out that way for you in the long term. What's the story behind that?

Yes, I signed because they thought I could add extra quality to the back four. They already had Graham Roberts, Paul Miller, Paul Price and Gary O'Reilly, but felt that my presence would bolster the squad and create more competition for places.

My best position was as central defender, but not as the dominant presence. My forte was to read the play, clear up everything that my partner missed and to let him attack the ball. In all truthfulness, I got it wrong when I went to Spurs in that I felt I needed to prove to everyone what a good player I was. I started by attempting things that I needn't have done. This led to me getting caught out on many occasions, which ultimately caused my initial spell to be a very difficult one. I take full blame for that.

So how did the move to midfield come about?

Mainly because Keith Burkinshaw felt I'd become a liability in the back four. He even said as much. While reading the team out at training one morning, he announced that he'd moved me to the right side of midfield for our coming game at Anfield.

As the announcement was made, many eyes swivelled searching for reactions to my move, I remember feeling quite emotional about it. In truth, I welled up a little as the decision wasn't my own and it may have been seen that I'd let the team down. I didn't particularly agree with what he'd done, especially as it was being read out in front of all my team-mates, but Keith had a job to do and that was his decision. I had to take it on the chin.

With respect Gary, the fans had been at your throat at the time. It must have been a partial relief, especially as you still had a place in the team?

I knew that I wasn't playing well enough and had made a number of mistakes. Still, I felt I was good enough to turn things around. Keith didn't really give me an explanation why he'd moved me although I knew inside that things had not started well for me and that there was a certain element of dissent in the crowd.

I also believe that, in those days, a manager felt compelled to play his new signings regardless, to compound his choice. Maybe it wasn't always the same with an emerging youngster in the side, who always knew that, once the established face returned, he'd be packed off back to the reserves. There was a general feeling that the new signing had to be played and possibly that's why a new position was found for me.

Step forward Gary Stevens, the new midfield signing!

Ironically, I played very well at Liverpool in my new position. In fact I played a blinder, topping off the performance with a welcome goal. If I remember rightly, we were one up, played them off the park, and went in at half time two-one down due to a dodgy offside and even dodgier penalty. I believe it was that game that made Spurs see my value as a utility player.

How did you cope with the barracking from the boo-boys and did it affect any passion you felt for the club?

My feeling was that they had every right to be having a go as I wasn't coming up to standard. They were paying their hard-earned money to come and see me and I wasn't producing to the club's required level.

I'd be the same if I was paying to see a singer or band that didn't come up to scratch, but in reality, what I really needed was their help. I desperately needed the fan's understanding and backing, although the truth is that no football player ever gets it in similar circumstances.

I remember warming up before games and hearing the match-day presenter, Willie Morgan, going through the team. Everyone would receive his cheer, then, when it got to my name, I'd hear the negative response and feel quite low. It never effected my desire to play well, it simply made me more determined to prove them wrong.

It takes a very strong personality to come through that adversity. What kept you going?

The fact of life is that many players in their time at Tottenham took stick, it's the same at all clubs. Steve Perryman took it, Glenn took it, even Ossie received stick at times. All I kept praying for was the time when the abuse abated and I could get on with the job of boosting the team and its fortunes. Again, I was only too aware that my form had to improve and that they'd react to better performances.

It now transpires that Keith's decision to move me to midfield was the start of better things to come, but I never let the boo-boys get to me, and always kept in the forefront of my mind that I was better than they'd witnessed to date.

To win the UEFA Cup in your first season at Spurs must have been amazing. What are your recollections of that run?

I always say that it was the UEFA Cup run that got me out of jail, having played some of my best football for Spurs during that awesome run. We played some excellent sides on the way with the crowd often acting as our twelfth man. In the final, I started off right side of midfield and played the extra-time period in the middle of the back four. It had already been announced, of course, that Keith was leaving.

Peter then informed me that I'd be returned to the back four the following season, because he felt that was my best position. As it transpired, he didn't, and I continued my good run in the place that Keith had found for me in midfield.

Many believe we should have won the League the following year. Do you agree?

Without question. I played that following season predominantly with Gary Mabbutt in midfield; sometimes with Ossie, and sometimes Glenn. But its funny how times change as some fans actually held my injury against Manchester United up as the reason we didn't win it [smiles wryly], not that I could have done much about that.

My own form until then was excellent. I was exceptionally fit and strong and felt within that something special was on the cards. Then, with my injury, the team got shuffled around and everything went pear-shaped against Everton on that infamous night when Neville Southall played a blinder at White Hart Lane.

The team claimed a superb victory at Anfield in my absence, then got knocked out of the UEFA Cup against Real Madrid, culminating in that extremely disappointing night when the League title slipped through our hands. To this day, it still crosses my mind what might have been.

You went from being barracked at Spurs to the England team in double quick time. You must have been absolutely delighted?

During the course of my career, I would say that I always set my own personal standards too high. I sometimes regret not being more flamboyant and taking more chances.

Whenever I analysed myself or my game, I always tended to look at the negative side, dismissing what was good and positive. If I'd possessed the confidence and balls of say, Paul Miller, then I'd have done a lot better. Still, it was superb to finally make the schoolboy dream come true and turn out for my country in that fabulous white shirt. It kept running through my mind how proud my parents would be.

I remember coming on at half-time against Finland, replacing Mike Duxbury, the ex-Manchester United full back. There was a TV strike so the majority of the public missed the game. We won five-nil and Peter Shilton did nothing but moan at me for forty-five minutes.

In his eyes, I was getting forward too much and therefore not giving him the cover he required, although that was probably more down to the paranoia of the goalkeepers' union. In truth, he had little to do and I can't remember him having to save a shot in the second half. But that was Peter, the consummate professional, the master between the sticks.

What's the full story behind your injury against Wimbledon?

Matches against Wimbledon were always nasty in those days. Their attitude was that we were the fancy Dan's and that they were going to rough us up a bit. That's not to say that we'd roll over. We had a player or two who were more than capable of standing up to them, and their ways.

I remember a ball being knocked through the middle. After a bit of a misunderstanding between Ray Clemence and myself, they got a shot in, which ricocheted up in the air. As the ball was dropping, I'd already taken off, but John Fashanu had picked up more speed than me and came in leading with his elbow. Those extra few steps made all the difference to his momentum, allowing him to head the ball into the goal, while catching me square on the chin with his flailing elbow. The second he caught me I was out cold. I fell unconscious to the ground from a great height.

I landed on my shoulder with all my dead weight, dislocating my joint and breaking my collar bone. [Laughs] Ray Clemence later told me that I was making one hell of a noise! I was still unconscious as I was being carried off and came round in the treatment room of Middlesex Hospital.

Any grudges?

When I first injured my knee, I was sent to RAF Hedley Court rehab centre in Surrey. While there, John Fashanu was admitted and we roomed together. As you know he's tall, elegant, articulate, in fact a very switched-on kind of guy. Every morning they would sound the bugle and a cup of tea would arrive. Over tea, John and I would spend those early mornings chatting, then prepare for the day's rehabilitation. From that experience I can only assume that he's got a split personality. Such an impressive character outside of the game, but a totally different kind of man on the pitch. Of course, the physical side of the game has always been there. I don't for one moment believe that he intended to knock me out, but I feel that he certainly intended to give me a whack to gain an advantage.

Did feelings of revenge ever cross your mind?

As you know, it was never in my character to go around clogging or kicking people, but there was a situation in a later game against them. Fashanu was out on the wing when I sensed an opportunity to give him a bit of a belt. I'd never had the capacity to kick a fellow player for no reason, although Keith had regularly tried to instill in me that I needed to be more physical at times.

In this particular case, I didn't really play the ball, or him, but as we lay on the floor, Vinnie Jones came piling in through the melee and did my knee. I wouldn't go so far as saying I'm bitter about it, but Vinnie had no need to make that tackle. In fact, his actions could even have harmed his own player, they were that irresponsible. It has subsequently come back to me, admittedly third hand, that Fash and Vinnie would target individuals, and that for this particular match I'd been chosen!

If that's true, I find it hard to accept that they'd happily target a fellow pro and carry out what is tantamount to a premeditated assault. What irks me most is that I was pushed into thinking and acting that way when, quite clearly, I was never that type of player or person.

Injury and the boo-boy era apart, was it a happy time at Spurs for you overall?

Yes, I loved it. There's always a tendency to look back at your 'good old days', but they truly were happy ones. The club was a big name in European football, with some world class players. The facilities were also first class, especially with the eventual ground changes that were taking place.

They were extremely happy times that I'll never forget, or want to. Spurs were always generous and reasonable with any requests I may have had. The club were superb right from the beginning. They originally put me up in the Ponsbourne Hotel at Newgate Street Village for months, all expenses paid. Then, when I'd found a new house to buy, they let me stay on for a further month while the sale went through. Nothing was ever too much for them and I'll never forget their kindness and willingness to help.

Wembley 1983: Gary waves to the Brighton fans after drawing with Manchester United

Which characters had the biggest effect on your time at the club?

I'd have to say that Steve Perryman would have to be right up there. Steve possessed all the attributes of a superb club captain, which he proved over a long and successful career.

He once advised me to keep a dictaphone handy, in order to register my thoughts and anything that happened over my career. He suggested that I'd probably forget much of what happened, and come the end of my career, I'd have a first hand chronicle of all those events, especially if I wanted to write a book or articles about the game. Of course, I didn't do it, and I regret not having taken his advice.

Steve would often nab someone after training, sometimes it would be me. "What do you think would happen if you did that?" he'd say, or "What do you think you'd get if you did this?" He was constantly trying to make us think about the various situations we'd find ourselves in during games and possessed the most enquiring of minds.

To Steve, there was always a reason why something should be done a certain way and he was always trying to make the players around him see further than just the obvious. Nothing was ever too much for Steve Perryman. He always had time for others, from the Chairman down to the rawest recruit. All that mattered was the common good of Tottenham Hotspur.

Anyone else?

Ossie was another thinker who also had time and energy for everyone. I remember playing an away game at Derby once where I'd been hurriedly clearing every ball away quickly and uncompromisingly. Sometimes your frame of mind dictates your style of play and I had possibly been a bit rash in my distribution. Ossie grabbed me at half-time and told me to relax more, and to think about being a bit braver.

"Give it to me" he said. "I'll have it. Don't just boot the ball away in the air. Be confident and play it out yourself, or to any one of the lads who are here to help". Ossie rarely lost the ball and what he said helped to temper my overall game. It certainly was a huge coup for the club to have people of the calibre of Steve and him on board.

Glenn Hoddle was another great character. Everybody looked up to Glenn because of his amazing ability on the ball and the way he would always be available to take possession, regardless of how many of the opposition players were surrounding him.

Did you have much contact with Bill Nicholson after your initial tour of the back streets of N.17?

Not a great deal after I'd signed. Occasionally, he'd be at the training ground, or we'd bump in to him at the club. In those days we used to go in to the ground at the end of the month to collect our pay slips. Sometimes, while walking past the offices, Bill would say hello, or offer a social cup of tea and a chat. The man was deservedly an icon at Tottenham Hotspur, but was aware that he shouldn't get too involved with the playing staff. It was out of respect for Keith, and typical of the measure of the man.

How did Bill compare with the personality of Keith?

[Long pause for thought] I think in some ways they were similar in that both always had an open door, which was obviously superb for the players. I think Bill probably listened to many more opinions, whereas Keith was very single-minded. He could be a very blunt, straightforward person who spoke how he saw.

Keith was also a stickler for timekeeping and often reminded us that, when he walked out on that training ground, he expected all of us there by his side. Then you'd hear a loud, "Cum'on then", and we'd all be off to a man on our circuits. It didn't matter if you were a World Cup Winner in Ossie Ardiles, or a spotty-faced youth trying to break through the ranks. You didn't mess with Keith. The man commanded, and got, total respect.

Your career at Spurs coincided with huge upheavals in football as a game. Did those changes effect your life as a player?

When I first joined Spurs, Douglas Alexiou was Chairman, with Irving Scholar Vice-Chair. In my first season that all changed, with the club becoming a PLC. We were all offered shares and there were various meetings being held all over the place. In those days, the club directors tended to travel on the team coach with us and mixed with the players at the team hotel. Like Brighton, it was very much a family oriented club, only many times bigger. I thrived on that family feeling, but soon after the change it was becoming noticeable that financial matters were much higher on the agenda than before.

Does anything still stand out that compounded your views?

I remember the filming of an advert at White Hart Lane, which extolled the virtues of Spurs as a family club. Historically, players hadn't grown up with this kind of outside influence to their day, and some commented on how strange it all seemed.

Suddenly, events like this were detracting from our day-to-day football duties, and becoming distractions. To me, first and foremost, a football club should be exactly that. Of course, it's okay to run those things along side, but they should never be allowed to interfere with your reasons for being there. We spent four hours in the ground that afternoon trying to film a twenty-second TV commercial.

All the lads were passing confused glances at each other and wondering what the hell it was all about. Of course, future generations of players have grown accustomed to this kind of thing, but it often makes me wonder how the Beckham's of this world cope with the intensity of it all.

Maybe you noticed it more because you were the first generation of players to be effected by the new commercial football revolution?

Yes, that's fair comment, and it is a vastly different game today. To be honest, the emergence of commercialism, Sky TV, and all the other outside influences scared the hell out of many players, although ultimately, its been a financial godsend.

In our defence, we didn't have the benefit of hindsight at the time and clearly didn't understand the implications of the new changes. All we could see was an outside interference to our football. But in many ways, Spurs were pioneers, and like Martin Peters, a few years ahead of the times. Unfortunately, where Spurs took the initial plunge, others came along behind and speculated, which may be one of the reasons why we've faced problems in later years.

Irving Scholar; Saint or sinner?

I think he had great hopes and visions and was genuinely passionate for the club. I'm also sure he was as disappointed as any fan when the financial side started to go wrong. Incidentally, every Christmas, we used to have a lunch at the training ground and the Directors acting as our waiters for the day. The Chairman would be hovering around the table in an apron, carving the turkey and serving chipolata's and vegetables.

Did you have to tip the waiters?

[Laughs]. Err, no. Although I'd have liked to see that.

Once you became established and more content with your form at Spurs, when did you sense the boo-boys stop barracking you?

I'd say it was after, or maybe during the UEFA Cup run. If you remember, I took one of the penalties in the final, which I believe put me in good stead with the fans. The next season we were right up at the top of the League. I'd had a personally rewarding time, had played very well, then got injured against Manchester United.

Things changed to such an extent that people now welcomed my return to a team that was showing immense promise. I remember feeling so proud when I won the London Evening Standard 'Player of the Month' award, which was awarded to the best player in the capital at that given time. How things change around.

And so, on to the come back trail?

What a heartwarming return it proved to be. It was in front of a huge Spurs contingent at Coventry. I'll never, ever forget the cheer I got as they read out who was playing. They didn't stop during the game either.

I remember getting booked for a mistimed challenge right in front of our supporters. The applause and affection I received from the Spurs fans that day genuinely moved me. It felt great to be back and representing those people under such totally different circumstances, especially having come through the rocky period when I first joined the club. I then sensed that things were starting to change for the better for me, which in turn boosted my confidence and performances even more.

Was quitting ever an option?

Never. I don't quit, it's not in my nature. To a certain extent, the barracking at home games was louder, whereas at away games it was only ever sporadic.

I've always believed that travelling fans are maybe a little more forgiving and supportive, but either way, I wouldn't let it get to me. After all, it was merely a bad start, not a bad career.

Who were your friends at Tottenham?

Probably my closest mate then was Danny Thomas. We signed for Spurs at the same time and stayed in the Ponsbourne Hotel for a few months, followed by coincidental house moves to Broxbourne. With Danny just a few hundred yards around the corner, we started out by travelling in together and I ended up godfather to his daughter Sacha.

So you must have felt it more than most when he missed that infamous penalty in the UEFA Final?

Without a doubt, I felt for Danny as a friend, as a team-mate and fellow professional. But having said that, to some extent you have to be hard and concentrate on your own game first, just remain focused. It was awful seeing Danny's disappointment, but after his penalty was missed the main concern was that we won.

After all I'd been through, missing my own penalty was never an option [laughs]. To be honest, I was damn glad to see that one go in. God knows what would have happened had I missed.

The crowd were fantastic that night, immediately singing round after round of "There's only one Danny Thomas", which carried on for the whole of the next season. Critics have been very quick to slam Spurs fans in recent years, maybe they should remember occasions like that more often.

You must have some great memories of that particular evening?

Just sitting here talking about it has set off the goose bumps on my skin. It's amazing how one man's tragedy became another's chance for fame. Tony Parks became a real hero that night with his penalty save and sparked some of the most amazing scenes I've ever experienced in a football ground.

Obviously that night proved to be your own personal high at Tottenham, but what do you consider your lowest moment?

I would say it was my first season, with the fans constantly on my back. As I've said, I was so eager to please that maybe I over elaborated some things and didn't do myself full justice.

During that period, some of us younger, single ones went off to a club after a match. One particular night there was a documentary on TV about Spurs, where, apparently, I'd been heavily criticized. While innocently standing there, two guys approached and asked if I'd seen the documentary. I said I hadn't, to which they filled me in on the details and aggressively told me that they agreed with every word.

I felt dreadful. If bad form wasn't enough, those two guys wanted to ruin my only night out and it prayed on my mind for weeks after. I honestly just wanted to do my best, to deliver for them, but they weren't making it easy for me. That and the injuries made me very, very low.

What was the overall dressing room atmosphere like at Spurs during that time?

I'd say it was excellent. We had some real characters; people like 'Maxie' Miller and Garth Crooks. I'm not sure what others thought of me, but I like to believe that I got on with everyone. The only time there was a little ill-feeling it centred around Stevie Archibald, who was an extremely reclusive character.

Steve kept himself to himself, which of course, was his prerogative. I don't ever remember socializing with him much, but that's not to say that we didn't pass pleasantries or hug him when he scored one of his many goals. I'd say there was clearly some friction between him and a couple of players but we never let it affect the team.

I always felt that Steve had a selfish kind of nature being an out-and-out striker. He'd rarely track back to help out, which irritated a number of players and coaches. But in all honesty, I tried to keep out of that and was happy to leave it to Stevie and Keith to sort out. Overall, it was a happy, balanced set of players who worked well together.

Who do you consider as the great players you shared a pitch with?

Without a doubt, it was Mark Lawrenson at Brighton. At Spurs I'd say

Ossie, Glenn and Ray Clemence. I'd also put Gary Mabbutt in there too. It's actually very hard to pick out individuals and say that they were great as so many top flight players came and went during my time at the club. Don't forget; Gazza came too.

He was outrageously talented, and one of the most brilliant and naturally gifted players I ever saw. Chris Waddle was also very deceiving. Originally, he seemed sluggish but was actually one of the quickest players at the club. I also played with Gary Lineker. Gary didn't get involved in too much of the build up play, but what a great, great finisher. It was a pleasure to play with them all.

Was there anyone at the club who you thought highly underrated?

I genuinely believe that people still don't realize what a great player Steve Perryman was. The man was so knowledgeable and a key influence on us as a group of players. I can't believe that he only received one paltry cap. For a man of Steve's standing that can't be right.

How about the great opposing players?

I was lucky enough to play against Johann Cruyff towards the end of his career. I think it was his general aura on a pitch that set him apart from lesser mortals.

Even then, Johann still retained the balance and poise that had illuminated the football world. Karl-Heinz Rummenigge was another great, as were two of our Anderlecht opponents in that famous UEFA Cup success of eighty-four; namely, Morten Olsen, the Dane, and Enzo Schifo. Enzo was being talked of as the emerging talent in European football at the time.

Which domestic League players gave you the toughest time, apart from the ones we've mentioned?

Lou Macari was a clever player. He was small and nippy with great balance. Of course, there were many big strong powerhouse lads like Cyrille Regis and Garry Thompson, who were hard to play against.

Then there were the tricky, pacy lads like Peter Barnes. Peter Beardsley was in the Lou Macari category; very clever, with a top footballing brain. Those kind of players see things much quicker than most. To be honest, there wasn't a player that kept me awake at night thinking I'd be run ragged. Of course, games against Ian Rush and Kenny Dalglish were a battle.

I remember having a great game against Kenny once at Brighton, keeping him quiet for most of the game, then he popped up out of nowhere with two crackers. As they say, form is only temporary; class is permanent.

How did long term injuries affect you mentally?

The short answer is that I rolled my sleeves up and battled through. The first was sustained against Manchester United. We were due to travel to Cheltenham races the next day as a team, but I ended up on the operating slab. Luckily, if you had to be injured, Spurs was an excellent place to be as the club's medical back up was superb. The players visited you in hospital, and the general feeling was to wish you back to good health.

Mentally I always needed a target. As long as I saw that there was a start, a middle and an end to the problem, I'd graft at it and try and claim my place back in the team.

What programme did you adopt to get back to fitness?

They gave me a little bench and a weighted jacket, the latter full of sand. I'd then proceed to do upwards of five thousand step-ups every morning. Of course, the fans, and especially the boo-boys, don't see all of this.

As all the other players were going out to training, I'd be stepping up, stepping down, stepping up, stepping down. After training, when the boys returned, I'd still be doing it. I'd even be stepping up and down when they went home.

Any legacies of those injuries?

I guess I must have about a yard and a half of scars in total from my various injuries and operations. Added to the knee and shoulder that everyone knows about, I even had a spinal fusion at Tottenham, which kept me out for a number of games.

Mentally, I've always been very strong, although physiologically, I'm not sure that football, or any kind of contact sports come to that, were conducive to a tall and slender body. This view was compounded by John Browett, the surgeon who performed my two knee operations at Spurs.

When the surgeon compared mine with Graham Roberts' chunky, rope-like ligaments, he said they were obviously better suited to the rigours of the professional game. In truth, I probably wasn't built to take the hard physical knocks involved in professional football, but due to my love of the game, how could I possibly spurn an opportunity that every kid in the country would give a limb for?

You played under some great managers. Do any of their pearls of wisdom stick in your mind?

Bobby Robson once said that an intelligent footballer is better than a dull footballer. That may seem an obvious quote but it made me think about my application to the game. It made me fully aware that I should always think ahead, to be pre-emptive, and to use it to keep one step ahead. I'd

Best mates; Gary and Danny Thomas celebrate Spurs' 1984 UEFA Cup success

worked hard at school and left with nine 'O' levels, with my careers' master trying to influence me to stay on for 'A' levels. Despite my deep belief that I'd always make it as a pro, I always believed it was necessary to improve myself and not to take anything, or anyone, for granted.

Gazza. Were you ever victim to one of his pranks?

Oh yes. I once came back in from training to find that my trousers were now shorts. 'Someone' had cut the bottoms off, but of course, Gazza didn't know how they got that way and hadn't seen anyone doing it. This he explained with a huge beaming smile on his face.

The place was always buzzing when he was around and you had to be vigilant to save yourself from becoming his next victim. I wish I'd known that before, not afterwards!

As a man I liked him very much, and had a lot of sympathy for how and why he ended up suffering so badly. He was world class on the pitch, but, as is well documented, every genius is flawed. The rest we'll leave to history, apart from wishing him well in anything he does in the future.

What kind of things did he do?

Let's start with the itching powder in everyone's pants... Everyone played his part in creating that great atmosphere, but nobody else was as extreme as Gazza. Sometimes you'd just pray that you weren't next on his hit list.

You must have experienced some great times with those lads?

I'll always remember a tour to Scandinavia to play some friendlies. After one match, we were invited back for a social evening at one of our opponent's homes. It had been a really friendly trip, as you'd expect over there, and the tone of the conversation was along the lines of, 'You may have thumped us on the football pitch, and seemed more interesting to our beautiful Nordic girlfriends, but you'll never beat us at drinking'.

Clearly news of the English drinking culture had travelled far, although our squad weren't boozers by any stretch of the imagination. Unfortunately, the gauntlet was already down and we were suddenly representing our country [laughs]. They set up an obstacle course on a green with the idea being that both teams would relay-run the course, stopping to jump hurdles and dodge bollards, whilst gulping the strategically placed beers that littered the circuit - Like 'It's a Knockout' but with drinks.

Did our boys take one hell of a beating?

No, we thrashed them! We did beat them at footy, we did chat up their women, and we did beat them at drinking. It was a thing to behold!

Was there a big drinking culture?

No, not at all. But in that particular case, it was a more relaxed situation, as opposed to the rigours of a tough League season. The atmosphere was incredibly friendly too. That squad was so close, we believed we had to play together and socialize together, doing more or less everything as a team. That's why we got the results when it mattered.

The drinking was really quite innocent. After an away game there'd be a bottle of wine on the table to enjoy with a meal. Then, when we got back to London, we'd all go off to The Bull at Turnford. Invariably, we'd have one drink and some would drift off home. Others would stay and socialize but not to the extent of getting drunk and falling over. Socializing breeds a good team spirit.

Given the chance, do you think you'd have done anything different to improve your lot?

Maybe I could have chilled a bit more; not been so eager to please. That may have taken a certain amount of pressure off me and allowed me to show my true self. Obviously, the injuries didn't help, but that was largely out of my hands. And maybe I should have been more prepared to fail, whereas in my eyes that was never an option.

I remember David Pleat ringing me one Friday evening to find out if I was in, which of course I was. I'd never go out on a Thursday or Friday night before a match. I felt I was dedicated to my job and at that stage desperately wanted to show the Spurs fans the real Gary Stevens.

In terms of style of play, I've often thought that maybe I'd been better suited to a more continental game. In fact my Dad was actually offered a job in Holland when I was about ten. Life may have been totally different had I been bought up at say, Ajax, Feyenoord, or PSV. That's not to say I have any regrets on that score. I was the proudest person on earth when I walked out to represent my country.

How would you sum up your seven years at Tottenham?

Easy, I loved it. Despite all the early problems, I'd change little. Of course there were difficulties, but everyone out there in every day life, everyone reading this, will have experienced some form of adversity in their lives. My personality dictates that my nature is one of extremes. Things are either fabulous, or really bad. Summing up, how many millions of people would have loved the experience of what I did?

I can now pick up books, videos, and memorabilia that have my name or achievements across them. Nobody can ever take that away, and my time at Spurs helped make it all possible. Tottenham Hotspur will always have a special place in my heart.

On hearing of your England inclusion, did your mind go back to the dreams of the small lad who was so adamant that he'd go on to represent his country?

I think my first thought was that my Dad would be pleased. In those days, the FA informed your club, who in turn would tell you of your international selection, and that you'd be getting a letter of confirmation. I think it was either Keith or Peter who made the announcement in front of the whole squad at training. The lads seemed genuinely happy for me and I remember 'Maxie' [Paul Miller] jokingly saying, "F..king hell. They'll pick anyone for England nowadays". We all laughed, but deep inside I was as warmed by my team-mates reaction as I was by the actual selection.

Had you baled out at any stage, what were the alternatives for the young Gary Stevens?

I could have taken up an apprenticeship as a draughtsman in my early Ipswich days. Maybe I'd have had different aims if I'd done that and ended up being a stalwart of say, Sudbury Town or Bury St. Edmunds.

We see you on Sky and hear you on TalkSport Radio. Do you have any other outside interests?

Yes, I'm in the throes of setting up a local soccer school, which will trip over into other sports eventually. It's been a passion of mine to get involved in training youngsters. One, because I love being out there working with them, and two, because I genuinely love the game and being in contact with it on a daily basis.

I've recently established www.theballschool.co.uk which is the cornerstone of my coaching business alongside football and sports summer camps. It's fantastic to have the opportunity to pass on all the experience I picked up in my career. I feel a duty to pass on those tips to the next generation.

Keith
Burkinshaw

Era July 1986 - May 1984

As fans, we are quick to criticise the actions of our club when things go wrong. Sadly, there now lives a culture of media and agent-driven change-for-change's sake, none of it really benefiting the game itself. Take the case of our most recent demotion from the top flight - then imagine it now. Spurs are relegated in a hail of inglorious bullets and flak – and keep their manager! If that seems as likely as a sleaze-free parliament, a free lunch, or a massive cut in your Council Tax bill, I can assure you, it actually happened - And thank God it did.

Keith Burkinshaw joined Tottenham as quietly as he'd conducted the rest of his career. Brought in by then-Spurs Manager Terry Neil [with his dubious red connections] Keith's arrival was almost lost under an avalanche of negativity towards the man who had secured his services. Neill's investiture at White Hart Lane had not been universally accepted, representing the most unpopular decision in most supporter's living memories. Yet if anything came out of his brief tenure at Spurs it was employing the [future] second most successful manager in the club's history – A man so true to the Bill Nicholson mould it was scary.

Before joining Spurs, Keith's career had centred wholly around his northern roots. After spells with Wolves, Denaby United, Liverpool, Scunthorpe, and Workington Town, he moved on to coach Newcastle United to a famous, yet disappointing, 1974 Cup Final. United froze on the day and became yet another victim to the great Liverpool side of that era. There were still few signs of what was to come...

I have heard the term 'Dour Yorkshiremen' applied to both Nicholson and Burkinshaw. While that may well be true, I prefer to remember them in other ways. Both were as honest and hard working as the day is long. Both enjoyed the strength of mind to instill much needed beliefs and confidence where previously there were none. And both conducted themselves in the most dignified and diligent of manners.

Dour maybe, but certainly characters who changed the belief and credibility of one of football's ailing institutions. These were the qualities instantly recognised by the Spurs board of the time, and the reasons why Keith was given his chance, and further persisted with even after the spectre of relegation had dealt its worst hand.

There are many opinions on Keith Burkinshaw's success; some glowing, some not even warm. There were those who immediately questioned his ability to run a club the size of Spurs, while others questioned his characteristic northern bluntness. But whatever they initially thought of Keith Burkinshaw he was about to prove everybody wrong - and with a style and panache that Spurs people hadn't witnessed for years.

Keith's perception of the game was anything but dour. It was he, of his own volition, who flew to South America to conclude the most famous deal in our history. It was he who gave back the pride to a club that was still reeling after losing its most famous son. And it was he who insisted on carrying on 'the Tottenham way'. Keith Burkinshaw, you are a true Spurs legend.

Where did football fit in to the life of the young Keith Birkinshaw?

I was born in Higham, Barnsley in 1935 and there wasn't a great deal to do other than join the local lads in a game, we were always kicking a football around. I left Barnsley Grammar School with six '0' levels and represented Barnsley Boys, which was a great honour for me at the time. I enjoyed myself at school.

Was it clear to you then that football was going to be your future?

I wouldn't say it was clear, but I definitely loved the game. Employment was limited in the Barnsley area at the time but I ended up working for a spell at the local Dodworth Colliery transporting coal from the pit face.

Unfortunately, that was the only future for many of the boys then. It probably would have been the same story for me if Wolverhampton Wanderers hadn't come in for me. Fortunately, they agreed to place me with their Yorkshire nursery team, Wath Wanderers. I was still an amateur at the time and ended up moving on to Denaby United who were in the Midland League.

Where and when did you become a pro?

That was back in the November of 1953. Liverpool, who were nowhere near the status of the modern day club, came in for me. It was still a great feeling to be recognised by a professional club especially after previous uncertainties. I seem to remember Liverpool finishing bottom of the old First Division in 1953-54, but I didn't make my League debut until April 1955.

Do you remember much about the day?

It was a Second Division game against Port Vale. Unfortunately, that proved to be my only first team game for the club, but I did pick up a Central League Championship medal with their reserve team in 1956.

How would you describe yourself as a player?

I was dependable but never what you'd call a top-flight player. I enjoyed a reasonable amount of success in the lower leagues but in all honesty, I probably rose as far as I was going to go.

As a player I was always trying to work out ways to out-think the opposition. I loved the strategy side of the game and I think it was always in the forefront of my mind to leap into coaching or even management. In that respect I can say I got what I needed out of my career and couldn't have enjoyed it more.

So where to after Liverpool?
In December 1957 I moved on to Workington Town, who were a League club at that time. That was for a whopping transfer fee of £2,500. I spent eight happy seasons there scoring nine goals in 293 League appearances. In those days I was a jack-of-all-trades, I even filled in as player-manager from November 1965 to March 1966. I had a Testimonial with Workington against an All Stars Team.

Did you finish your playing career at Workington?
No, I still felt I had something to offer and moved on to Scunthorpe United where I spent three more happy years. Ten months of that I spent as caretaker-manager, so I was picking up bits and pieces of experience on the managerial side as I went.

There were some quite well known faces in the ranks at the time. Ray Clemence was coming through and a small up and coming kid by the name of Keegan.

You spent the majority of your playing career in small clubs in small towns. Where did your full-time coaching career begin?
Another small town, with another small club. Newcastle United. [Laughs] Joe Harvey was Manager at the time and he invited me up as Assistant Coach. I filled that role for three years then stepped up to the position of First Team Coach. I believe we built up quite a reasonable side there and even reached an FA Cup Final.

Unfortunately, we froze on the day and finished runners up to that marvellous Liverpool team of the time. That was in the 1974 Final at Wembley; the boys just didn't do it on the day.

What did you get for getting them to Wembley?
The sack. [Laughs]

And then on to 'little' Tottenham?
[Smiles] Yes. I arrived in 1975 and worked under Terry Neill and his Assistant Manager, Wilf Dixon, who was at Hull with him.

Being a Yorkshireman, and having played your career wholly in the north, was it a big wrench to go down south?
No, not really. I'd travelled south on many occasions with various sides before and didn't consider it a major move. We were fairly open-minded as

to where and who we would go to, so geography wasn't a major problem. In fact, as the years passed, I grew to really love the place and still live in a village near Welwyn to this day. My life is here now, it's peaceful, and of course, Tottenham isn't too far.

Wasn't Tottenham in a bit of a mess when you arrived?

Not really. Terry Neill was busy stamping his own personality on the job, although in truth, he had a tough act to follow. Of course, all managers have their own idea of who they want and don't want personnel wise. Terry had certainly swept through the club with a new broom dispatching some pretty well known faces. We finished ninth in that first season yet I never felt that the Spurs fans had really taken to him, which was probably much to do with his playing background.

When Neill returned to Arsenal, you were offered the Spurs managerial post. What's the story behind that?

To be honest, I didn't think I'd get it. I applied in the usual way, along with all the other applicants, but there were two important factors that helped me get the job.

Firstly, we'd been on a pre-season tour of Sweden, where we'd tried a few different moves and strategies. We won the competition and I believe the Board were impressed with the way I handled both the players and the circumstances.

Secondly, by then I'd built an excellent rapport with the squad and their input went some way to convincing people that I was the man for the job. But it came as quite a surprise when they told me I'd become the latest manager of Tottenham Hotspur Football Club.

Spurs had been through managerial torture for a few years. Did you feel it may be a poisoned chalice in some ways?

No, not at all. As a new Manager you have to go in and stamp your own authority on the position. It's no good going in as a shrinking violet and worrying what people think or stumbling over what went before. None of those issues had anything to do with me anyway.

Was the gravity of following in Bill Nicholson's footsteps a worry?

No, never. In fact, I worked with Bill later on when he returned to the club and we always had a good relationship. We both believe in good passing football and both wanted the best for the club. I believe the board brought some form of continuity in appointing me. They saw the respect shown by the playing staff towards me and they recognised that I was both diligent and had a strong character.

Keith Burkinshaw, was certainly a manager with the ear of his players

Your first season saw relegation for the club, how did you feel?

Like everyone else I was mortified, but we didn't just become a bad side. The threat of relegation had been creeping up on the club for some time. In many ways, the club recognised this by keeping me for the Second Division campaign and showing faith in my beliefs and man management. In that regard I don't think I let them down in the long term. In truth, I was planning to go straight back up long before we actually hit the wall.

What was going through your mind on that last day of the season when the fans flooded the pitch after the Leicester game?

I wasn't there. I was actually up in Blackburn looking at a player. Like I said, relegation had been all over us for a season or two. I had been meticulously planning my future squad for the next season for some time before the fateful day. The thought of two campaigns in the Second Division wasn't an option.

A club like Spurs deserves to be at the top table and I had to raise heaven and earth to get them there. If you remember, we were already down, so I chose to look at new players in an attempt to win automatic promotion.

I heard later that it was a highly emotional day and that there were lots of tears. That's what you grow to expect from the Spurs fans over the years. They are magnificent fans who wanted to prove their backing for the team. I'll never ever forget them for the way they loyally supported the team, and me, on that most unfortunate of days.

There were some special games the season Spurs spent outside the top flight. How do you remember that year?

I remember most of it. We'd been up there for a long time during the season and Bolton were looking like they'd finish top. That left us, Southampton and Brighton to fight it out for the remaining two places.

The last day of that season at The Dell was a nail biter, but I always felt confident that the boys would get us back. We played some great stuff overall and the game against Bristol Rovers particularly sticks in my mind. Winning that game nine-nil certainly boosted our goal difference.

Bolton eventually took the division with 58 points when it was still two points for a win, Southampton came second on 57, and we beat Brighton on goal average, both on 56 points. See what I mean about the Bristol Rovers game?

That was a good season for the Second Division. We took huge travelling support wherever we went and most of our hosts enjoyed their best gate of the season. With Spurs in town it was certainly entertaining. We scored 83 goals that year whereas Bolton and Brighton hit 63 each and Southampton 70. Because of the way we encouraged them to attack we also managed to leak 49 at the other end. Of course, I'd rather not let in that amount of goals, but it was better than boring the pants off people. Spurs have a tradition of entertaining; a tradition that's part of me too.

How did you pull off the coup with Ossie and Ricky?

I heard via Harry Haslam, the then Sheffield United Manager, that Ossie was available. We'd all just watched the two help Argentina win the World Cup and I couldn't believe my ears when I heard Spurs had a chance to get them. They weren't that expensive either, so I phoned the Directors and asked for permission to go and speak to Ossie first.

Around the same time I heard that Terry Neill at Arsenal had got wind of his availability, so I flew down there as quickly as possible and made contact through Antonio Rattin. Of course, Rattin was the man at the centre of a World Cup controversy back in '66, but I found him extremely helpful and an extremely welcoming person.

What was your immediate impression of Ossie?

I found Ossie extremely intelligent and personable, and very amenable to coming to Spurs. Word had got back to me that Neill had decided not to make the trip, so I felt I had a fairly clear road. Whilst talking through the details of Ossie's transfer it transpired that he had a friend he wanted to come with him. Ricky had replaced Ossie in one of their World Cup matches and I remembered them both as excellent players. The fact that they were both exceedingly nice people was the icing on the cake.

I quickly phoned back to London and asked the Board if there were any more pennies in the coffers. I also explained that buying the pair of them would help them settle into London life a lot quicker and save the embarrassment of potential homesickness or feelings of being estranged.

That was an extremely astute move on your behalf Keith. How did the Board react to your request?

They were very much in agreement with me and told me to carry on with both deals. You wouldn't believe how quickly everything was wrapped up. Argentine football was suffering very badly financially at the time and the whole package suited both sides. All parties involved moved very quickly to secure their transfers, and both men were happy to come to England.

So everything moved extremely smoothly?

That is, until it came to getting their transfers agreed by the PFA. At first they refused to sanction the deals but I moved heaven and earth to win their approval. Few transfers are conducted without problems, but I just didn't expect what we ran into when we got to England.

Did you make big change in the team's style of play to accommodate the two South American boys?

We had to change styles for the Second Division campaign. We adopted two over-lapping full backs who whipped the ball in for our forwards to use, or for Glenn to start attacks. When we went back up, things had to change again. Ossie and Ricky were now playing through the middle and Steve Perryman was playing out from the back, a rank behind where he'd played most of his career. Many players made compromises for the overall style of the team.

What did you think of your captain Steve Perryman?

I'd worked with some very good people and had an excellent skipper at Newcastle in the shape of Bobby Moncur, but I think Stevie was better. Steve was more of an all rounder; the man who took my ideas on to the pitch with him and gave inspiration to everyone.

The job he did around the club with players, trainees, and the supporters alike was quite amazing. He was always willing to give a part of himself, or time to anyone who needed it. He had endless patience, and for me, there was never a better captain than Steve Perryman. He is a very strong and determined man, and is still a great ambassador for Tottenham Hotspur Football Club.

If Steve had a weakness it was his left foot, although I always felt he was clever enough to make up for that deficiency. He was a battler who was in fact probably more skilful than most people gave him credit for.

Steve took no nonsense on the pitch and always knew how to look after himself in a battle. You need that toughness to rub off onto other players, especially some of the younger ones.

Who were your own heroes in football?

As managers, people like Sir Matt Busby and Bill Shankly. Both were incredibly strong characters and built up their clubs as icons for others to look up to. Both built teams that played great football and were respected and idolised by fans of all clubs.

There were many players that I particularly liked myself, including our own Ossie Ardiles. The man had something that set him apart. Aside from being his manager, it was a pleasure to see him float across the pitch. Obviously Glenn Hoddle must come in to that category and there was a lad in the 70's at Blackpool called Tony Green. Unfortunately, Tony's career was cut short by injury but up to the time he stopped the lad was a goal machine.

I guess my earlier recollections are of the great Real Madrid side with Puskas, Ghento, and Di Stefano. Those names influenced and affected a generation and certainly made me think more about how the game should be played. My own attitude is that fans want to be entertained, I hated the thought of my teams boring the pants off people.

The early days of Ossie and Ricky weren't fantastic. How did you turn things around?

It's the word that has totally engulfed Spurs since I first encountered them - 'expectation'. Having bought in two World Cup winners, I'd say the expectation was even higher than in other years. Still, we had to bed the two guys down and get used to playing another system. It's extremely difficult moving countries. It takes time to get used to another way of life and a totally different way of playing the game.

Nottingham Forest away was our first game of the 1978-79 season and Tottenham's first back in the top flight. Were you nervous?

No, not nervous, I was more hopeful and expectant. Forest had been League Champions the year before and Cloughy had built up a top squad. They had names like Shilton, Kenny Burns, Martin O'Neill, Archie Gemmill, Tony Woodcock and John Robertson. Ricky scored our goal in a well deserved one-all draw that day and it crossed my mind that if we could get such a good result at Forest, we could get results anywhere. Maybe we expected too much too quickly.

The following Wednesday brought us all back to earth. Did that worry you bearing in mind you'd stuck your neck out to bring the new lads in?

Again, no. Losing four-one in front of your own supporters is never nice, especially after that fantastic ticker-tape welcome, but we had a short-term job to do in restoring confidence and a long-term objective in bringing success back. No single result was going to get me down.

A two-all home draw with Chelsea followed, then that fateful afternoon at Anfield. Your heart must have dropped?

Strangely enough, there were signs in that game that we'd get it right eventually. Unfortunately, we were ripped to shreds seven-nil by a magnificent performance and a magnificent team. They'd have played any team off the park that afternoon, so I wasn't totally distraught at what I'd seen. Of course, for the fans it was a nightmare, but little things started to happen that afternoon and we learned a lot from the experience, but I knew I had to make changes.

You built an incredibly strong squad of players for Tottenham. Can you tell me about some of them?

It was a matter of completely overhauling a club that had been on the slide for a while. In those days the Board gave me carte blanche to run things, including the handling of all transfers, which I did happily. It wasn't until later on that the interruptions started to occur rendering my job almost untenable.

Tony Galvin was a tireless worker on the pitch. He'd link up a lot of the play and was as intelligent off the field as he was on it. With all players you have to work out the most efficient way of extracting the best from them. Some need an arm round their shoulder; others need to be handled a little firmer.

Graham Roberts was one such character. I found that if I was on his case a lot of the time he'd play out of his skin. He wasn't lazy and always trained well but I think his character determined that he needed someone to roust him up a little. I like to think that, after a player's career is over, they fully understand why coaches and trainers treated them a certain way. We have a role to fulfil and man management is certainly a big part of that.

Crooks and Archibald were both strong and quick. Archie did a great job of holding up the ball and both knew where the net was.

Wasn't Archibald a little difficult to handle by all accounts?

Funny you should say that as many said he was aloof and kept himself to himself, but I never found him like that. We always had a good relationship and I believe that I found the way to get the best out of him. There were others who proved much more difficult than Steve, and you'll never guess who I'm talking about either [laughs].

The Cup wins in 1981 and 1982 were very special nights for Spurs fans. What are your memories?

Yes, they were fantastic events and especially the 1981 replay when the fans were just amazing. There are simply too many individual memories from the FA Cup to recall except that it rankled away at me that we hadn't added the League title to our haul. It seemed we were at Wembley every other week then, what with Finals and replays. Yet it was the big one that always eluded us.

The Cup Finals were superb events but it meant that we had to work hard and keep the player's feet on the ground. In those days there were special squad pools where players worked together to boost the pot with personal appearances and cup final songs, etc. It was important that they remained focused on their game with all those peripheral issues going on. That's where Steve Perryman was great, he used to organise anything to do with the players pot, and they clearly trusted him to do so.

I understand Steve Perryman advised you not to play Ricky in the Manchester City replay. Did you consider his thoughts?

Whenever Steve came to me I invariably agreed with what he had to say, but this time I felt that Ricky needed a lift. Yes, I know he trooped off the pitch in the first game with his shoulders bowed, but I felt that by lifting him we'd get the best out of him. In this case I walked back into the changing room after the first match and told Ricky that he would be playing on Thursday night. You should have seen his eyes light up. I like to think he proved the decision right.

Did the backlog of cup games in 1982 ultimately cost you the title at Spurs?

In retrospect, yes, I would. In 1981-82 in particular we were scrapping for the League title, the FA Cup, the League Cup, and the UEFA cup. In the end it proved too much and we ended up retaining the FA Cup at Wembley against Queen's Park Rangers. I strongly believe we were good enough to win the title at the time. The players certainly deserved it.

You set a few managerial records at Spurs didn't you?

Yes, I became the first manager to lead his side to two major cup finals in one season and we reached the Football League Cup Final without conceding a goal. Keeping clean sheets all the way to Wembley was music to a coach's ears, our success was built on a rock of strong defence.

"There used to be a football club over there." Those words have haunted the club since your departure. What were the emotions behind that now legendary quote?

For the first few years at Spurs I was allowed to run the club from top to bottom. I ran everything from the youth to the first team and worked feverishly on bringing in the right faces to make Spurs successful again. The Board had stood by me after relegation and wholeheartedly backed me to bring the club back and take it on to further success. I wanted to repay that faith, but felt that the new regime were restricting me in what I could do. Suddenly, the great atmosphere that prevailed before was being replaced by something alien.

No longer was the talk of football, but money. Okay, you can't run a football club without it, but it suddenly seemed an overwhelming obsession and I felt that the football side was being left far behind other new priorities. I also felt like I was being watched, and anyone who has experienced that in their work will tell you that it destroys what you are trying to achieve and spreads ill feeling. This did nothing for interpersonal relations, and after much thought and not a little grief, I decided that my position was now

Keith holds up his White Hart Lane leaving present: The 1984 UEFA Cup

untenable and that it was time to leave. Of course, I never wanted to go in the first place but it was being made quite clear to me that I wasn't the person they wanted to take us forward and that they were looking to turn us into a European-style club. The Chairman of the time decided that he wanted to be more hands on, therefore my role started to diminish.

You resigned in April announcing that you would leave at the end of May. That must have been an emotional time for you especially with the pending UEFA Cup Final against Anderlecht?

Yes it was. I loved the vast majority of my time at Tottenham. I'd grown very fond of the group of players we'd bought together, and felt we'd grown as people and professionals.

Having experienced the ignominy of relegation, and then taken a step or three upwards, there was a great feeling in the camp that more success was just around the corner, but some people had other ideas.

On that particular cup run I felt that the players were trying to say a big thank you for the years we'd spent together and for the successes we'd brought to the club. More than one person asked me if I was absolutely sure I knew what I was doing, but being a man of principle, I'd made up my mind, and as far as I was concerned, that was that.

Unfortunately, there was also a niggling feeling that their heads were being turned by promises of a richer future by people who didn't really know the football side.

After an impressive one-all draw in Brussels, the return leg became one of the greatest nights in Tottenham's history. What were you feeling personally?

As you can imagine it was a night of mixed emotions for me. There had been some confusion about bonuses before the game, which Steve Perryman helped put to bed, and obviously everyone knew I'd resigned.

We put out a strong side for the first leg but were decimated by injuries and suspensions for the second. Losing my skipper wasn't the easiest thing to contend with. The opposition were no fools either. They'd won the cup the year before and were determined to hold on to it. It was a night of great passion, tears, and another fantastically vociferous crowd. It was a great way for me to say goodbye to all those wonderful Spurs fans, people who'd supported me and the team for a good few years.

It didn't end quite there, you had a testimonial match a week later?

Bobby Robson brought an England XI to play us at White Hart Lane, including a guest or two. Pat Jennings and Peter Taylor came back, alongside Liam Brady, Brian Talbot and Trevor Brooking.

It ended up two-all in front of over 20,000 fans and that was the end of my Tottenham career.

Much is made of the fact that you released Pat Jennings. How do you look back at the transfer?

Yes, you're right. Much was made of that situation, but there was more to it than met the eye. People criticise for how that situation panned out. But I had to make a decision based on the future success of the club and the facts to hand at that time.

There just wasn't the feeling then that players could go on forever back then. Ironically, it was probably because Pat played on to forty that changed people's minds, but up to that time it just wasn't the way.

The hard facts at the time were that Pat was thirty-one and had suffered a reasonably long injury. In that time, Barry Daines had ably replaced him on nineteen occasions. It looked considerably promising that we could move on with the younger lads, especially with Mark Kendall's progress as an up-and-coming Wales under-21 international.

There was also some confusion at the time about Pat's wages. He'd just enjoyed a testimonial and I believe he was in discussion with the Board regarding this. Maybe we got our wires crossed but it just seemed to me that Pat wasn't happy with the situation.

To this day I still don't know whether he was in dispute with the board or whether we both misread each other's intentions. But despite all that, I like to think that he's a friend now and that there are no hard feelings. I was doing what I felt best at the time for the club.

Tell us about your career after leaving White Hart Lane?

I enjoyed a two-year stint coaching the Bahrain National Team, subsequently moving on to Sporting Lisbon, where I stayed for another two years. We won the Portuguese Super Cup in 1986-87 and I enjoyed learning the cultures and languages. They were great experiences.

When I came back to England I was offered a Managerial post at Gillingham, which lasted six months, then I became Chief Scout at Swindon, before moving on to become Assistant Manager at West Bromwich Albion. When Ossie left the Hawthorns to go back to Tottenham in 1993, I took over as boss there.

In 1997 I was appointed Director of Football at Aberdeen and resigned in December 2000. More recently, I've done some scouting for Stoke City and have assisted the League Manager's Association, but my latest role is as a match delegate for the Premier League.

Morris
Keston

Era 1942 - Present day
Appearances Still counting **Goals** To carry on

I t may seem a little unconventional including a fan inside a book of legends, especially considering the many great individuals that donned the white shirt over the years. Yet, as my research unfolded, Morris Kestons' story stood out above all others. The man is a walking, talking, sixty-year plus tour of World football, its famous names and places. In Hunter Davies' excellent 'Glory Game', Morris perceptively quotes that fans never get any recognition for their travels and tribulations. Well this time Mr. K. it's your turn!

In compiling these stories, three names constantly reoccurred; those of Nicholson, Baily, and the most surprising, Morris himself. This intrigued me. Eddie was a marvellous player for club and country, as well as a brilliant foil to the most successful manager in our history. It's clearly no coincidence that the club enjoyed its most memorable times when illuminated by those two names. Both fell from player's lips with equal measures of respect and regularity.

Morris never played for Tottenham, or coached or managed them, even so, his name has honourably represented Spurs in many more ways than meets the eye. On meeting the man, it becomes abundantly clear why a whole generation of sportsmen trusted and befriended him. He is as modest as he is approachable; loves Tottenham Hotspur deeply; and has a heart the size of the passionate side of north London.

If compiling these men's stories has been a long journey, it was nowhere near as long as the one experienced by Morris Keston - Spurs very own Super fan.

Morris, you started in humble beginnings back in Stepney, the son of an East End tailor. What first attracted you to Tottenham Hotspur?

I wasn't really interested in football. Two cousins kept pestering me to go so I attended my first match in 1942, when Spurs and Arsenal shared the ground. There wasn't the same animosity that exists now. Had I left it a week later; who knows. I may have supported Arsenal [laughs]. Football was localized during the War. My first game was at the Lane, only because it was closer to my Hackney home, and simply fell in love.

What were the fortunes of the two clubs in those days?

Spurs were better than Arsenal then, although both were top four, as were Aldershot, who had all the stars who'd joined the Army; People like Tommy Lawton and Raich Carter. I used to take my place in the ground at about half twelve. It didn't feel the same if I didn't get my regular viewing place. By the late forties, we were attracting crowds as big as 65-70,000. Season tickets were like gold dust. I got my first one in 1962 for something like three or four pounds.

Travel must have been a nightmare then. What was it like and how did you find time to mix with the players?

Journeys up north could sometimes take more than two days to complete in those days. There were no night buses so we travelled up on George Ewer coaches, which later became Grey Green. I first travelled to Grimsby away with Reg Drury, the reporter, leaving at midnight, and arriving next morning at seven. It wasn't until 1959-60 that I ran in to Terry Medwin and Ron Henry, who then introduced us to the others. Until then, we used to stroll around in the freezing cold until kick off.

The year after my conscription, Spurs won the old Second Division, when I saw about nine games. The following year they won the First, when I saw none. Although serving in Egypt at the time, I could tell you every result and scorer thanks to the four newspapers I'd ordered. I returned in 1951, when only a handful travelled away, while the team had a regular pre-match routine. Half went to Friday night pictures, and the rest went dog racing.

What was the drink culture then?

People often accused me of taking the sixties players out drinking, which was pure nonsense. Incidentally, the way some of our teams have played since, they looked like they could do with a good drink!

Players simply didn't abuse themselves then, trouble is, some people just have to think the worst. Take the Greaves saga. I travelled all over the world with Jim, with England and Tottenham. We were very close. He wasn't in to drinking, and because we travelled regularly, the dining car attendants knew us and would keep us some seats. We always had dinner together, but Jimmy and the others only ever drank socially.

What was the reaction of the management to your friendships with their players?

Bill Nick was very reserved and kept his distance. The Director's didn't like me, but in reality they didn't like anyone in those days. We toured Switzerland in '62 or '63, and Chairman Sidney Wale was on our plane. He didn't say a word all the way home.

People always highlight the party I threw for the '67 Cup Final win as the reason for the board's attitude, but I assure you they were cold towards me long before that. I suppose it must've been the times, but they saw me as some kind of threat to the players, even though I'd never abused my position, or the players' trust. They simply liked me as a friend, and to be honest it wasn't even the social side that attracted me. I just wanted to witness some of the fabulous football played in those days.

My earliest friendships were with Terry Medwin, Bobby Smith, Cliff Jones, and Jimmy Greaves. In fact, the whole forward line. [laughs]

So if Tottenham didn't score, you'd get the blame?

[Laughs]. I hosted three big parties based around the Cup Finals, which were planned meticulously weeks beforehand. Fortunately, Spurs managed to win all three of them. I remember once having a social night in with all five of those lads and their wives. We were playing at West Ham next day and won six-one. Each one of the boys scored, except Bobby who was injured. Of course, it's never the same if you lose.

I understand you hosted Cup Final luncheons and parties?

I'd built some excellent relationships on my travels, having been invited in to many Directors boxes, and always received the warmest hospitality. I simply wanted to reciprocate the fantastic kindness I'd received from people like Peter Robinson at Liverpool, Dave Sexton and Tommy Docherty at Manchester United, and George Hardy at Derby County. It's not in my nature just to take without giving something back.

If you win the Cup, you want to be with your friends and loved ones, not in a banqueting hall with a load of strangers listening to a lot of dull speeches. I specifically told the players to come to my party after the official one. What went wrong was they left too early. I'd have genuinely preferred them to have attended the official one for longer, but it was their choice, not mine. Mind you, it was a great do. I'll never forget Stan Flashman and Dennis Howell's [the then Sports Minister] sauntering up and down arm in arm. What a great picture that would have made in the papers. [laughs]

I understand Bill Nicholson phoned you one day?

Until the 1971 League Cup Final, we'd literally only said passing hellos, although ironically, I helped out on his Testimonial committee years later.

"Mr. Keston" he started. "This is Bill Nicholson from Tottenham Hotspur. I'd just like to inform you that the party you're throwing for my players..." I interjected.

"Mr. Nicholson [and I called him Mr. Nicholson] with respect, I'd like to tell you that I'm not throwing a party *for* your players. It's a party for my friends in football. If your players choose to come along they're very welcome. If they don't, my party will still go on". It was all exceedingly amicable and he told me it was not a problem and that he just wanted to let me know not to expect them early. This proved to me that the negative stories about my parties were a lot of nonsense. I believe even the club started to realize that by then.

Did he carry on acknowledging your presence after that?

He'd always say 'hello' or 'how are you', but from a distance. That was Bill. He wasn't a flamboyant kind of character. If he had been I'd have known it was me he had a problem with. He always stayed in the background and was a totally dedicated man. I never had a problem with Bill. It was more with Sidney Wale and his impression of fans, any fans.

Was there a defining moment where it came to a head with Wale?

Yes, it was a Friday evening Manchester in 1963. We were due to play Bolton the next day and United in the Cup Winners' Cup on the Tuesday. Rather than go up twice in a week, I decided to stay, whereas the team returned on the Monday night. Whilst sitting in the hotel lobby, the players started to drift in. Suddenly, a local news photographer approached and asked for some pictures. Sensing what could happen, I moved my chair away and let him get on with it. Just then, Sidney Wale walked by and made a point of saying that I wasn't with the official party.

Jimmy Greaves was furious with him and wanted me to confront Mr. Wale to tell him that it was the players who had sat with me, not the other way round. In fact, Jim was so incensed I thought he was going to have it out with him there and then. So something developed between Mr. Wale and myself, although in later years he realized it was innocent and that I wasn't trying to takeover the club. I do believe he was like that with everyone, not just me. My only interest was to offer the club I loved my full support.

So he initially saw you as a threat to the club?

Yes, and not just me, anyone who got close was similarly shunned. They were aloof in those days. They didn't give tickets away like they do today. The Directors box is usually full nowadays because you can either buy tickets... Or you can buy the club if you have enough money to pay!

It was a unique situation then. They were there, and we were here. I remained convinced that they'd have played in front of empty seats such was the disdain for the supporters. Some clubs welcomed them. Many didn't.

Being so close to other boards, allied to your obvious business acumen, were you ever offered positions with them?

I was offered Directorships at Derby, Stoke, and Fulham, with the carrot of possibly replacing my friend Ernie Clay at the latter. Ernie was planning for retirement and thought I'd make an excellent replacement for him in a year or so. I accepted with one proviso - that he allowed me to watch Spurs every week!

We laughed and Ernie retracted his offer. Later on, he visited Tottenham as my guest. It was obtuse really. It wasn't as if I was trying to get on the Spurs board, although, if I'm honest, I can't say I'd have turned it down. Who wouldn't?

Old friends, Morris and Terry Venables share a joke after a charity football match

Your 'feud' with Wale eventually cooled. How did that come about?

Unaware of the stand off between the Spurs board and I, George Hardy had invited me in to Derby's Director box at White Hart Lane. 'County were Champions at the time, but unfortunately, I felt I had to turn it down because I didn't want to antagonize or cause any embarrassment to Spurs. George understood, but asked me to join him at a Derby game.

On arrival, I was having a drink at the boardroom bar with one of their Directors, while unbeknown to me, Sidney Wale was having drinks with George. It later transpired that George had told Sidney Wale, "If Derby had a fan like Morris, I'd have him on the board immediately". And with that Mr. Wale introduced himself, and asked for bygones to be bygones. The strange thing was, we'd never had an argument. That's what I couldn't understand.

Maybe a mixture of your business acumen and proximity to players worried him?

I'm not sure really. I don't know what started it. I guess you're right, but he'd clearly misread my intentions, and made up his mind oblivious to the truth. I put a lot into football.

In fact, I was so intent on registering my thanks to players that I started to organize and run committees for benefit nights and Testimonials. I didn't receive a penny out of those games and actually used to buy my own tickets regardless of whoever's night it was.

Whose testimonial's did you manage?

I worked on Bobby Moore's, George Cohen's, and Harry Cripps' of Millwall. Then I chaired Geoff Hurst's, and a few of the Chelsea lads, like Ian Hutchinson, Eddie McCreadie, and John Hollins. I helped five or six Spurs players including Greavsie, Alan Mullery and Phil Beal, and was also Vice-Chair on Gordon Banks'. I probably served on twenty all tolled.

The players were only too pleased to reciprocate though, like the do we staged for the Handicapped Children's Committee at Barking Town Hall, attended by George Graham, Bobby Moore, Terry Venables, and Geoff Hurst. My wife worked on that committee. You should've seen the kids' faces when all the boys walked in. Each and every one joined in with them. The satisfaction derived from helping far outweighed the work involved.

How do you go about setting up a Testimonial, or is it simply down to the fans' passion for that player?

A lot of work goes on behind the scenes. For Gordon Bank's game I introduced a special prize for the winner of a draw. The only way you could enter was to buy a pre-match ticket via the local paper. The prize, which I'd arranged via friends in New York, was a trip to see Muhammed Ali fight live, plus a meeting with Ali himself. They sold 8,000 pre-match tickets, which was unheard of then. Sadly, the weather was atrocious, although I missed the game myself. Spurs were at home and I couldn't break my record of consecutive matches. Fortunately, Gordon and the committee understood.

Did you ever regret the one week delay where you could've become an Arsenal man?

No never, although the rivalry was different then. Of course, as a Spurs man I always wanted them to lose, but it wasn't a deep hatred with me as I was very friendly with many of their players, and those of some of the other London teams. I believe the rivalry is essentially at fan level.

I recall attending George Graham's wedding on the morning of a 'Derby' game once. Afterwards, everyone was invited back to the celebrations, though Terry Venables and George had been kicking lumps out of each other during the match, and Terry had been George's best man the very same morning!

So how do you feel when Arsenal win something?

I'll never forget when Arsenal lost that European penalty shoot-out against Valencia. I was sitting at home willing them to lose, which they did, yet we all spoke to each other on the telephone next day.

Equally, when George Graham won the 'Double' with them at Anfield, I sent them a message of congratulations. I wasn't happy about it, but once the game is over you have to take it on the chin. After all, it is only a game.

Tell me the story of you, George Graham and the toilet?

I first met George via Terry Venables, a friend of many years standing. Our early meetings had been restricted to the days leading up to 'Derby' games, and George soon realized that they coincided with Arsenal victories. Eventually, we both started to believe in the coincidence and were convinced that our respective chances of victory depended largely on coming face to face. I became George's talisman, and a full-blown ritual was born.

On one famous occasion, I'd managed to avoid him for a fortnight. It was the eve of the big game and Sylvie and I were at home watching TV. The doorbell rang. It was George, so off I scuttled off to the toilet and crouched on the floor to hide. Ignoring Sylvie's protests, George systematically searched the flat, eventually finding the toilet door bolted.

He pulled a chair, stood up to peer through the glass above the door, and banged very loudly. I looked up to see his grinning face. "Seen you" he shouted – and Arsenal won again the next day.

When the hierarchy at Tottenham changed, how did they treat you then?

When Irving Scholar arrived little changed for me. I knew Irving when he was a small lad and sometimes he'd invite me into the Director's Box. I remained an outsider, although Terry was keep to install me on the Board as an adviser. I believe Mr. Sugar vetoed that idea, although that's never really been confirmed either way. Then there was the time when I nearly became acting Chairman...

How did that come about, and what were your feelings about the situation?

Phillip Green rang me on the eve of the 1991 FA Cup Final and asked if I'd come to his office in Baker Street. This was years before he became as prosperous as he is now and I asked what it was all about. "Morris, don't ask any questions, just come in" he said.

On arrival, I looked around his office and saw Tony Berry, Terry Venables, Phillip, Irving Scholar's lawyer, and, I think, Douglas Alexiou. Phillip was either going to buy Spurs from Irving, or at least try to get them out of trouble. Bearing in mind that the team had already arrived at their pre-match hotel, there we sat, discussing a potential purchase, and its future!

During the meeting, Phillip mentioned that he was making me acting Chairman. I replied, "Phillip, I can't be acting Chairman of Tottenham Hotspur."

Characteristically, Phillip calmly assured me that we'd negotiate the situation together and that I wasn't to worry. We had a big debt to Midland Bank at the time, Irving wanted to sell his shares, and Phillip had a large cheque sitting in front of him. Irving was away on the day but the lawyer had power of attorney to approve any deal, and to sign if required.

What happened then?

Phillip wasn't in the position he's in today, but he'd agreed to buy the shares providing Midland accepted him as guarantor the following Monday morning. With Irving still insisting the deal had to be concluded before we all left, Phillip reiterated his stance, while the deal hung in the balance for hours. Suddenly Terry took to his feet, stating that he needed to get back to attend to the team. It was now gone nine o'clock on the Friday before Cup Final day. Proceedings turned into a game of chess, with Irving persisting and Phillip quite rightly pointing out that he could lose all his money if the bank turned him down.

I don't know if Irving was changing his mind, or maybe he felt he could get out trouble by other means. Either way, it all collapsed and I lost my chance of sitting in 'The' chair.

When he said that he'd make you acting Chairman, what went through your mind?

[Pause] I'm going to meet the Queen tomorrow at Wembley, and it's *my* team that'll be there. [Laughs] Actually, it wasn't true about the Queen, she'd be there anyway, all that mattered was the team, and all I could think of was watching Spurs carrying off the FA Cup from the Royal Box. And I didn't say that I couldn't do the job, it just came as a massive shock. You might say, on the spur of the moment.

So the football side prevailed over the financial situation?

Of course, I've only ever thought of the football side, otherwise I'd have accepted a Directorship elsewhere, had I simply been interested in finances or massaging my own ego. Yes, I have one like everyone else, but it didn't stretch to being power-crazed or going over to a club that might compete with Spurs.

You used to follow England as well in those days?

Yes, I was friendly with Don Revie and a few of the managers who followed him. I also knew Ted Croker, the secretary of the FA. In fact, I was one of the few allowed to travel with the official England party at the time.

What do you remember of that infamous Feyenoord game in 1974?

We stayed in the Hague with Terry Venables and his wife. Terry and I went as fans, as did my kids and my nephew, who came to look after them. Terry's always been a big Tottenham supporter, so we drove to the match on the day and agreed to meet the kids outside the stadium after the game, or before in case of any problems.

Once we saw the trouble happening [and something had told me all day that it was going to occur] we shot away twenty minutes from the end, put the kids in the car and left for the airport. Unfortunately, I don't believe the courts and government do enough to stop this problem. Now they fine them fifty pounds and they come out laughing.

But don't you think that away supporters feel safer in numbers?

Yes, and segregation on the terraces I understand, but what about the Corporate Boxes where a number of heated exchanges and fights happen most years? Nobody ever mentions that. Some of them get fired up with booze and then the barriers come down.

Football is 75% finance these days and 25% the old feeling that we used to have. It doesn't seem to occur to some that they are guests and should behave as such.

Morris, what contact do you have with players now?

I have no contact with the modern squad. All my contacts played, coached, or managed in a different era. I've never met any of the newer guys and mainly because they're kept away from the fans, although I'm not convinced they have the same feeling for clubs anymore. Players move around; fans nearly always stay with their club.

Who were the other characters behind the Tottenham scenes?

Cecil Poynton was a dour, yet lovely man. He and Eddie Baily always shared little chats with me when we met, In later years I helped Eddie with his Testimonial game, and to sell most of his memorabilia. Unfortunately, there are many sharks out there preying on unsuspecting ex-players and their naivety of those markets. For me, it was a pleasure to able to help such special men.

You knew John White and Cliff Jones too. What were they like?

John was a lovely man. A great joker, and he and Cliff always were a great double act. I remember returning on a night train from Preston once. The pair of them went into the kitchen, put on chef's outfits and came out serving the whole party. They had a joke and smile for everyone.

When we stayed at the Midland Hotel they used to serve us dinner covered by large silver domes. Ron Henry was there and it just happened that he was a pigeon-fancier. As they lifted the cover to reveal our food, they'd replaced it with a packet of budgie seed. John was a lovely, lovely man. I got on very well with him and his wife, and of course his father-in-law, Harry Evans, the old Tottenham Assistant Manager.

You were also close friends with Bobby Moore. What was he like?

We had a small, men's suede and leather business together. Bobby was a great lad and was in fact, very shy. With mates, 'Jack the lad', but put in front of strangers his innate shyness came to the fore.

I phoned Bob two days before he died and asked him how he was. Despite his obvious pain, all he could think about was asking how my wife's bad back was. That was Bobby – always thinking of other people. He's sadly missed.

What's your record at Spurs?

I missed one home game from 1959 until 2000, because of my triple heart bypass operation. "Let me go. I don't want to lose my home record", I remember saying to the surgeon. "If I let you go we'll lose you!" he replied. I recently missed a home game due to a bad shoulder accident, and yes, I argued again with the same outcome.

I understand you were instrumental in changing a career or two in your time. What were the stories behind those?

I advised Dave Webb to take Heybridge Swifts 'keeper, Simon Royce, to Southend, and Tony Waddington to sign Geoff Hurst [for Stoke] and Phil Beal [for Crewe]. Geoff actually signed for City in my old flat in Orchard Court, London, with Tony and I mediating between the two.

What do you think of the youth set up at Spurs over the years?

Once upon a time, almost all of our players came from the youth ranks. In later years it didn't work out that way as even our excellent Youth Cup winning side of 1971 only really produced Souness and Perryman. United are really the only club to have nurtured a strong youth policy with Scholes, Butt, Giggs, the Neville's and Beckham coming through together. At one time we had Hoddle, Hughton, Hazzard, Perryman, Brooke, and the underrated Mark Falco, and many others that were reared by Ron Henry and co.

Did you know much about the Souness situation and why he left?

Yes, I knew both Graham and the circumstances. In fact, it was partially down to me that he went to Middlesbrough, as I knew their vice-Chairman Harold Shepherdson.

I'd already mentioned Graham to Tony Waddington at Stoke, advising that Graham was a confident lad and had only played half a game in Keflavik in the UEFA Cup. Graham felt strongly that he was definitely good enough for the first team, and I know it was put around that he left because he was homesick - I know for a fact it was because he wasn't getting a first team game. Rightly or wrongly, Graham felt he needed a move, even at seventeen years of age.

As a member of London's Sportsman Club you met some incredible people.

It was like an extension of football in that I had a capacity to make friends wherever I went. I enjoyed extensive business travel then, and was a regular visitor to Las Vegas and Caeser's Palace, where I made friends with owner, Bill Wynberger.

I met boxers, film stars, businessmen and many famous sports stars, and was a guest at Zsa Zsa Gabor's sixth wedding. I even met Frank Sinatra, a great man who clearly remembered our meeting and sent a telegram inviting me to see him perform on a pending two-week booking at Caesar's Palace. Yet with hand on heart I can honestly say that, although it was great meeting all these superstars, I was never happier than when watching my Spurs back home in London. Yes, it could be expensive, but I didn't look at the cost. It genuinely gave me a tremendous amount of pleasure. I had a successful business and it was my intention to spend it as I made it. That's what I earned it for!

Did anything strange ever happen on your travels?

I'd travelled all over the world, but this particular story took place in Glasgow. I was booked into the Central Hotel, but wandered over to the North British to find the players. It must have been around seven in the morning. While there, I thought I'd ask if any rooms were available. They said they had one left and I agreed to take it. My luggage was back in the Central, I was unshaven, and unbeknown to me, there had been an armed robbery in the Co-op in Claremont Road, Cricklewood the day before. Unfortunately, my ugly mug fitted the description perfectly.

After changing hotels, my door suddenly burst open, and there stood three burly Police officers who told me I was under arrest. Fortunately, the guy who had committed the robbery had a finger missing so we all had a good laugh, and met up later at the game.

Your love of Spurs got you on TV a few times. Which shows did you appear on?

I appeared on Michael Wale's early evening news show once. Then I was invited on to 'The Big Match' with Brian Moore and Jimmy Hill, who had rung me to say he was in trouble. ITV were compiling an edition of the show and had decided to introduce a new feature where a fan interviews a manager. Jim asked me if I'd go on and interview Keith Burkinshaw.

Jimmy, a good mate, was clearly in a panic and a tad confused as to how he'd find another Tottenham fan to do the show in such a short time. Spurs were due to play Forest, and after the edited highlights they intended to show Keith and I walking across the pitch, with me questioning him. Keith made it abundantly clear that I wasn't to ask him any leading questions. I nodded, and off we strolled across the White Hart Lane turf with the cameras rolling...

You did it... didn't you?

As we walked, I expressed my disappointment at the defensiveness of Brian Clough's team, and then, as we hit the centre circle, I turned and asked, "By the way Keith. Every Spurs fan would like to know why you sold Pat Jennings?"

Keith was brilliant, coolly and professionally explaining that with Barry Daines and Mark Kendall coming through, that it was the right to let Pat go. I went on, "But why to the Arsenal. We hate them y'know?" After that I received abusive phone calls until all hours of the morning, until I just felt that something drastic had to be done to stop the nightmare. Then

Cup of Cheer: Glenn Hoddle and Sylvie Keston toast another Spurs Cup win

one night the phone rang. It was the same guy, and as he finished his usual tirade of abuse, I shouted, "OPERATOR, CONNECT", which had enough impact to stop him calling as he thought he'd been traced by the Police.

Ironically, what was quite a lengthy interview got cut on the day. There had been a fire at Bristol, and most of the smaller clips were huddled together towards the end. This meant that they put me on last and just for the briefest of moments. I wonder why? [Laughs]

How did all the football travel affect your relationship with the family?

Funnily enough, nobody had really been that involved with football before me. My Dad liked the game but I was the first to take it to heart. Now it's the whole family that's involved; my son and daughter, two grand-daughters, nieces and nephews. There's a big circle of us who are all Spurs mad. Everybody got drawn in because of my involvement and now every single one is a Spurs fan, even the wife, who originally came from Arsenal country [Laughs].

So what was your own crowning moment in a lifetime of following Tottenham?

Easy - Wembley 1961. In those days when the League title was over, that was that. Then you had the build up for the Cup Final, with the news-papers, special editions and everything. The FA Cup Final retained all the glamour, and all you wanted was to see your team there. I'd been to three Semi-Finals defeats in '48, '51, and the '56 game against Manchester City. The elation of winning 'The Double' was incredible, but the build up to that Wembley game will always stay in my mind. Looking back on it now, we just didn't realize at the time how good the 'Double' team was. It was years later that the whole thing sunk in.

Who were the best three players you ever saw at Spurs?

Well, if you're talking about my three favourite players you'd have to include Ron Burgess at number one for his overall game, Jimmy Greaves for his goals, and for one season at least, Jurgen Klinsmann.

To me, Klinsmann was the greatest professional we've had in this country for the last thirty years. The man arrived with everything against him; The Press hated him, he'd joined what is assumed to be a predominantly Jewish club; and at the end of his career when everyone thought he'd come for a final payday.

In the end he proved the opposite of what everyone had painted him. The man chased lost causes that lesser mortals would have left, turning many to our advantage. He was no mercenary seeking a last hurrah at our expense. Klinsmann faced many battles on his arrival - and to his undying credit, he won all of them.

What do you think about the loyalty factor in football now?

Personally, I don't blame players. They've a short career and they're entitled to move, whereas fans normally stay loyal to their clubs. Foreign imports simply cannot have the same initial feeling for Spurs as, say, a local lad. Equally, a fan gets nothing for swapping clubs. For supporters, it's all about the love of the team they follow. Of course, there are players who settle somewhere for a long time and build up a love for it; players like Pat Jennings and Cliff Jones, who are Spurs men through and through. Both desperately want to see us win. Then there are players who'd run through walls for the club. Players who may not have been the most skilful but you certainly knew when they weren't out there. Guys like John Pratt, and my ex son-in-law, Paul Miller. Put them in a white shirt and watch them spill blood for the cause.

You've witnessed many changes in the game. What's changed the most?

Of course, salaries have rocketed but I get particularly despondent about the way the game is reported nowadays. When Jacques Santini joined, I barely knew his name, yet I could recall snippets of news from sixty years ago because we felt more part of what was going on then. Journalists simply write up stories to a deadline now.

Years ago you had Reg Drury, Peter Lorenzo, Ken Jones, Desmond Hackett, Geoffrey Green, Laurie Pignon; they had strong relationships with players, whereas today there are Press conferences. Therefore, every paper has more or less the same story. There are no individuals anymore. That's not being old fashioned, they simply phone each other up to confer tales. Before, you had to use your wits or your contacts, whereas today, stories revolve around the rich players; the Beckham's of this world, instead of interesting stuff about our teams.

Football clearly changed your life Morris, but it seemed you had principles and stuck by what you thought was right.

Yes, my whole life changed. Football came first... and last. In the early days, I just wanted to travel to see my team and mix with the great friends I'd made. Of course, it made life easier being able to afford the parties and the travelling.

I once asked Terry Venables if I could sit on the bench at the Spurs-QPR Cup Final in 1982. As Rangers Manager at the time, he asked what I would do if Spurs scored. I truthfully replied that I'd jump up and down and celebrate. Terry laughed and told me I couldn't sit on his bench but invited me to Rangers' banquet at the Royal Lancaster Hotel. Of course, nobody knew it would be a draw then, but I turned the opportunity down, because if we won I'd be gloating, and had we lost I wouldn't want to go to any parties.

Yes, it was always important to do the right thing, even though it cost me Directorships of other clubs, and possibly even the chance to become a Chairman. My love of Spurs took high precedent over all of that, although I did do one thing that was a little naughty. Eager to see Spurs play a friendly in Egypt in 1963, I marked 'Christian' on my visa, thus allowing entry to the country and the game. It was another extremely sensitive time in the Middle East and Jewish people were banned entry.

You've experienced an amazing life Morris. Do you have any regrets, and is there anything you'd willingly change given the opportunity?

My only regret is getting old knowing those times won't happen again. Overall, no, I don't think so. I had a wonderful time, and if I'm totally honest I enjoyed the glamour, the glitz, and being the centre of attention. Who wouldn't?

I loved appearing on television and in the media, and felt proud when my name was connected with helping players and charity funds, especially those for kids with illnesses who were worse off than ourselves. I was fortunate in many ways, bumping into the players and a few well-connected characters, but no, I don't regret a thing.

Photos
Every effort has been made to trace the copyright holders of the photographs in this book - some have been unreachable. We would be grateful if the photographers concerned would contact us.